GOING SOLO

Everything You Need to Start
Your Business and Succeed
as Your Own Boss

GOING SOLO

Everything You Need to Start Your Business and Succeed as Your Own Boss

**JULIE BARLOW &
JEAN-BENOÎT NADEAU**

sh.

SUTHERLAND
HOUSE

TORONTO, 2023

Sutherland House
416 Moore Ave., Suite 205
Toronto, ON M4G 1C9

First edition, May 2023

If you are interested in inviting one of our authors to a live event or
media appearance, please contact sranasinghe@sutherlandhousebooks.com
and visit our website at sutherlandhousebooks.com for more
information about our authors and their schedules.

We acknowledge the support of the Government of Canada.

Manufactured in China
Cover designed by Jordan Lunn
Book composed by Karl Hunt

Library and Archives Canada Cataloguing in Publication
Title: Going solo : everything you need to start your business and
succeed as your own boss / Julie Barlow & Jean-Benoît Nadeau.
Names: Barlow, Julie, 1968- author. | Nadeau, Jean-Benoît, author.
Description: Includes bibliographical references and index.
Identifiers: Canadiana (print) 20220496072 | Canadiana (ebook) 20220496137 |
ISBN 9781990823114 (softcover) | ISBN 9781990823152 (EPUB)
Subjects: LCSH: Self-employed. | LCSH: Success in business.
Classification: LCC HD8036 .B37 2023 | DDC 658/.041—dc23

ISBN 978-1-990823-11-4
eBook 978-1-990823-15-2

Contents

Introduction

The oldest profession in the world

Believe it or not, this book was inspired by Greek philosophy—and not just because the authors met in a History of Western Thought class at McGill University. We actually learned a lesson in that class that turned out to be fundamental to our future work as freelance writers.

We were reading Xenophon, a Greek citizen-soldier-philosopher-mercenary and student of Socrates who lived from 425 to 355 BC. The work was *Economics*, and our professor explained that the original Greek word for economics, *oikonomikon*, from which the English derived, had nothing to do with multinational corporations or GDP, which hadn't arrived in ancient Greece. The word means, "order in the house." The original meaning of the English word "economics" was something akin to "running a farm."

At the time, Jean-Benoît was a budding freelance writer who spent the bulk of his spare time not studying, but getting articles published in local newspapers and magazines. It took him a few years to make the connection between freelance writing and the class on Xenophon. Farmers, of course, are self-employed, like freelancers. For that matter, Xenophon himself was self-employed. And as a matter of fact, so was most of Greek society at the time—almost everyone except the slaves.

It could be argued that throughout most of history, self-employment has defined humanity in its natural state. People have been working independently since before humans could walk upright. No one can put an exact date on the appearance of the world's first self-employed worker because they have always existed. People were self-employed long before anyone came up with the brilliant idea of a payroll or a head office. The history books are overflowing with self-employed heroes (as well as anti-heroes, villains). Christopher Columbus and Galileo are two examples that jump to mind. But behind the scenes, farmers, shopkeepers and the oodles of skilled tradespeople backing them up have been woven into the fabric of history for millennia.

Historically, "having a job" was the anomaly. The notion of full employment—meaning the idea that everyone who *can* work *should* have a job—is quite recent. It dates to the beginning of the 19th century when the Industrial Revolution and agricultural mechanization pushed agricultural workers to throw in their hoes and flock to factory jobs in the cities.

The fact that "jobs," or paid employment, became so highly valued was a stunning reversal. Throughout most of history, the people who controlled their means of production sat at the top of the social ladder. And workers, who owned nothing and sweated for their wages, were at the bottom. Those were hard times (in many places, they still are).

Henry Ford was one of the first industrialists to understand that if he didn't share his wealth with his employees (by paying them good salaries and giving them time off), they would eventually push back and revolt. He was not the only one who had this bright idea: in 1889 Germany, Chancellor Otto von Bismark invented old age social insurance for the same purpose. The whole 20th-century history of liberal democracies was about governments and companies buying political and social stability by protecting people's jobs. Organizations became technocratic and work became Labour. In the process, for some reason, self-employed people became a footnote, or were forgotten—except, of course, for the ones who ended up running companies, creating jobs and providing security to their peers as entrepreneurs and employers. And even then, we forget that they started out as, "self-employed."

Skip forward to the end of the 20th century: people of our age (post Baby Boom) were all raised to believe that the goal of our lives was to get a good job. Even today, stable employment is so highly valued in our society that people tell children it's the main reason they should get a higher education. People without bosses—unless they *are* bosses or recognized professionals—are still seen as outliers or even second-class workers ("the ones who couldn't get jobs"). Which is strange when you think about how recent salaried work actually is in history.

Curiously, the proportion of self-employed workers in the workforce has actually risen over the past five recent decades. It's around 15% today, up from 12% in the 1970s. Is the pendulum swinging back to life before employment? What's changing?

Lots of things. Machines are more efficient than ever. Countries seem to have less money to hand out to their citizens (or at least that seemed to be the case before the COVID-19 pandemic). Financiers, who can invest anywhere and are not limited to their own countries, are hiring labour wherever it is cheapest. And now, with our shared experience of health confinements, many of us learned that we can do our jobs as well—if not better—from home or from the office. That alone appears to have gotten more people thinking about working for themselves. Two studies in 2021 found that about a third of the Canadian population was thinking of making the leap to self-employment. Statistics Canada reports that "the desire for freedom" is the primary driver behind Canadian workers' decision to become self-employed.

Basically, jobs across the Western world are becoming less and less permanent and workers are striving for more flexibility. That means that more people will turn to, or at least consider going all the way and becoming self-employed, like Xenophon. The point of his work, *Economics*, was explaining how to be a good citizen, and it all started with being good at "keeping your house in order," which was, in essence, being a self-employed worker.

How we became self-employed workers

We would be rewriting history if we said that either of us really "chose" self-employment. It was the inevitable product of being creative. Coming to terms with our job status was actually a bit of a struggle for both of us, mostly because we had been raised by parents who valued education but believed the primary goal of education was to get a good job (we're not blaming them, lots of people still believe that). This was all the stranger given that Jean-Benoît's father was actually an entrepreneur. Yet, neither of us grew up with the foggiest idea of what being "self-employed" meant.

Jean-Benoît became self-employed by accident one January morning in 1987 when the temperature in Montreal hit –20 °C. He was twenty-two years old and standing on top of an oil tank at a refinery on the east side of the city where he had been working for three months and had an epiphany. After a three-year rollercoaster ride of university studies that had swung from civil engineering to literature to playwriting, he finally realized what he wanted to do: do a degree in political science and become a journalist.

Jean-Benoît started working as a freelance journalist before the first semester of his political science degree at McGill University had even started and he never quit. The early years were intense while he worked under the double pressure of going to school full-time while starting a career. He made a lot of mistakes, tried various types of writing, got some good advice and some bad. But by the time he finished his degree in 1992, he had a few journalism awards under his belt.

The next year, he got a job, then became a "born-again" freelancer, this time by choice. In early 1993, he was hired as a reporter at *L'actualité*, Canada's premier French-language magazine, sister publication of *Maclean's*. He eagerly accepted the position. What young journalist in their right mind would turn down an offer like that? Thirty days after he started, he handed in his resignation. He just couldn't see himself working for a boss.

That was when he signed up for a life of hustling and insecurity.

The same year, Julie was wrapping up her Master's degree in English literature (she was a far more assiduous student than Jean-Benoît). Whereas Jean-Benoît grew up as the son of an entrepreneur, Julie was raised in a middle-class/working-class family where "running your own business" was not on the list of options for adulthood, even though her grandparents had run a farm and her uncle was a successful agribusinessman. It was graduate studies that opened Julie's eyes. The Ivory Tower was not her place. She wanted to be a writer. So she started pitching ideas to magazines and is still doing that thirty years later.

Julie had only one actual job over her writing career. In 1998, she worked for six months creating and running an English department for a French-language publishing company in Quebec. But even that "job" was an idea she pitched to the company, who she had discovered writing a magazine article. And although she worked in their office, she billed her hours as an independent contract worker.

Freelancing—a term used for self-employed writers and creators in general—is probably the only way for creative types like us to make a living. Basically, we forego a guaranteed source of income because we have too many projects on the go. Freelancing is the only way we could have written a dozen or so books and thousands of articles between the two of us, produced a radio show, taught workshops, done translations and created a documentary TV series while managing to move around between Montreal, Paris (twice), Phoenix and Toronto. Over the years we have learned how to manage clients, stay organized and keep on top of invoices and bills, to negotiate and run a website, some of the many "other" skills you need to make a freelance writing business viable and profitable.

Of course, there have been moments when being self-employed has seemed like a really stupid idea, even to us. The middle of the Y2K scare, the tech bubble crash in the early 2000s, the months following the 2001 terrorist attacks, the 2008 stock market crash and the early months of the COVID-19 pandemic are a few such moments that jump to mind. And that's not mentioning the ongoing destabilizing effect social media would have on the writing industry. Whenever the economy tanks, or even hiccups, or our business is shaken up, stable employment suddenly looks like a much wiser, safer option.

It is and it isn't.

In times of trouble, no one knows better than a freelancer how businesses rally to protect their employees and how contract workers become secondary concerns. However, disasters come and go, and if you play your cards correctly (by reading this book, for example), you'll bounce back from adversity—and often learn valuable lessons from it. We always have. It's called being adaptable. That's because, while salaried workers may lose their job, freelancers only lose clients. And there are more out there. Over the past three decades we have seen countless employees with so-called job security get fired, but we never have. We're the boss!

Sure, about once a year some disappointing professional experience makes each of us wonder why we don't just go get a job. But every time we imagine ourselves having to go to work and act according to someone else's decisions—or worse, having to give up our plethora of projects—we renew our vow to stay self-employed, for better or for worse.

Figuring out what we do

In some ways this book is the product of thirty-five years of trying to understand and explain—to ourselves and to others—what we do, what self-employment is and how to make it work.

A little secret: we chafe at the term "self-employed worker," which has a clinical sound to it. In English, the term comes from tax jargon: it defines taxpayers who earn revenue without having an employer. Other countries (with other languages) have more dignified terminology for self-employment. The French (from France) call a self-employed worker *une entreprise individuelle* (an individual enterprise) or *un travailleur indépendant* (independent worker). These sound more respectable to us, and a better reflection of what we actually are. For this book, we could have adopted a new term, like "solopreneur," or even invented a new one of our own, but we decided to stick to the term self-employed because it's recognizable.

It was Jean-Benoît's father who introduced the idea of self-employment to us. During Jean-Benoît's political science studies, when he was going through a particularly rough patch in his freelance career, he ran the idea of getting a job by his father, who was a partner in an engineering firm at the time.

"You might want to think about your situation differently," his dad explained. "For one, there are a lot of tax advantages to being self-employed." To which Jean-Benoît replied with another question. "Uh, what do you mean by self-employed?" And that's where we started.

As we would learn, we belonged to a category of hybrid individuals: half person, half business. Being "self-employed" means you are a sole proprietor. You may or may not have invented the activity you are performing, but you own your means of production (your skills, your tools) and you call the shots.

Understanding what you are is the first challenge any self-employed worker has to overcome. Contrary to what you might have believed if you were previously an employee, self-employment is not just a backup plan for when you get laid off. After a century and a half of worshipping "jobs," most people have come to think of a self-employed worker as someone who "scrapes out a living" doing "something," and doesn't have "the stuff" to be interesting to employers. Unfortunately, many self-employed people who were raised in the same job culture think this way too—and they entirely miss the point.

If you carry out your self-employed work feeling like a subpar worker and only hoping it will lead to a job, your clients will pick up on your insecurities, hone in on your weak spot and take advantage of you. As a result, you very well may end up leading a precarious existence.

But if self-employed workers are not just failed employees, what are they?

One of Quebec's comic geniuses, Yvon Deschamps, famously described his mother in a sketch that perfectly summarizes the meaning of self-employment. He said, "My mother doesn't have a job. She has too much work."

This, in a nutshell, summarizes all there is to understand about self-employment:

- You don't have a job, you have work.
- You don't have a boss, you have clients.
- You don't have a salary, you have income.

Let's break these ideas down.

Work. Your job is to look for work contracts or produce a service or units to sell. Once you become known for what you make or do, word will get around and people will call you. This idea may sound far-fetched to a committed employee. But the fact is, a person's know-how becomes valuable when it is scarce and in high demand. If you are skilled, reliable and do something useful, you will have more than enough work to fill your schedule—and your bank account. You may even have enough work to share with other workers (more on this in Chapter 6). Your skills and the demand for them are what gives you "job security."

Clients. You probably won't see them every day but don't worry, that's normal—and desirable. First, because you should have many clients, not just one. And second, you don't want them on your back telling you how to organize your office or your schedule—that's your job, not theirs. The only thing that matters to your clients is whether or not you deliver what you have promised, on time. From a business point of view, clients are your equals. They're not your boss.

Income. A self-employed person earns income from the sale of a good or service. Whereas wages are governed by strict laws and in some cases, by collective agreements, a self-employed person's work is governed by contracts. Clients only pay when you send them a bill. They don't make source deductions for the Canadian Pension Plan, for Employment Insurance, for your pension plan or for anything else. You collect the full amount you bill, plus sales tax (see Chapter 19), then you decide how to manage your money (see Chapter 23).

Think of it this way: as a self-employed person, you have to work with a different operating system than an employee does. Self-employed workers who talk about their "job," their "boss" or their "salary" are just not getting it. They will end up losing out on the advantages of being self-employed mostly because they fail to understand what they really are: a business *as well as* a worker.

From time to time, organizations in Canada try to unionize specific categories of self-employed workers, but most of these attempts have ended up as associations of workers in a specific field. The Canadian Media Guild (the union that represents CBC employees) now has a thriving freelance guild, the Canadian Freelance Guild (CFG), of which Julie is a member. The CFG helps writers with contracts but has no collective bargaining powers. The Canadian government has long considered legislating and regulating self-employment. But real change, if it comes, is decades away. In the meantime, the only way self-employed workers can thrive and protect themselves is by sharing wisdom and experience and better understanding the powers they do have.

The Five Functions of your business

One characteristic of being a freelancer is that you're constantly on the lookout for novel information, even when you are in the middle of producing and delivering. Jean-Benoît was working on a magazine assignment when he had his second epiphany about self-employment.

It was the summer of 1989 and he was interviewing a professor at Montreal's prestigious HEC business school. The fellow was running not just one, but five summer theatres in Quebec simultaneously. When Jean-Benoît interviewed him at his office, the professor-cum-businessman showed him how his whole business was organized in forty-nine folders on top of his desk (this was the 1980s, PCs were still rare). Jean-Benoît still recalls the conversation that ensued.

"Running this business is pretty easy," the businessman explained.

"Really, running five theatre companies at the same time is easy?" Jean-Benoît replied, incredulous. "Most producers go crazy running just one."

"Sure," the businessman answered. Then he explained: "It all boils down to the fact that there are only five things involved in running a company: Sales, Operations, Research, Finance and Management. They are the fundamental functions of any business, whether for a multinational, a start-up, a non-profit organization, a boutique, a variety store or a writer. If you neglect any of them, the business will get into trouble. But if you mind them all, things should run smoothly."

Jean-Benoît was still not convinced. "Maybe that's true for multinationals," he said, "but how about grocery stores or anyone who is self-employed, like me, a freelance journalist?"

The businessman's answer changed Jean-Benoît's whole philosophy about work, if not about life. "The self-employed worker is a researcher, sales manager, publicist, chief negotiator, accounts receivable manager, financial controller, accountant, president and CEO, chairman of the board of directors and his own press attaché. You are also your own secretary! In short, you are the business. Buy yourself some folders."

In other words, being self-employed is the ultimate role play game, and here we are, over thirty years later, still playing all those roles (now using computer folders)—plus new ones that have popped up since the 1980s, like being our own webmasters and social media coordinators.

But let's go back to the five business functions, which, as a self-employed person, you will have to perform just like the owner of your local convenience store does.

- Research
- Sales
- Operations
- Finance
- Management

These roles are all vital. Neglecting any one of them will put your entire business at risk. Which is why they are at the heart of the structure of this book, adapted to the specific needs and requirements of self-employed workers.

For example, by Research, we mean "research and development," good old R&D. This involves finding good ideas, asking yourself what you want to do about them, what purpose they serve and what you have to do to make them work. And even when you are in the thick of a project, you have to have a special folder in your brain for new, promising ideas. They can pop up any time. A self-employed worker should always be getting ready to do something else.

Operations is also hard to understand because it combines production and exploitation. Most successful self-employed workers are good at production, but they are often not as good at exploiting their work and skills to the fullest. If you put in 100 hours designing software for one customer, you might as well sell the software to a hundred other customers and multiply your profits. Of course, this process is not as straightforward in all fields. As writers we often have to sign exclusivity contracts that limit our ability to resell our writing. But we find other ways to maximize the benefits of our original work (like being paid to translate our own work for a different publication). That's the difference between producing and operating. Learning how to operate your business is what makes it grow.

It took us a long time to understand that a person who earns $250,000 doesn't necessarily work ten times more than a person who earns $25,000. Virtually all self-employed workers fall into the trap of believing that the only way to earn more money is to work harder, to put in more hours. We all know that there are a limited number of hours in a day. While those who earn ten times more might simply be in a more lucrative field, chances are they are ten times more organized—that is, they have figured out how to multiply their income without multiplying their working hours. They have found stuff that works *for* them.

That multiplier effect comes from performing—well—all five of the functions of your business. Your goal is to get the most out of all aspects of your business: research, sales, financing, operations and management. Being the creative type, we are naturally inclined towards research and operations, but over the years we have become quite astute at sales, finance and management. And it has paid off.

Who should read this book

Going Solo was written for all types of self-employed workers, with special guidance for creative and enterprising types like ourselves. In other words, this book is for anyone who earns a living (or wants to) but doesn't get a pay cheque every two weeks. Whether you are a lawyer, actor, barber, photographer, illustrator, salesperson, manufacturer, craftsperson, machinist or truck driver and whether you work in a metropolitan area or a small village, this guide is for you. By "creative" we're not limiting our readers to "artistic" people. Taking an existing business in a new direction is very creative.

The advice we offer in this guide is in line with what numerous associations for self-employed workers recommend. We have also added tips we have developed, tested and taught in workshops on self-employment over the decades. We are not promoting any particular doctrine, lifestyle or ideology here. We are not arguing for a bohemian lifestyle over a consumeristic existence. That's your business.

We wrote this book because so many of the practical advice workshops we have attended over the years—and so many of the books and articles we have read about being self-employed—have left us feeling like something was missing. And that would be the basics. Workshops and roundtables on self-employment almost always have a tax specialist who talks about financial issues, or an accountant to discuss how to incorporate. But these specialists rarely explain the basic things self-employed workers need to know when they are starting out, like how to properly invoice a client or how to recognize a client who is treating you like an employee (see Chapter 11). How you are supposed to start without the basics?

How to read this book

Although this book explains some principles that are taught in business schools, it is not meant to be scholarly. Our goal is to provide simple effective answers and solutions to problems that can seem (and actually sometimes are) complicated. We use as few buzzwords and as much common sense as possible.

So, you can read this book either from cover to cover, or starting wherever you want, according to your topic of choice, or your immediate needs. We included a very detailed Table of Contents so you can quickly identify questions for which you need answers (you might be in a pickle when you are picking this up).

Each chapter starts with a quasi-universal "myth" about the issue of self-employment at stake. These are beliefs we have heard participants express over and over in our workshops. The chapter then explains the challenges you will face, the mistakes you should avoid and how to overcome obstacles with information, advice and other tricks of the self-employed trade. We include some external references, but we find other writers tend to overdo it with references.

We divided this book into four parts that roughly correspond to the five basic functions of a business—research, sales, financing, operations and management. But we combined sales and financing in one chapter because separating them seemed artificial. Unlike Tesla owner Elon Musk, who worked at a loss for ten years before churning a profit, the only financing most self-employed workers can dream of will be their sales.

Part 1 is about research and preparation. This is where we address the business plan, how to develop ideas, understanding intellectual property and how to structure your business and your office.

Part 2 is about sales and financing. We discuss sales and publicity, but also negotiating and contracts. That's where your ideas, your clients' expectations and your ability to deliver on them, come together.

Part 3, about operations, is the shortest, because it's almost impossible to generalize. Hairdressers, computer programmers, personal trainers, human resources consultants and graphic designers have very diverse activities. What they do have in common are issues about communicating, after sales service, billing and collecting, and that's what we focus on.

Part 4 is about managing. This is where we deal with taxes, deductions, insurance and the nitty-gritty details of managing numbers and columns.

Bear in mind that these divisions are somewhat artificial because so many sections are linked. Negotiating, for instance, to which we devote four chapters, is part of sales and financing, but also of operations. Invoicing and collecting, at the end of Part 3 on operations, is also about financing. This is very natural. The different parts of self-employment work together like the organs in your body: the pancreas and the liver go hand in hand. So do your stomach and intestines. Not to mention the heart and lungs.

We have also spread "Questions from Readers" throughout the book to explain to readers how to start out in specific situations: being unemployed or a parent, or a student.

We hope that using this book, enterprising creative types will be able to use our advice and guidance to make the various parts of their business "body" work together so they can turn their desire for freedom into a successful business.

Research and Preparation

The Killer Plan

Asking the hard questions

Myth #1: "I just have to dive in and start."

The newly self-employed often put the cart before the horse. Jean-Benoît was a typical case. Fuelled by youthful naivety, he plunged into freelancing in his 20s without doing any research to figure out what it actually involved. Naturally, he made some classic beginners' mistakes, like trying to sell a magazine article that still had a previous editor's comments on it. Pretty amateur.

Fortunately, Jean-Benoît got a few things right. For one, he started freelancing while he was still in university—and he still managed to finish his studies more or less one time. Studying full time had an advantage: it forced him to take his time breaking into the writing profession. It also took the financial pressure off for a few years: Jean had enough money to get by on his college fund and he lived a student lifestyle like everyone else, so he didn't feel pressure to earn a lot. But he had a lot on his plate. So he needed to be both ambitious and pragmatic to pull it off. These are exactly the qualities a self-employed worker who is starting out needs in order to survive.

One thing Jean-Benoît had going for him was a set of goals. The most common mistake people make when they start out as a self-employed worker is failing to define their objectives. You need to ask yourself some hard questions before you dive in. The most important one to start is: are you treating self-employment as something to "fill the time" while you actually look for a job? If that's the case, you might not succeed at either. No one hires a self-employed worker because they see "potential" in them. They hire them because they know they will deliver. So you need to be able to explain (first to yourself, then to others) exactly what you are offering and how much it will cost. You also need to know how you will produce your good or service.

This is already hard enough when you have defined skills and are working in a territory or a market you know. If you are setting out to be a hairdresser, actor or mortgage broker, you definitely fit into recognized professions in an established industry. The challenge in those cases is proving you are good or better than your peers.

Things get more complicated when you are pioneering, creating a new or unusual profession from scratch or entering a new market or sphere of activity. These days, there's nothing unusual about working as an independent web consultant, but fifteen years ago, plenty of people had never even heard of such a profession. The obstacle in cases like this is not beating the competition, but showing a client why they need what you are selling. To do that, you have to make sure you know, yourself.

But in both cases, you have to grasp the basics of your industry. Jean-Benoît knows this better than anyone. It took him three years to understand what magazines expected of him as a freelance contributor. With hindsight, he knows he could have figured this out in a few months if he'd taken the time to talk to people in the industry—in short, to do his research Julie learned from Jean-Benoît's mistakes and did do her research. She went as far as meeting with editors who were interested in her ideas before writing for them to better understand their expectations. In any field, spending time doing research upstream is time-consuming and even tedious, but it is always a good investment. Very few self-employed workers can get by without doing this. For a budding self-employed worker, haste is your enemy.

Defining your activities, doing market research and a feasibility study all at once might sound like a tall order. Luckily, there is an accessible tool for this that anyone can use. It's called a "business plan." Whatever you are planning to do, it's a business. You should think of writing a business plan as going on a kind of retreat where you ask basic questions about yourself and your goals. The most important questions are not about the business. They're about you.

The thirteen questions a business plan answers

When you present your business plan to the public, or buyers, you need to answer four basic questions. They are the same questions that a website answers:

- What is my product?
- Who is it for?
- How much am I charging for it?
- How will I make/deliver it?

To answer those four questions, you need to back up and first answer thirteen questions with sub-questions.

Here they are:

1. What is my current situation?

- Why exactly do I want to start a business?
- Do I have enough money to finance it? (If you don't, there are other solutions, but you need to know.)
- What is my financial track record? (see Chapter 5)

2. What are my personal and business goals? (Answer this as freely as possible; we'll come back to it.)

3. In practical terms, what do I want to do or make?

- What will I sell?
- How much should I charge? (see Chapter 5)

4. Am I cut out for this? (This may require some hard thinking.)

   - Am I suited to the working conditions of being self-employed? (e.g. lack of security, competition, working alone)
   - Do I have experience in the area?
   - Will I enjoy/tolerate the tasks involved?

5. Is my project viable?

   - What do my friends, colleagues, future customers and future competitors think about my project?

6. How will I go about it?

   - What tools do I need?
   - What skills are required?

7. Who can help me?

   - Am I good at sales, management and production?
   - What friends and allies can I count on to help me?

8. What is the market for my product or service?

   - Who will buy what I am making or pay me to do it?
   - Where will I offer my product or service: in a local, international or virtual market?
   - How much do customers want to pay for this service?
   - What are the standard rates for the industry?
   (This is called market research: see Chapter 5)

9. Who are my competitors?

   - What services do they offer?
   - Are their customers happy?

10. Where will I get the money to start?

- Where will I get money now? A year from now? Two years from now?
- How long can I survive before I have to start generating income?
- What will my expenses be? (see Chapter 5)
- Which expenses can I eliminate or reduce?

11. What problems should I foresee?

- What could go wrong?
- What is most likely to go wrong, and how bad will this be?

12. How often will I need to revise my plan?
- What is my plan B in case things don't work?

13. What deadlines will I set for myself?

- What regulatory deadlines apply?
- When do I have to start selling?
- When will I start having income?
- What are the best- and worst-case scenarios I can foresee?

Do the questions sound overwhelming?

If they do, don't panic. This is why making a business plan is so important: it forces you take a hard, honest look at your business idea from all angles. A business plan can take several months to put together, but you can see why it's necessary. You will have to face all these questions at some point while you are running your business. It's better to have thought about them before you are in the middle of an emergency. You can't set out on a transatlantic sailing expedition without making sure you have enough food. Yet many people start a business without taking the time to think through how they will navigate the inevitable ups and downs. Although it can be hard on the self-esteem, think about the business plan like a professional version of Socrates's famous words: "know thyself."

Magical thinking does a lot of damage to businesses. It's very common to hear people say things like, "I'll find the money when I need it," or "I know people will buy this." But that kind of thinking is why only one in five companies survive their first five years of business. Optimism is a must when you start out, but blind ignorance is almost always fatal.

Of course, anyone can become a victim of their own wishful thinking. Very large companies survive on average only two or three generations, often because their leaders haven't anticipated problems that arise (like succession). Take the Reichmann brothers, Nortel, Steinberg's or Eaton's: many well-established companies ended up self-destroying because their projects were either not well thought out, overly ambitious, simply grandiose, over-financed or just poorly timed. Your business plan can help you avoid this. You need to smash those rose-coloured glasses so you can see things clearly.

You might have noticed that the list has few "yes or no" questions. There's a reason for that. When you are making a business plan, you have to rack your brain. The business plan forces you to either specialize or define a realistic approach to your field, one that will appeal to clients, banks and future partners. It also forces you to think of backup solutions in case your first idea fails. It forces you to really commit to your ideas.

Your business plan also has to be written down, not just thought over. There are three reasons for this:

1. Writing requires you to think in a disciplined way. Very few people can actually sit and think methodically without getting distracted and letting their thoughts wander. Just try thinking about a problem, sitting by yourself, without a pencil/keyboard at hand. What happens? You get distracted after about thirty seconds. Writing makes you commit to your ideas. It makes it possible to engage in prolonged analytical thinking without your mind running off on tangents. It requires effort, but it will save a lot of time in the long run.

2. Writing things down frees your mind. Nothing is more exhausting than trying to juggle a bunch of ideas in your head at the same time. Creating a document lets you nail down your ideas so you can avoid constantly questioning them and rethinking things as circumstances

change. It's a record of what you have thought and you can refer to these thoughts as you go along.

3. When things are written down, they can be shared with others. You can run your business plan by a consultant, friend or veteran worker in your area. That person can then comment on the plan and even challenge it. If you try to get that kind of feedback by talking in person, comments might come across as overly negative or just insensitive and make you uncomfortable. Writing gives you that little bit of distance you need.

The basic business plan

But be careful: don't let your business plan turn into a 500-page autobiography. The business plan is a tool to help you think. A detailed twelve- or thirteen-point business plan, like the example above, makes sense when you're looking for partners, associates or bank financing. If you are planning on working solo, the business plan really only needs to answer five basic questions:

- What?
- For whom?
- How much?
- How?
- To what end?

You can answer the rest of the questions as you're going along.

Don't be too rigid or detailed when you are writing your business plan. It shouldn't be treated as scripture. Many people actually succeed after they tear up their original business plan because it wasn't working. The business plan will also become outdated at some point, and the conditions under which it was written will change. Yet even in these cases, would the person who tore up their business plan have succeeded had they started without one? Probably not. The failure of the business plan forces you to approach your business a different way. When a new idea comes along, the business plan has to be adapted.

You will notice that the second question in the business plan is not about your business, but about your personal goals, what *you* want to do, what *your* dreams and aspirations are. The reason is, the thousands of choices you will make when you are self-employed—whether about big issues or small—will all be driven by your personal goals.

For instance, imagine you love social dance and want to make a living from it. Maybe you want to open a social dance school because you love to teach it, or because you're looking for a partner to teach it with. But maybe you want to become a social dance champion, or want your students to go to the social dance Olympics. Or maybe you really want to create the ultimate social dance shoe. Or maybe you want to run a multinational social dance company with franchises on five continents.

These are *all* legitimate reasons. But identifying your motives and your ultimate goal will guide all the choices you make when you are starting out, and, more importantly, as you go along. You will not choose your students the same way if you want them to win the social dance Olympics, as you would if you want to design and create a new social dance shoe. You can become a hairdresser because you want to run a small business on your own, or because you want to become Vidal Sassoon and revolutionize the hair-care industry. Either way, you should know before you start.

This question of personal goals is, well, personal. You are the only one who can decide on these. It's essential to know what those goals are and then to follow them. Take a good look at the people around you. A lot of people feel like they are standing still, going nowhere. That's usually because they are working towards goals that aren't their own, but those of their parents, or spouse or boss. When you are self-employed, you are your boss. Your goals are the only goals that matter.

Greek philosophy applied to the 21st century

Question 1 (What is my current situation?), question 4 (Am I cut out for this?) and question 6 (How will I go about it?) can be hard to answer. They force you to look objectively at your situation and ask yourself how you got there.

Although the goal of making a business plan is to get you to think about the future in concrete terms, there is an introspective element to the process that many people find unsettling. Do you really have the stuff to fly on your own wings, without a safety net? It's better to answer these questions before you start, because they will force themselves on you very quickly once you do start.

In addition to time and talent, succeeding as a self-employed worker requires good judgment and the ability to work alone. You won't have a supervisor organizing your days and telling you what to do. There will be no sales team to go out and shake clients down for money, or tech team to solve the glitches you are having with Zoom. You can't just mosey over to the office next door to get feedback on a submission or talk over a problem. You'll take coffee breaks alone.

This book, like many courses and support services, was written to help you anticipate and manage the challenges that come with being self-employed. But in order for a self-employed business to take off, you have to meet some basic requirements.

Imagine a Boeing 747. The jet is you, carrying your two children, but also your mortgage and a few debts. If the Boeing tries to take off on a runway designed for a Cessna, it will crash. To take off, the jet needs a long enough runway to be able to reach take off speed. The same goes for an aspiring self-employed worker: some training, research and advice could certainly help you get up to take off speed, but you still can't avoid basic facts about yourself and other constraints like the laws of gravity.

To succeed, you need talent, time, judgment and an ability to make decisions on your own. Willpower is essential, but it's not enough. You have to have ability. An aspiring jockey who is two meters tall and weighs 100 kilograms should consider a career breeding horses instead. An architect who doesn't like to draft will not enjoy their work. Of course, great architects all get other people to do the drafting for them anyway, but first they have to become great. And to do that, they need to have drafted. You won't become a great mortgage broker if you don't like working with numbers or talking to people.

And while talent is essential, you also need to back it up with a certain number of hard skills in public relations, sales, accounting, taxes, interior design, planning and so on. Luckily, these things can be learned.

However, if you don't have anyone to give you financial support, or don't have some capital saved up for the first year or two of your endeavour, you might want to rethink your plan. The only thing that might save you is landing a first big client as soon as you leave your job—but that rarely happens. You might consider getting a part-time job to put bread on the table for a while.

It will take time to get your business off the ground. And why wouldn't it? An engineering student works very hard during their studies only to be paid peanuts when they graduate and start working as a junior. But how could it work any other way? Society needs properly trained professionals who can build airplanes so they won't fall out of the sky. If a student fails an exam, they're not ready. Why would it be any different for a self-employed person who has to produce quality goods or services for clients who need them?

What we think about those studies on self-employed workers

Many reports have been made on the "insecure working conditions" of self-employed workers. It is a fact that many self-employed workers "struggle" financially. But it's worth asking: which self-employed workers are we talking about, exactly?

Many—we would even say most—self-employed people go into business for one of two reasons. They have either lost their jobs (or can't find one) or they want to "try something new," usually in a field they are not yet qualified to work in.

In either case, most beginning self-employed workers are looking at a learning curve that will last from six months to three years, even longer if they haven't yet mastered the required skills necessary in their field. These workers are financially insecure because they are still learning.

We don't need studies to tell us students are usually poor. Yet everyone knows the more people get educated, the better societies function. With rare exceptions, students don't stay students forever. The same thing goes for the self-employed: some succeed and start businesses that grow. Some succeed but go on to do something else. Some fail and go on to do something else.

When you think about it, every company in the world, even the biggest multinationals, started out as a successful self-employed worker. IBM and Apple are both good examples. These companies ended up being run by accomplished entrepreneurs or technocrats, but that doesn't change the fact that they all started out as self-employed businesses.

In other words, the vast majority of self-employed workers are in transition: they are experimenting and learning and will move on to something else, whether that's a new job or their own business. That means reports on the "insecurity" of the self-employed are skewed. They only look at all categories of self-employed workers as one, including those who are starting out, and those, like us, who deliberately stay small. Studies and reports on insecurity fail to look at the most spectacular success stories of the self-employed and those who have used the opportunity to do something else.

If you work as much as an engineering student studies, for five years, you will be able to earn as much as a salaried engineer does, provided, obviously, that you have talent. Also, if you succeed, you can be sure you will work more than your eight hours a day, like any successful engineer.

When Jean-Benoît started out as a freelance writer, Montreal had a weekly cultural magazine called *Voir* that paid him $20 per sheet of copy (about 8 cents a word). Jean-Benoît was very proud of this rate at the time. He managed to earn $2,000 in his first eight months of freelancing. Two thousand dollars! (As we mentioned earlier, it helped that he was in university, socializing with other students who were as poor as he was.) In reality that was peanuts, but he learned—a lot. He really didn't know much about journalism when he started out. A self-employed person who already knows their trade can certainly expect to earn more than $2,000 in the first year, provided they prepare ahead of time.

In short, if you really think you will make a fortune overnight, you're probably not serious about being self-employed. The first year, like Jean-Benoît, you may very well work for peanuts. And your first goal should be to earn enough to live. It won't be the Klondike, but if you can survive a year without champagne baths, you'll be fine after that—unless, of course, champagne baths are your goal. In which case, you should consider that when you're writing your business plan.

2

The Head Office

What you need to know about setting up a space

Myth #2: "I don't really need an office. I can work anywhere."

There are a lot of things to do before starting a business, but organizing the physical space of your office, workspace or workshop is one of the most important. The space you create will either make it easy to work, or make it hard. If you make the right choices, your office will put you in the mood to work. If you don't, it will be a thorn in your side. These are the "realities" you need to consider to make a workable workspace.

Getting the space right is crucial, especially if you work from home and have the challenges of separating work from life. If you are in that situation, you need to be able to send a strong signal to your spouse, partner and/or children that the office is not just another room in the house. No matter where you set it up, your workspace has to be a territory that you "stake out" as your own.

The location

To work at home or not to work at home. That is question, or at least the first question you have to answer.

A rented office makes a good impression on customers and can protect you from all sources of domestic interference: the sixteen-year-old who wants to use your printer, the spouse who wants your opinion on dinner plans, that sink full of dirty dishes that you think you can get rid of before your 2:00 meeting.

The drawback is cost: the outside office will have a considerable impact on your operating expenses. Bear in mind that offices rarely come with fridges or stoves, so renting a place might also add to your food costs if you end up ordering in, or eating out as a result.

Of course, there's also the option of the so-called virtual office: in theory, it only requires a computer, a phone and a seat at whatever café you fancy on any given day. We can recall the time, about twenty years ago, when everyone rhapsodized about "the paperless office," which is sort of the same idea. Now they're called virtual offices and could—again, in theory—exist inside a laptop, iPad or iPhone, with some help from the Cloud.

The paperless office turned out to be a bit elusive and the virtual office is pretty much an urban legend if you want our opinion. In our whole circle of self-employed friends, we only know one person who actually works from different locations without a home base—he travels between Hawaii, Montreal, Brazil and Germany with a laptop. However, he only works part time, doesn't have a family and does a job that mainly requires communicating. He doesn't make anything.

Very few of us have the personality, talent and inclination to work effectively week after week, constantly changing location. We know people who have tried it, but most realized they needed a minimum of office furniture and equipment in order to be productive day in, day out, year-round. Technological advances of the last ten years, particularly cloud computing, have slashed paperwork. But many self-employed workers also end up realizing they like a bit of routine more than they thought they would.

The bottom line is that wherever you work, you need to have a certain number of things on hand to do it efficiently and safely, not to mention comfortably. We have a twenty-nine-year-old colleague who's a bit of a bohemian: she didn't have a very good office and sort of worked anywhere. After a couple of years, she starting having serious back problems and actually became near-sighted—at age twenty-nine. She finally understood that she needed to take a hard look at her work habits and her office setup, spend some money and get a proper desk. If you work without an office, without a filing system or a decent chair or any kind of organized space, it eventually catches up with you, or at least your back. Without a decent office space, you will suffer and eventually your business will too.

The notion of a virtual or paperless office is also presented as a fashionable way to save money. Not surprisingly, it's almost always touted by people who sell computers but aren't self-employed themselves and don't know what it involves. Don't buy it. You need a physical space to run your business.

One option is to rent a space with some other self-employed workers. This has some added advantages, like giving you some built-in exposure (among colleagues and their contacts) and cutting down on the isolation that is the bane of many self-employed workers. Coworking spaces, which are essentially commercial co-ops, are, of course, becoming more and more popular (or bouncing back, anyway, after the pandemic sent their occupants scrambling back home). You can rent a work space and pay for any other services you need *à la carte*. These might include a reception desk, a secretary, data entry services, Internet access, office automation, translation, accounting, bookkeeping, bookbinding, a database, conference room, mail counter, courier, office supplies, kitchenette, security guard or parking. In most cases, you can take what is convenient for you and pass on the rest. But you may end up paying for services you don't need.

Although actual home offices are the least expensive option, include the comforts of home and in many ways are more convenient, they do have what could be two serious drawbacks, depending on your field. They don't look serious to outsiders the way a rented office does. And a home office will necessarily take up space in your house. Having a home office means a section of your house becomes off limits for everyone else you live with (because your office *really does have to be* off limits).

For many people, the low cost of running an office out of their house amply compensates for any drawbacks it entails. You can deduct some of the expenses related to your home from your income tax (see Chapter 18). The home office also offers the possibility of working in your pyjamas if that's your thing, reducing your monthly clothing bill. When we need to meet clients online, we put some clothes on our upper bodies and comb our hair. In extreme cases, we might invite someone in, in which case we have to tidy up the house: unmade beds are a no-no in most professional situations. If keeping tidy sounds like a hassle, you can set your home office up near the main entrance of your residence so clients will never see the rest of the house. But wherever you choose to work, remember that working from home requires some discipline, probably more than you think. Some home office workers even find they have to start their work day by taking a shower and putting on work clothes, just so they will feel like they're "going to work."

Home offices are also more suited for some businesses than others. Some types of self-employed workers, like lawyers, have no choice but to set up shop outside their home. For some reason people don't take lawyers seriously if they work out of their home. Maybe it's just TV, but we tend to associate law offices with swivel chairs, tailored suits and reception desks. There's also the fact that we feel like confidential conversations are better carried out in a professional space, not someone's house. Home offices are not ideal for engineers, either. Since their professional culture is very team-oriented, loners working from home will raise eyebrows among colleagues and customers. Inside the profession, they are dismissed as "basement engineers."

But there are a few tricks you can deploy to make working from home seem less makeshift. Some self-employed workers systematically have meetings in restaurants to avoid inviting clients in. Others use a post office box address, but you should be careful about this: it can sound sketchy to some. Another idea is to have your professional mail sent to a business centre that can also provide a receptionist and photocopying services, or courier and parcel delivery if you need it. And then there's one last trick, although this one requires a bit of acting talent: you can answer your phone in the voice of a secretary, put the call on hold and return with your normal voice. Probably not a viable long-term solution.

At any rate, before setting up a home office you should check your municipal by-laws. Some municipalities actually prohibit residents from running a home office. Most of these by-laws were put in place to prevent junkyards and escort services from popping up in "good" neighbourhoods. But they may apply to a graphic design business too.

The City of Toronto, for instance, has different rules for separate categories of businesses: group homes, music teachers, personal services (hairdressers, seamstresses) and so on. You can run a doctor's office, with certain restrictions; a dance studio but only in a detached house; you can't operate a kennel.

But even if there's no law forbidding home businesses where you live, doing so can be unpopular. Your neighbours will complain if your business makes garbage, noise, odours or if you park a tractor trailer in front of your house, for example. For information about by-laws, check online or call your city or, but whatever you do, don't supply your name. Then, if it turns out that you need a permit, remember that obtaining one is generally a matter knowing *how* to ask: for example, in some residential areas, jewellery making is prohibited, but not *artisanal* jewellery making. It's best to figure these nuances out ahead of time.

Generally speaking, if you use your home to carry out quiet, solitary work (like we do, as writers) no one will complain about you. If some neighbours grumble, you should use this as an opportunity to explain that working from home allows you to keep an eye on the neighbourhood and potentially ward off burglars or vandals. We're not making this up: years ago, Julie was sitting at her desk in the middle of the afternoon when she noticed a couple of teenagers trying to break into an apartment across the street and called the police. Living as we do in a snowy city, we have also been available to move our neighbour's car out of the path of snowploughs while she was at work, or accept delivery packages for her. As long as neighbours don't have unreasonable expectations of you, it can work for everyone.

Office decor

It's always possible to decorate your home office on a shoestring budget, but you should carefully consider the pros and cons of this. If you are going to have customers or suppliers visiting your office on a frequent basis, appearances will count a lot. Even if you are planning to do most of your business online, people are going to see where you work. Where home offices are concerned, the advent of mass video-conferencing has turned previously hidden horrors into universal eyesores.

But no matter how much you spend—or don't—on office decor, no one wants to see you working on the kitchen table between stacks of plates. Temporarily working on a makeshift desk during a pandemic is not the same thing as running your office out of your house. If you're teaching small groups at home, you should set up a separate classroom. If you are running a consulting service for business executives, you should probably be ready to shell out $15,000 for some slick office furnishings. Some clients might even want to see your office before they sign a contract with you, just to get a sense of how legit you are. Most of all, it's important to think of how your office will look ahead of time, not when you are in the middle of giving your webinar on recent trends in the real estate market.

However, remember that when it comes to offices, "beauty" is rather relative. Some clients are put off by lavishly decorated offices. It's like when hairdressing salons splurge on marble sinks and offer you espresso: you know that's going to be added to the price of your haircut. Julie has switched hair salons because of the "espresso tax": if your decorating choices come across as overly luxurious, clients may run from you too. Original artwork on the wall behind your desk sends a message. Just make sure it's the message you want to send. So before you head to IKEA, think about what your clients will expect and what will probably make them comfortable. Who knows, maybe a state-of-the-art office is less appealing than having an aquarium in your office—some Asian cultures, for that matter, consider fish a sign of good luck. In short, when you're putting together a workspace you should aim for "suitable" rather than "beautiful."

We moved on a regular basis when we were in our 30s, running around the planet following fellowships and researching books, so were constantly setting up new office spaces in new places. Jean-Benoît boiled it down to a science, scavenging the streets of whatever city we were living in for tables and shelves, or things he could turn into tables and shelves. Though functional, our jerry-rigged work spaces were pretty ugly. They were composed mainly of items we acquired on garbage day. At the time, we figured it didn't really matter. It was before video-conferencing and as self-employed writers, we rarely, if ever, invited outsiders into our offices. So, from a business perspective, spending money on aesthetics was just not a good investment.

Our ideas changed as we got older, and for equally legitimate reasons, as you'll see.

Creating an image

After comfort and functionality, "seriousness" should be your guiding principle to create a workspace.

What defines successful people? They all look "serious." Customers evaluate your seriousness at a glance. So, what does a "serious" office look like? It doesn't require expensive art on the walls. Mostly, it means looking like you are organized to do whatever you do. It should look permanent. Improvising an office space is not serious.

Once upon a time—actually, not that long ago—we told young journalists that to look serious, they should carry a conspicuous scheduling tool, like an agenda. That might be going out of style with the advent of online calendars, but it still doesn't hurt. Whether you choose an electronic or paper agenda is up to you. Personally, we have stuck to paper agendas over the years. People laugh at flip phones, but surprisingly, paper agendas still command respect. They even have a certain nerdy coolness to them. The other reason we like our little booklet agendas is that they give our eyes a break from screens—and frankly, you can pull out an agenda and scribble down a time, date and address more quickly than you can create a calendar invite on a smartphone. But basically, it's up to each individual and entirely dependent on the image you are trying to project.

Which brings us back to the question of offices. After spending years working in very practical, often makeshift offices that "did the job," we decided to change our tack in 2007. Having adopted twin girls from Haiti the previous Christmas, we decided to take advantage of parental leave and build an annex on the back of our house. We opted for an open, airy space that we would share. Instead of our traditional dumpster-dive decor, we took the leap and hired a carpenter to build us custom desks and bookshelves out of Russian plywood. At moments it felt like we were living beyond our means, but then we reminded ourselves that the real motivation for having custom-built furniture was to make the most out of a relatively small working space of twenty square metres. That often counts for something when you work at home. In our case, it was worthy paying someone more gifted with spatial organization than we are to come up with good ideas about how to make the most out of a small space. In the end, the furniture cost us $3,000, which was less than our new website. And our office really is quite smart-looking, for a change.

But even today, we think it's smarter for most freelancers to invest in good software tools (like the proofreading software Antidote and Quicken for book keeping) and good desk chairs, than to indulge in expensive office furnishings. The new office is a pleasant place to work and looks more professional than past versions. But its main qualities are still: it's comfortable, functional and has lots of light (our architect gets the credit for that).

In general, when it comes to furnishing an office, self-employed workers are better to err on the side of modest: there's nothing sadder than watching a great restaurant close after six months because the owner overdid it on chic decor. Atmosphere is important, but not if the food doesn't follow. Same thing goes for the home office. Unless your office is, itself, a sales tool, you're probably better off spending your money on marketing than on a mid-century modern coffee table.

That said, you should never compromise on personal comfort. No one should spend eight hours a day on a folding chair in a dark corner of a small room squinting to read a screen that's too small. You're the boss, so give yourself the respect you deserve. Work somewhere pleasant, with a good window and, if possible, a balcony. It's the least you can do. Offices should be pleasant-feeling places because they are, after all, where you're going to spend most of your waking hours.

If you're short on ideas, hiring an office designer is not too onerous: they charge about $150 per room and can come up with economical, aesthetic and ergonomic solutions to many problems. You can also get ideas for inexpensive solutions from office furniture rental companies.

The starting point is a dedicated room or well-defined nook. Having a space exclusively devoted to work is what allows you to concentrate on whatever you are doing. Tax authorities also prefer to see a separate room for your rent deductions. Having a defined office space also provides your spouse, children and friends with build-in boundaries and reminds them that even though you work at home, that doesn't mean you are on call to run out to the drugstore (or the liquor store) at the drop of a hat.

Once you have your space, the first thing you will need is a table or desk with a good surface area, well-arranged lamps (on the left if you are right-handed . . .) and a good chair. Many people are seated more comfortably in their car than they are at their desk: a $600 ergonomic chair, which can be tilted, swivelled and rotated, might seem expensive at first, but, trust us, it's money well spent. It will save you much more in chiropractor bills down the road.

Having some sort of small cabinet for your printer is also ideal. The printer should not be on your desk. Even the best ones are noisy and make it hard to hear people talking during phone calls or videoconferencing. Also, no matter what the people who sell computers tell you, there is no such thing as a paperless office. We have five filing cabinets of different sizes where we keep correspondence, research files, tax files and routine paperwork. Maybe it looks old-fashioned, but it makes our office neater and more functional. Although we receive far fewer letters than we used to, the amount of mail coming in each week is still impressive.

Because like everyone, we are ultra-dependent on our Wi-Fi networks and electronics in general, we have made keeping an eye on the electrical supply part of our office management routine. With at least a half dozen different electrical devices in your office, you need to make sure you have a good power supply. A dedicated power line is best. Now is not the time for your printer to stall because your eight-year-old blew a circuit doing an experiment with lightbulbs. At the very least, use power bars with quality surge protectors for all your equipment: it would be a shame if you accidentally fried your hard drive when lightning stuck a nearby transformer.

Communications tools

Communications tools have evolved more quickly than any other aspect of the home office over the last twenty-five years. Jean-Benoît recently had a hilarious exchange with a receptionist at McGill University, our alma mater. When he called to get a copy of his transcript, the receptionist asked him for his McGill email address to identify him. Jean-Benoît, who graduated in 1992, explained to the receptionist that email hadn't yet been invented when he was at McGill. Having grown up with email, she couldn't seem to get her head around that.

Everyone over forty today has first-hand experience of the series of upheavals the communications world has gone through over the last three decades. We actually sent our first magazine articles to editors by fax. Email didn't become a regular tool in our business until 1995. Cell phones only became common in the second half of the 1990s and smartphones, only in 2012. Over that period the concept of "a computer" expanded into hybrid tools that includes a keyboard, a phone, a camera, an agenda, an entertainment system so much more.

When will all these wild transformations slow down? No one knows, but Jean-Benoît has a theory that they will peak, functionally. History is a good indicator. If you look at early pictures of cars, they evolved from horse carts into the familiar car shape over a generation and a half. Designs are still evolving (or regressing, depending on your point of view) but the basic shape of a car isn't being revolutionized any more. Computers and mobile phones evolved from typewriters, TVs and landline phones over a generation and a half as well, so while they are bound to get faster and more powerful, this might be where we get with the basic technology and design.

That's good news for people who work at home. For once, we will be able to buy a shoe that fits and wear it for the next ten years, instead of having to throw it out as soon as the next model arrives. It will be nice to not have to update and revolutionize our communications tools every six months.

The Zoom (or FaceTime) invasion

It's important to think about Zoom, Teams and FaceTime when you are putting together a home office. If people didn't use these tools much before 2020, they sure do now. Video conferencing is a great alternative to long-distance phone calls (as well as travelling) and is certainly here to stay.

As many people in improvised home office-setting discovered, videoconferencing is easy and cheap, but it has the drawback of being incredibly invasive. Strangers who live hundreds or thousands of kilometres away suddenly get to see how you look, dress and the conditions in which you live, up-close. They get to hear your family dog barking in the background whether they want to or not. Everything in the camera's range (plus the noises in the range of your microphone) becomes elements of the image you are projecting. Phones had their limitations, but at least they had the advantage of not exposing your environment to outsiders. With Zoom, everything is on display unless you turn off your camera and mic. And you can't always do that.

So, think carefully of what people will see behind you when you are putting together an office. If your workspace is in the living room, consider putting a room divider or screen behind your desk to limit sneak peeks of your loved ones coming and going during online calls or meetings. Virtual backgrounds are a great solution but as we discovered during the pandemic, not all computers have enough processing capacity to create them, and they can be distracting. Tropical beach scenes rarely send the right message during business calls.

And they don't eliminate noise. Visuals won't be a problem if you use Zoom with only the mic turned on, but keep in mind that your computer's built-in, omni-directional microphone will pick up and sometimes amplify other sounds in your home—even a head-set doesn't completely solve this.

A self-employed person's communication tools are not radically different than those of an average person these days. Chances are you already have a computer, a high-speed Internet connection, a smartphone and perhaps a telephone with a landline (we've hung onto ours for its reliability). Those are the basics.

Will you need more? It's a matter of the image you want to project, but it's also a practical question.

The key is to buy just enough equipment so you can work efficiently, and not to end up being over-equipped. The "looking serious" factor should only apply to what your customers receive, or see. The self-employed worker who banks on impressing their clients by spending $10,000 on state-of-the art office equipment—without first thinking about what they need—may be in for a disappointment. Ask yourself, will your customers know, or care, if you are using a ten-year-old desk phone or computer? Probably not. Generally, what matters most is that your equipment does its job.

But a landline, seriously? In our case, it makes sense. We are frequently interviewed on radio and we also interview people ourselves. Nothing beats a landline for sound quality and reliability.

That said, having reliable office electronics is a must. You won't last without your computer, printer or scanner for very long. These are likely to be among your biggest investments. Still, you should start by identifying your needs and evaluating your skills (notably, in trouble shooting and fixing computer problems).

We once purchased a colour printer/scanner/fax machine, then spent many years hiring technicians to repair it. The machine was so big we nicknamed it "the dishwasher." After multiple breakdowns, and after we had spent hundreds of dollars on expensive printer cartridges, we decided to reassess our needs. How important was colour printing to our business? In the end, not very. So, the last time the "dishwasher" broke down, we replaced it with a smaller, less expensive black-and-white model that doesn't use nearly as many cartridges and still does 99% of what we need day-to-day. And we saved space: it's more like the size of a microwave oven.

Computers have brought about a revolution that is as important as the automobile once did, with one difference: if your car needs to be repaired, you can take it to a garage. It's never that simple with computers. Few can figure out what's wrong with a computer when it freezes or breaks down, let alone fix it. Computer viruses generally require treatment by a specialist. Our solution has for many years been to purchase our computers through an excellent, friendly, reliable technician who sets them up for us and whom we can call whenever we have problems. We pay him for his time but he gets back to us and usually solves our problems the same day. Compared to ten years ago, you can solve a lot of software problems over the phone, or through videoconferencing or TeamViewer. The hard part is finding someone who will pick up the phone and help you in the middle of a crisis. And let's face it, when the computer doesn't work, it is a crisis. So, it's worth having someone who can do that and staying in their good books.

Computer choices are personal. We've always preferred Mac over PC. The machines cost more, but they are more reliable and much less vulnerable to viruses (and we have our Mac technician friend to fix them if there is a problem). We did use PCs for five years, but, having "grown up" in the sheltered world of Apple electronics, we resented the viruses and all the choices we had to make about software with our PCs. The PC is a hacker technology. We felt like we wasted a lot of valuable work hours attending to security risks.

That said, the Mac environment works well for us because we are in an industry where everyone else uses Mac. The drawback with Macs used to be that some software, like FileMaker (database management) or the accounting software like Quicken didn't work as well as they did on the PC, but Apple has solved that in recent years with special versions (the Mac version for Quicken is wonderful).

We've always found it was worth investing in a good printer and scanner. It is almost impossible to work without a scanner these days. Faxes (thankfully) seem to have finally become extinct. For a long time, our philosophy was to have separate devices for printing, faxing (at the time) photocopying and scanning. That's mostly because of Julie's childhood: her father, a mechanic, warned her about machines that do too many things, like integrated entertainment systems. "If one part breaks the whole thing might as well be broken," he told her. But Julie grew up in a big house where there was room to have a lot of machines doing different things. That has never been the case in a single moment of her adult life. We have never had space to spare. And at any rate, printers these days do almost everything you need, anyway: print, scan and photocopy. That helped Julie to get over her hang-up with multifunctioning machinery and we adopted the all-in-one printer.

Whatever technology you use, make sure you back it up. Too many self-employed workers neglect good backup systems. This is a MUST. It's amazing how many people overlook, or actually skimp on proper backup systems. They often live to regret their oversight. When our external hard drive recently gave up the ghost, we had the choice of switching to a cloud-based system for doing backups or buying another external hard drive. Our much-appreciated computer technician recommended we buy an external hard drive. That's what he uses and he runs a computer business. It turned out to be the simplest, most affordable solution for us as well. (See why we love him?) In our case, it made sense for two reasons. First, we work 95% of the time from home. Second, the highest risk of data loss for us is not from fires, but from computer breakdowns. If you are not sure which direction to go, ask other people in your industry what they use.

In some fields, it's even a good idea to have a battery pack and a small power generator on hand, especially if you are working from an area where the power supply is unreliable. Remember that when you're employed by a company, it's the boss—or property manager—who takes care of the generator and backups. Now you're the boss so it's on you!

Finally, if there's one thing that we've learned over decades of experience with office electronics and connectivity, it's that things only work well . . . when they work. A computer scientist friend once told us:

electronics are 100% reliable, but they only work about three quarters of the time. A quarter of the time they cause headaches. He was exaggerating a bit, but we live by his words anyway. Computer bugs, breakdowns and mysterious malfunctions happen, sometimes at the worst moments. The volume on a computer stops working when we're about to launch Zoom for an important magazine interview, or the printer gives up two days before a book deadline when we are in the middle of doing page edits. Something that was working beautifully suddenly turns into an ugly mess. It happens. To everyone. Reliability should be your top criterion when you are shopping for electronic equipment for your office. And if you ever replace a device that's not broken, make sure you keep the old one around just in case. It's another good reason to put a few filing cabinets in your office.

QUESTIONS FROM READERS

Self-employed with children

How does it work when you have kids?

Everyone is a prisoner of time, but for self-employed workers with children, time can be a fearsome enemy.

That's what Jean-Benoît learned in 2006, when we adopted our twin daughters, who were three-and-a-half-years old. After twenty years of working on his own, Jean-Benoît would spend the next five years in a state of professional shock.

Don't get us wrong: being parents is extraordinary. Our lives started operating on a new logic that had nothing to do with success, or money—you don't become a parent for either. Still, Jean-Benoît (more than Julie) found that kids turned his habits upside down. Adapting his schedule to school hours, the demands of making meals, packing lunches, organizing school trips, handling school holidays—every element of the new time-management regime was a challenge for him.

Things have improved radically in recent years as the girls have become more independent and Jean-Benoît can work eight-hour days without (too) much interruption.

We both had to form new habits in the early years but it was extra challenging for Jean-Benoît because his best, most productive hours are in the early morning, between 6 and 9 a.m. As we would discover, these are peak service hours for parents with school-aged children. Our kids always had to be at school by 8 a.m. Before that, we had to wake them up, feed them breakfast, make sure they were dressed for the elements (quite the undertaking when you live in Montreal) and supply them with a nutritious lunch. Sure, one parent could have done that alone, but who wants to systematically miss seeing their kids in the morning?

Adjusting to kids was a little less of a struggle for Julie since early mornings were not her prime work time. But we both had to reorganize our workday and work in conditions we didn't always control. (And every summer when the girls went to camp, we instantly reverted to our old ways.)

By a strike of good fortune, a self-employed neighbour of ours was in exactly the same situation at the same time (in fact, we had coincidentally adopted girls from the same orphanage in Haiti, who arrived within a few months of each other). So we improvised a sort of childcare "kibbutz" between the three of us: during the summer the girls could roam freely between the two houses, keeping themselves busy so we could spread out the responsibility for watching over them. They went to the same day camp so only one of us had to go pick them up. It was informal, but practical and the girls wouldn't have had it any other way.

The challenges of working independently with kids aren't the same for everyone. Many people are already parents when they become self-employed. If that's your case, count yourself lucky in one way: you are pre-adapted. You won't have to endure the effects—torments, for some—of the parental metamorphosis. But the lack of pre-existing structure may be more of a challenge for you, especially if you're used to it.

In any case, don't fall into the trap of thinking it's easier to raise kids with a schedule you control. Few self-employed workers actually control their whole schedule. You won't be able to make do without childcare of some sort, whether it's a nanny (our choice when the girls were very young), shared childcare (like our kibbutz system), daycare (which we also used part-time) or an available relative (we had that blessing too). We went back to work full time ten months after the girls arrived and hired a part-time nanny to come three days a week, but kids are kids and there were still interruptions.

If you are working at home, it's crucial to set limits on your working hours. As important as it is to block time away from kids to work, you need to be able to see your kids without being constantly interrupted by work. When we're with our girls, we're never working. We don't answer the phone if we know it's a work call and we don't attend to work emails—or we keep it to an absolute minimum anyway, just handling emergencies and urgent issues. We also have a policy of never talking about work in front of the kids unless it's educational for them, or just interesting, like when we interview a Governor General, or the Premier, or a rapper. We are disciplined about respecting those limits so that the girls, in turn, respect the fact that we are working and can't solve a problem they are having with an app during office hours. They know they can come into the office for a limited number of things, like picking up something from the printer, or telling us they are going out. Otherwise, they don't even tell us when they get home from school (we put a jingle on the door so we could hear them come in).

Guarding your work territory does take a certain amount of work. Children are an invasive species. They need to be taught, very young, not to touch the computers without asking us first. Young children will quickly delete documents, invoices, PowerPoint presentations or customer accounts if you let them.

It takes a while for kids to get the hang of work-at-home parents. Our biggest problem when they were small was that they constantly "borrowed" our office equipment: pens, pencils, scissors, Scotch tape and staplers were highly coveted items. We stocked the kitchen with three pairs of scissors so they would go there first. As they got older, phone chargers and USB keys disappeared without a trace. We started putting labels on the cords but USB keys and phone chargers are endangered species in our home.

Jean-Benoît once lost track of his stapler for an entire month. He searched the basement, the girls' bedroom, the living and dining rooms and even the bathroom, but to no avail. When he asked the girls about it, they responded with the classic: "We didn't take it."

Really.

Eventually Jean-Benoît gave up and bought a new stapler. Then, three months later, one of the girls brought the original stapler back to the office.

"Where was it?" he asked.

"At the neighbour's," she answered, as if that was self-explanatory.

As the twins morphed into teenagers, the problem went from office supplies to telecommunications. It took years to solve that one. When you work at home with kids, it's best to have a dedicated phone line for your business (although people, of course, have less and less "phone lines" to begin with). Children answering phones can really throw customers for a loop.

The other challenge children bring, of course, is financial. Kids cost a lot. To afford them when you're self-employed, you have to accomplish the difficult feat of earning more without working more. You won't have more hours—except from the time you used to spend commuting. This is a challenge for anyone working in a business that bills by the hour. You'll have to increase your rates.

We are fortunate in our business, the writing trade, because of something called intellectual property. Thanks to royalties, our books continue to earn revenue for us long after we've stopped working on them. We still have to put in hours promoting them, but not nearly as much as we do to get them published in the first place.

But it's not all uphill. An old friend of ours, a well-known actor, had his children quite young, while he was still starting out. We thought that took guts, but he used to drag out the old expression, "Every baby come with a loaf of bread under their arm." We thought that was a bit corny until we had kids and realized it was true. There's no magic at work. What happens is that when you are a parent feeding kids, you develop a kind of killer attitude. You don't have time to waste fooling around. Each hour we spend at our desks is hard-earned and precious, and has to pay off. Basically, with kids, we had to stop working on things that weren't worth it from a business perspective. That meant choices. We had to give up certain clients who just didn't pay enough.

It was only later that we realized we could have made these choices earlier in our careers, anyway. Our actor friend was right: our daughters really did arrive with a loaf of bread under their arms.

3

Brainstorming

How to build strong ideas

Myth #3: "My idea is so good it will sell itself."

Mr Freelance: *Hello, Madam President, I'm calling to offer my services.*
Ms President-of-a-Large Company: *Really, and what would those services be, exactly?*
Mr Freelance: *Well, um . . .*
Click.

This conversation was over before it even started. Ms President isn't going to wait around on the phone while Mr Freelance figures out how to explain what he wants to sell to her.

Self-employed workers need to be able to define what they do before they start selling. If you are working in Flin Flon, where the pool of communications consultants is probably rather small, you might get away with presenting yourself to potential clients as a "communications specialist." People might be willing to let you explain what you do and what you have to offer them. But if you live in a city where "communications specialists" grow on trees, presenting yourself as "a communicator" or "a communications consultation" is just inviting your potential client to quickly end the call.

So, you are, indeed, a communications specialist. What do you communicate about? What kind of consulting do you offer? What sets you apart? You need answers to these questions. This is the first step in putting together a solid business plan.

The challenge is to make sure you stand out, but just enough. You need to be able to fit into a category and match a known need. Consider a potato grower. Potatoes are the perfect example of an undifferentiated good. They grow everywhere but in Antarctica. Some years, growers in P.E.I. end up with so many potatoes they have to throw out half of their crop to avoid flooding the market and driving down prices. In business lingo, the potato is a "commodity," a basic good that is sold by the ton. But people who buy potatoes usually need a specific type of potato. So, a grower will offer potatoes that are washed, sorted by size, pre-cut, pre-pealed, pre-baked or fried.

The McCain brothers really got this concept. Instead of selling dirty potatoes in twenty-five kilogram bags for $10 each, they figured out how to sell French fries in one kilogram bags for $3 each. Of course, McCain's competitors eventually figured this out and started making their own French fries. But that didn't stop McCain's, who then introduced "wavy" fries and other variations on the theme. When those weren't enough to stay ahead of the competition, McCain's started making frozen pizzas. And so on. Business magazines call this phenomenon, "value-added." The price of potatoes is no longer based on supply or even on the size of the tubers. It's based on how much people want them and how much they're willing to pay to get them.

A self-employed worker cannot afford to just be a "commodity," or just one undifferentiated potato among others. You need to be a specialty, like the frozen pizza, which has a lot of value added.

Martin, a childhood friend of Jean-Benoît's, started his own business a few decades ago after thinking the idea over for years. He did well to take his time and think it over carefully, because he had two children to feed and a mortgage to pay by that time. A skilful man, Martin wanted to build custom furniture for the self-care industry. He didn't have a specific idea, he just wanted to match his skills to a product. After much soul-searching (and research), he narrowed his field down to designing and producing wooden cases that travelling nurses could use to carry their instruments—his wife was in the business so he knew there was a need for them. It was such a good idea that one distributor he consulted during his research offered to sign an exclusive contract with Martin before he had even seen the prototype of the case. It's a very specific product for a very niche market but it turned out people needed it and were willing to pay for it.

So, what exactly makes an idea "good"?

The question is not as naive as it probably sounds. Ideas are a dime a dozen. But some are better than others. The only criterion for a good idea is: it has to be INTERESTING, both for you and for your client. A bad idea might find a buyer anyway, but the buyer will pay considerably less for it than they would for a good idea. A good idea will take you further than the most powerful network of friends will. You will recognize it by the excitement it generates when you talk about it. You will find yourself scrambling to find your tablet or a notepad to jot down notes about your idea that come to you while you're eating breakfast. Soon after that, you'll be writing a business plan about your idea and talking about it even more. Just don't forget to protect it (more on that in Chapter 4).

One of the best "good ideas" stories we ever heard came from Quebec entrepreneur Paul Gallant. It was good enough to get a business magazine interested in it, which is how we heard about (we both ended up writing stories on it). In the mid-1980s, Paul Gallant was working as a small international TV merchandizing consultant—already a pretty good niche. This micro-business was working well. But one day Gallant stumbled on a strange new material, a kind of flexible styrofoam that didn't break or crumble. Gallant realized he had in his hands the perfect material to solve a problem he'd been grappling with for years: he wanted to design and produce three-dimensional puzzles. It took Gallant one evening to design the assembly system, which he quickly patented. The company that he created to sell the puzzles, Wrebbit, had its heyday in the 1990s. It hit a snag around 2000, but expanded again after 2013. The ups and downs, which are inevitable in any business, didn't change the fact that Gallant's idea was a great one to start with.

The three-dimensional puzzle is an example of inventiveness, but you can have an excellent idea for a service, as well. Just take a look at the membership list of any association of self-employed workers: it will include members who sell high-end shoes in old people's homes, rent board games and host game nights, record books in digital audio format, write estimates and supervise construction sites, cook traditional meals for people in their homes. For that matter, before Paul Gallant hit the jackpot with his 3D puzzles, he earned a comfortable living with an interesting niche of his own: designing derivative products for television.

A good idea must be an idea you like. You have to be happy working on it. You can't be in it for the money, alone. If you're working strictly for money, you should get a job.

For that matter, it's no coincidence that many freelancers start out doing something they used to do as a hobby. Are you passionate about photography or baking muffins? Think about it and think about what might be missing in the market. You probably know a fair bit about the market already, because it's your hobby.

But you should really do something you love. A computer scientist who spends all her free time building beautiful furniture will gain a lot by following her passion, as opposed to being an "okay" computer scientist (unless, of course, she's primarily motivated by money). If you enjoy the outdoors, plus sewing, a repair service for camping equipment could turn out to be a very good business, especially as the ecological benefits of repairing things (as opposed to throwing them out) become more prominent in consumers' minds.

You can also look at it this way: why would anyone try to develop an uninteresting idea when there are so many good interesting ideas to be had? We learned as business journalists that companies have trouble finding employees who can do mental math. It appears that calculators have made us all forget our multiplication tables. Why not start a company that teaches mental arithmetic? People write books about it. It wouldn't require much investment and could turn out to be a great business.

But even very good ideas take a lot of work to get off the ground. You can't just pull good ideas out of a hat. Thomas Edison, the father of both the light bulb and the phonograph, famously said that "genius is 1 percent inspiration and 99 percent perspiration." It takes a lot of thought and effort to come up with a sensible and feasible idea and turn it into a business plan. The three-dimensional puzzle is a great example of good idea, but as we learned when we were writing about it, Paul Gallant had mulled the basic concept for ten years before he found the material he needed to make it happen. It was the same story with Joseph-Armand Bombardier, who invented the snowmobile. Bombardier spent thirteen years (from 1922 to 1935) working on the concept of a mechanical dogsled design but it took another twenty-four years before he found an engine that was both light and reliable enough to equip a small single-seat snowmobile. And so, the Ski-Doo was born, in 1959.

Three approaches to creativity

Creativity comes about via three different processes: analytical, synthetic and iterative.

The analytical approach starts from the cause of a problem (e.g. a headache) and finds a solution (e.g. acetylsalicylic acid, which stops the pain). The synthetic approach takes an idea and figures out what problem it can solve: for instance, someone discovers a new molecule and it turns out to be a miracle cure for headaches. Successful pharmaceutical companies use both these approaches simultaneously.

The third approach is called iterative (referring to repetition): you create a new product or idea through trial and error, by making changes as you go along. Computer programmers are familiar with this approach: by tinkering with existing software, they sometimes end up with a whole new piece of software or a new version of the old software. The book you are reading is a good example of how iterative creativity works. The second edition was slightly different than the first edition (published in 1998) and the third edition was a bit different from the second. This version is a quite different from the third edition because it has been translated and adapted from the original French work and includes Julie's input and experience. So because of iterations, this edition is no longer really similar to the original one. But it also wouldn't exist without the original one.

Every creator puts these three approaches to use in varying degrees. What this means is that in your day-to-day life as a self-employed person, you will no longer listen to a program, read an article or visit a trade show as a mere consumer. Instead, you will develop an insider's eye and a killer instinct about everything out there that relates to your project.

If you are going into advertising, you can no longer ignore commercials on TV or go get a snack while they are running. You'll need to be listening to and comparing commercials to understand what works and what doesn't, and imagining how you might do things differently. It's your job to come up with new ideas that your future clients and associates will love.

A smart person is an informed person. Whenever we hear people complain about "not getting enough information" about something, we wonder whether they have a newspaper delivered or subscribe to an online information source. It's amazing how many people don't adopt the easiest technique for staying informed (i.e. reading what's out there). No one is born knowledgeable: you get that way by making sure you get information. Informed people inform themselves. This quality is essential for the self-employed worker. You can't afford to be clueless, especially about anything that might affect your business.

When you start to get informed, of course, you realize that the number of articles out there on any given subject is absolutely colossal. Industrial spies today don't use special techniques. They just read a lot. Turn to experts in your field to "curate" it for you. Visiting or subscribing to the newsletter of a specialized web site in your field will keep you up to date on the latest news and probably most significant trends in your area. We religiously read the newsletters of the writers', freelancer writers' and journalists' associations to which we belong. They follow the most recent developments in their fields.

Naturally, you'll need to organize your information. That requires some discipline and a method, but it's mostly a matter of getting into the habit. Are you interested in Chinese medicinal plants? Clip (or save) and file articles you find about them or save them as PDFs in a special folder. Even if the information you collect doesn't turn out to be key to your specific project, staying up to date on news is important. If nothing else, your clients need to see you as someone who is proactive and well informed.

The Iceberg Theory

Exactly how much research do you need to do? Can you overdo it? The iceberg principle should help you decide. During a break one afternoon at a convention in St. John's, Newfoundland, Jean-Benoît craned his neck to see an iceberg floating near the harbour. He was astonished by this mammoth, dazzlingly white beauty that looked like a floating tower. Of course, the really amazing thing was how little of it he was actually looking at. Research is like the part of the iceberg that's underwater. To keep your project afloat, you need to have a hefty amount of research under the water supporting it. If it turns out that the original idea wasn't the right one, the research can morph into another project. The iceberg analogy fits this too: when they become unstable, icebergs topple and take on a different form.

The project of a poorly informed person runs the risk of sinking like the Titanic—whose design flaws only became apparent after it sunk. You are going to have a hard time doing PR in the pharmacology business if you don't read up on human biology: if you don't know what an enzyme is, your clients won't trust you. Scientists, like all specialists, quickly assess the knowledge base of people they talk to. You don't need to be a specialist yourself, but you should master the basic concepts, even if you are being hired by people in a specific field to communicate their information to an outside audience.

A graphic designer hoping to land a contract in the pharmacology sector should review their biology lessons as well. They should know what a mitochondrion looks like. A hairdresser who understands what the ingredients of dye are, as well as how they interact—even if that doesn't change how it's used—will earn the confidence of their customers. Customers faced with an obviously uninformed provider will end up wondering if the person is even interested in what they're doing.

The same would be true for information technology, or any technology for that matter. It's sometimes a matter of knowing the jargon: in the writing world, we often have to interview engineers. Their technical and scientific training is the antithesis of what journalists do (we synthesize information and boil it down to what's understandable). As a result, engineers seldom trust us. They aren't entirely wrong: journalists tend to be weak in science and math. So to compensate for this and get engineers to trust us, we make sure we learn at least some of the basics about their fields before interviewing them (this also makes our questions better). For example, when we started writing about hydroelectricity, we made sure we understood the difference between "energy" and "power": 99% of journalists confuse the two concepts, which, in the field, is akin to not knowing the difference between a waterfall and a lake. Over the years we've seen that when we do our research and acquire a bit of knowledge about a field, engineers—and all specialists for that matter—trust us more. As result, they loosen up and talk more freely, which makes our job easier.

That said, you need to set limits on your research too. It's important not to pour all your time and energy into gathering information—which is, after all, the passive part of starting—and not have any left over for the active part of running a business, like knocking on doors, approaching new clients, breaking into markets, preparing pitches. If you don't know where to stop, you run the risk of over-researching and even losing focus on your goal. Remember, there are two types of research: the research you do about your field and your market and the research you need to do to get the job done. The first type of research is encyclopaedic: you need to be interested in learning about the field for its own sake, including who its main players are. The research you need "to do the job" means gathering the knowledge you need to fulfil the contract you have or are trying to get. And stopping once you have a little bit more than enough.

Testing your idea in sixteen steps

So, you have a good idea and you are doing the research you need to make it viable. The next question is: does it meet a need? Does the consumer want a snowmobile that can climb cliffs? Or a turkey recycling service?

Probably not. So here are the questions you need to ask in order to test an idea:

1. Is the potential market small or large?
2. Is it a physical or a virtual market? Local or foreign?
3. Is this market growing or shrinking?
4. What's the expected lifespan of this product, this service?
5. Will it become outdated quickly?
6. Will I be able to develop other products or services based on this idea?
7. Is my idea revolutionary?
8. Will my customer require special training to be able to use my product?
9. Is my idea dependent on another product? (e.g. like the CD depended on the CD player.)
10. What economic, emotional and human needs will it fulfil?
11. How do competing ideas on the market work?
12. Should my advertising be aimed at a few, or a lot of customers?
13. Will I need an elaborate distribution network?
14. Will I have to comply with standards and/or obtain permits?
15. What are the shortcomings of similar ideas on the market?
16. How many people/companies can benefit from this idea before it loses its value?

To answer these questions, you will have to interview potential customers or future competitors. You might hesitate, thinking it's bad form to ask a potential customer for their opinion. But don't worry, it's perfectly acceptable. You are not asking anyone for a job. You just want to find out what they want or expect, so you can figure out how to best meet that need. When the time comes to sell your product, a professional, well-informed approach will be invaluable. Some people may refuse to answer your questions; others will gladly take the time to help you out. If you have friends in your field, get their feedback. The same goes for associations and chambers of commerce. You'll be surprised how willing people are to help someone with energy and a great idea.

Sometimes it doesn't take a lot of effort to establish a trusting relationship. When Julie started her freelance writing career, she reached out to other experienced writers and editors who, like her, worked in both French and English. It's a pretty small group, so she didn't have trouble finding them. Perhaps because bilingual writers are such a small niche in the writing field, the ones she spoke to were uniformly interested in a young writer joining their ranks and in talking about their rather unique skills. One editor Julie contacted even invited her to dinner and they remained on friendly terms. He later helped her with press contacts to promote her books. People are generally happy to help as long as they don't feel like they are wasting their time. Basically, all they want back is the assurance that you will make good use of their advice. And they will always be more apt to help if they see you are serious and have done your homework. One editor Julie discovered was so impressed she gave Julie one of her first magazine assignments right off the bat.

When you reach a customer or competitor who is friendly and willing to answer your questions, ask for his or her name and title. If that person is in a management position, his or her point of view will carry weight.

You can also gently question your future competitors, although that approach requires a great deal of tact. It's probably simpler to be up front about it rather than using ploys, like pretending you are a potential customer who is looking for a good price or for information about a service, or asking a friend to inquire for you.

When we were starting out, we tried to always be straightforward and transparent with our competitors (i.e. other writers). We told them we were just people starting out and needed advice. There was the odd person who truly shut the door in our faces, but most were comfortable talking. They could probably see we both had potential. Beginners always imagine that veterans will clam up because they want to protect their turf. That's probably why so few beginners dare to reach out to veterans in their field (and as veteran writers, we are impressed by the few young writers who do reach out to us for advice): if nothing else, it shows they have confidence. Exposing your vulnerabilities can be uncomfortable, yet recognizing your limits is also a sign of wisdom. The best people in any field won't see beginners as competitors. They spontaneously know that they have to help them, *because they have been helped.* So, of course, they'll take the time. As older writers we also know that we need to have younger writers in our network, sometimes to do the kind of work we don't have time to do, or to do work that they do better (like social media posting, for instance). Competent, well-established self-employed people often have too much work on their hands, so you can bet they'll be interested in a promising newcomer who can help them finish a contract. It's a good way to get started and to get training all at once.

However, if you decide to open up and talk about your idea to a competitor, even one who seems sympathetic to your cause, you should certainly take steps to make sure they don't steal your idea (see Chapter 4). Think about it. If you want to have a frank discussion with this person, you will have to show your cards: you can't very well ask someone for advice but refuse to say what you are planning to do with it. There are all kinds of legal means you can use to protect your idea, including trademarks, patents and copyright. However, the best protection is talking to trustworthy people of good character. In other words, use your better judgment.

If it's clear that you've worked hard to develop an idea and that the project fits your own specific skills, your competitor won't even consider stealing it. Sure, there's always a risk, especially if it is just an idea, which can't be patented or copyrighted, but you will run the same risk when you start selling your idea anyway. People will hear about it! On the other hand, if your idea is really good one, a veteran in your field may introduce you to their business circles or even offer you a partnership, which would make it possible to solve two problems at once.

Put those algorithms to use

At the very least, you should know how to create an "alert" to flag online content relevant to your project. Using keywords that you choose, search engines like Google or TalkerWalker find new pages and blogs related to your idea and send you a list of links as they come up, once a day or every week—it's your choice. We each have a set of Google alerts on topics we are following, as well as for our books (so we see new reviews or mentions when they appear) and for ourselves (to see when and where our names pop up). We sometimes create new temporary alerts for short-term projects we are working on. A tip: create your Google alert from the Google country site relevant to your needs. If your idea is about American or global markets, use google.com, but if it's about the French-speaking market, google. ca or google.fr will give you better results. Alerts are also good police: one of ours turned up the case of a publisher who had sold one of our books to a third party without informing or paying us.

However, the web does have some flaws you should be aware of. There is a lot of unverified, inaccurate information out there. The best way to avoid being a victim of false information is to identify and use good sources. Traditional media and Wikipedia (which is built on references from traditional media) are good bets. They both have established mechanisms in place to verify the information they are disseminating.

And don't get caught in an information bubble. Algorithms can bring you huge quantities of material but if you rely on them exclusively, you can get caught in a kind of information echo chamber (hearing the same information in different packages). Information is our business, so we make a point of reading general news sources in addition to any specialized reading about particular topics. The reason is simple: everyone needs some information they haven't "chosen" from a specialized source on a specialized topic. Casting a wide net for news feeds your intellect, your general knowledge and brings to your attention new factors and ideas that might influence or impact your business. Algorithms do many things, but not this.

Three tips for doing your research

From the time of Gutenberg (who invented the printing press around 1450) to, say, Bill Gates, the most useful basic research tools have always been a pair of scissors (or a knife), a notebook and a pen. Twenty years ago, we added the web—until 1999, Internet didn't offer access to anything you couldn't find on paper, like traditional archival databases. Now there's Wikipedia. The quantity and quality of information on the web have increased exponentially (see box below) and is still growing.

While the web has obvious advantages, like speed and ease of access, it also has limitations and several big drawbacks. The amount of information you can find online—about a trillion pages at the moment—is about as mind-boggling as the speed at which it can be found, which is now counted in milliseconds. The challenge is knowing how to find information. While Google clearly dominates, there are other search engines out there, like Bing. Whatever you use, don't forget: it's just a tool. To find the best information and make good use of it, you need to know how to ask questions. When we typed *robot crutch* into Google, we got 1.3 million results. But when we type "robot crutch," in quotation marks, we got 200 results. The quotation marks limit the search engine results to *only where the two words appear together*. You use quotation marks to find more precise results. You should go to the trouble of learning Google's advanced search functions. The Google guide explains the types of searches you can do. If you type crutch, it will bring up all the pages where the word "crutch" appears. But if you type *inurl: crutch*, you'll only get the pages where the word "crutch" appears *in the URL* (the web address), which are far fewer. There are about ten specific commands of this kind.

All non-journalists should consider taking one of the many courses offered in research skills (or interviewing, for that matter) by journalist organizations such as the Canadian Association of Journalists (CAJ) or the CFG. These are open to non-members for a fee (usually quite reasonable), often available online and offer excellent training.

Many of the information sources that good journalists use are available to the general public, including

1. Annual reports for companies or Ministry reports from the government. These contain information about the needs of a potential client or the specific information about a sector.
2. Courthouse docket lists of cases that are in front of a judge or jury. If one of your clients or competitors has been in trouble with the law, the case file and the testimony in the case file may help you identify information your competitor is hiding from you or from future customers.
3. Business registries: they hold a surprising quantity of information, including names and addresses of associates.
4. Access to information laws. Although they can be difficult to use, in practice, these laws allow private citizens to obtain all the documents

to which they are entitled from federal, provincial or municipal authorities. Such information might include studies by civil servants on landfills, expense accounts of BC Hydro executives or the amount of a competitor's bid on a contract. Every agency, department and municipality has an access-to-information officer. This information is available to ordinary citizens on request, so the self-employed worker will never have to justify getting access to it.

Save that thought

Whatever sources and methods you use to find it, the information you dig up will only be useful if you record it and use it properly. To do that, you need a method. Write all the information down. When you take notes, whether it's on a notepad or an app on your tablet or smartphone, be careful: use separate sheets or files for each idea so they'll be easier to file.

Ideas also pop up randomly during conversations or through an off-hand comment by your Aunt Grace or Uncle Raymond. If you can't make a note right away—we always have a pen handy, but most people don't—then record it as soon as you can. If you hear about an accountant who might have some valuable advice, write down her name. Same for the names of potential clients. Even having an empty Kleenex box on your desk to stash paper notes is better than having no place for them at all. A "notes" file on your computer desktop also works well. Just remember that note taking is only a transitional step on the way to in-depth reflection on what you'll be doing. At some point you have to put your notes in order and act on them.

Organizing documents is one of the biggest challenges any self-employed person faces. When Jean-Benoît was starting out, one of his magazine editors, Pierre Sormany, gave him a simple trick for keeping things under control: only file what you have actually read (and only what you thought was worth reading). Unread material should be put in a "To Read" file.

Whether you use paper, a computer or a combination of both, you have to set up some sort of filing routine. It doesn't matter how you do it, as long as you do it regularly and it fulfils its objective: to keep valuable information somewhere you'll be able to find it quickly, when you need it. Jean-Benoît organizes most of his newspaper clippings by geographical location or theme, but he also has some folders and files where he puts catchy ideas or hot subjects. Julie organizes clippings by the publications she thinks might be interested in them, in paper folders, and has other paper files for specific projects, both prospective and ongoing. She has computer folders for different clients and according to different themes. You'll figure out what works for you with a little experimentation (if you are using paper, always keep extra folders on hand) and don't worry, changing systems every now and again is normal since your projects and focus will change over time.

However, every article and note you keep should have a date on it: after piling up articles for ten years, your oldest documents might start to turn yellow but that doesn't mean you should throw them out. On the contrary. That's sometimes when they become most valuable.

Go through your folders and files regularly (but not too often, that's obsessive). Like poor quality wine, weak ideas lose their appeal over time but good ones get better. If you trim the hedges too often, your ideas tree will wither and die. There's no point in collecting information in the first place if you purge your files obsessively.

Dear diary

You should keep a journal about your business idea, even if writing is not your strong suit. A journal is not a To-Do list or a novel. It's just an exploration of ideas, thoughts and observations. You should take the time to write these down every day even if you only have five minutes to do it: record developments and especially any new ideas that pop into your head. And this often happens by the miraculously simple process of explaining things to yourself, which is what a diary really is about. This is different than working on a business plan. It's exploratory, to help you in your research. As we mentioned in the previous chapter on writing a business plan, writing is the best tool for helping you think clearly and systematically. If you attempt to deeply reflect on an issue without writing anything down, you'll soon find your thoughts wandering. They will turn to your kids, your mother, your garden, the dishes, Canada's economic problems, Justin Trudeau's beard, whatever random data is rolling around in your brain. If it turns out that you can think about a single topic for an extended period of time without your thoughts drifting off, well, you're a genius.

For the rest of us, only writing makes it possible to think intensely about a subject for hours on end, without forgetting where you started. As we've said, it's impossible to write absentmindedly. We never think more clearly than when we're writing. The process itself is deliberate. The act of writing makes the brain collect, classify, connect and organize ideas that otherwise just slosh about in your head.

To make a concentrated mental effort, there's only one real alternative to writing: having a focused conversation with someone. Excellent ideas have a tendency of popping up when you talk to someone else. Talking forces your mind to organize thoughts so they'll be intelligible and interesting to an outsider. We do this naturally, though it requires a certain effort to stay on topic. The drawback of conversation, however, is that you can't control the whole process. Your interlocutor can ask questions and change the topic. Writing is more focused and allows you to explore subjects thoroughly and systematically, one at a time. You are totally in control. And you shouldn't be afraid to write down whatever is on your mind or might be worrying you, even if it has nothing to do with your business. Writing is like wiping your mind clear. And you'll be amazed at the connections you'll make.

While you are writing (or conversing), your mind will also do some housecleaning, sorting what's important and what's not. Have faith: when you write, the most important things always rise to the surface. And they may not be what you expected them to be, which is the mark of some good thinking.

QUESTIONS FROM READERS

Becoming self-employed after losing your job

It happened to a friend of ours. Michael had been working as a federal civil servant for thirty years when his job was abolished along with thousands of others. He was laid off without notice at the age of fifty-three. Michael thought he was protected by an ironclad collective agreement that gave him job security for life, but after eighteen months, he still hadn't gotten his job back. So, he started picking up some consulting gigs. But he found it slow and frustrating.

That's the rub in being self-employed: you can't pull a self-employed business out of a hat. That's why most consultants for business start-ups recommend you start working on your business *before* you quit your job. You need time to get things up and running. If you're unemployed and you really want to start your own business, you should still try to find a job anyway, even if it's only part-time.

There are some situations when it's okay to quit your job first: if you have enough money saved up, or a spouse who can support you financially, or if you're starting out in a field where you already know the ropes and have established a reputation. Some people also start self-employed businesses after months, or even years out of the workforce, say, caring for a family member or loved one. They don't necessarily have money, but they have had time to think the business through and secure the resources they need to be able to stick it out. The "involuntary" self-employed person generally has a steeper hill to climb. Life pushed them somewhere they didn't necessarily want to go.

Different government services and self-employment associations have programs to help people in this situation. The human resources department of the company that laid you off may also offer services to help former employees.

In addition to financial resources, the main question newly self-employed workers have to answer is, what are my goals? This was our friend Michael's main problem. His work experience qualified him to be an immigration consultant, but he was not particularly interested in being self-employed, per se.

What Michael wanted was another job. He had to decide if his priority was becoming an independent consultant or securing new employment. As it was, Michael wanted the best of both worlds: he thought doing contracts would lead to a job. But you won't be more than a "half" self-employed person if you aren't serious about building a loyal clientele.

Our friend Michael had this problem: he couldn't decide whether or not to really embrace the project of running a small business. You can't have it both ways: you won't succeed in being self-employed if you're really thinking of it as a stopgap measure. You need to be committed to the plan and ready to stick it out.

Another friend, Darrin, voluntarily removed himself from the job market. He quit his job at an assignment editor at a TV news chain to become a mortgage broker. Working in TV was too hard on his family life and he wanted a more flexible schedule. He considered a few possibilities before making up his mind to enter the mortgage business. He took his severance package from his TV job and put it towards training. It took him a good year to build a client list, but he was starting in ideal conditions: his wife was earning a good income and his sister was already an established mortgage agent, so he could partner with her.

To become self-employed, Darrin still had to learn the basics: he had to write a business plan to generate strong and marketable ideas, to calculate his hourly rate, to analyse his financial situation, to organize his office and to sell himself.

Another issue that affects many are basic skills. About 50% of Canadians between the ages of fifteen and sixty-five are functionally illiterate. Without being completely illiterate, they find it difficult to read. Many of them discover their problem at the worst possible moment: when they lose their job and are struggling to write a resumé and a cover letter. Of course, if you are reading this book, literacy is not one of your problems. Still, if you suspect someone in your network has this problem, you should refer them to a literacy centre for help.

As we explained in Chapter 1, the first thing you should do as a self-employed worker is to create your own workspace, office or workshop. This is important for both practical and symbolic reasons. Putting this off until you get your first contract is a big mistake. You need to stake out your work territory at home. You can't have half-dressed children running in the background of your Zoom meetings, or dropping half-eaten snacks on your contracts. You should also avoid washing dishes, going for groceries or helping with the homework during work hours. Easier said than done? Maybe. Essential? Absolutely. You need to stay "at the office" during work hours. Having a defined space is the best way to make that happen. When you're there, you're not at home.

One last piece of advice: the insecurities you feel when you start out your own business might make you willing to do anything. Offers to work on contract for a former employer are common and always tempting. Make sure you don't fall into a very common trap of being an employee in self-employed clothes. Many employers hire "bogus" self-employed workers and even force them to show up for work on time in the morning. This is the worst of both worlds, since the employer is illegally avoiding obligations (to pay benefits) to save money. If it happens to you, you should discuss this with a lawyer and tax authorities. In Chapter 6, we'll talk about how tax authorities define a truly self-employed worker. If you closely examine your situation and conclude that you are, indeed, an employee disguised as a self-employed worker, you should take steps to correct this situation either way.

4

Protecting your idea

Owning your idea and making it work for you

Myth #4: "If I talk about my business idea, someone might steal it."

Jean-Benoît once heard a homeless man tell a passer-by, "Why would I want to buy a house? My stuff would just get stolen."

Many self-employed workers think the same thing when they are considering making money from their idea. The fear of others stealing it prevents them from developing it in the first place. This fear is usually misplaced. Self-employed workers should strive to develop an idea that's so great, other people *would* want to steal it.

Advice books for the self-employed don't usually discuss copyright, patents, intellectual property and trademarks until the end, as if they are some kind of afterthought for businesses. And when they do talk about intellectual property, it's almost always from the angle of protection. But owning an idea is not just about protecting it: intellectual property is actually among the most potent leverage businesses have at their disposal.

Our favourite example of the potential of intellectual property comes from the career of George Lucas, the creator of Star Wars. In the 1970s, after he produced American Graffiti, Lucas approached a few producers about his new project, an outer space fairy tale that he had developed into a full-blown concept of seven films. Lucas was asking for a fortune up front. Producers were only willing to pay him half of what he wanted. So Lucas bargained to retain the rights for figurines. He also secured derivative rights over the name of the franchise itself, Star Wars, and the sequels. The producers agreed immediately. These rights seemed like a trifling matter to them, possibly because, at the time, they still were. Of course, Lucas went on to become very rich man thanks to the royalties he earned on Star Wars' action figures and the franchise. When the film's producers decided to make a follow-up, George Lucas could dictate the terms of the deal because he owned the Star Wars name.

It's disheartening to talk to self-employed people who have no interest in intellectual property rights and no idea about what they can be worth. It's like talking to someone who wants to be a real estate broker but who isn't interested in real estate law, or a prospector who doesn't care about mining laws.

Intellectual property is the equivalent of planting a fence in the territory of knowledge so you become the owner of a chunk of it. Like any owner, you can do whatever you want with your property as long as you respect the law while you are doing it: you can let people use your property for free or you can set up a ticket office where people have to pay to get access to your property. Naturally, the bigger or more beautiful or exciting your idea is, the more people will line up at the ticket office, and the more they'll pay to use it.

There is always a risk

But isn't there a chance your idea will be stolen while you are still developing it? Many people wonder about this. The answer is yes and no. The proven cases of idea theft that we've heard about were usually for unspectacular ideas about things that were sort of "in the air" at the time. If you come up with an idea about the Olympic Games three days before the opening ceremonies, you can be sure that someone already had the same idea and, as a result, didn't steal if from you. They just had it earlier, when they had time to put it into practice. For your idea to have been worth anything—and worth stealing—you had to have had it two years before the Games.

Here's a comforting thought: thieves are generally lazy. They are not going to sow seeds if they can just steal apples and get away with it. As a result, the risk of having your idea stolen increases not just in function of how interesting the idea is, but also how much preparation and work you have already put into developing it. An idea that is almost ready to be put into practice is more likely to be stolen. We see this in journalism. Clients occasionally buy raw ideas for stories and hire someone else to write them (and yes, sometimes they just help themselves to our ideas without remunerating us). Even if they paid a little for an idea of ours, the client would be more likely to pay (us) thirty times more for the finished product, the complete article. Why? The difference is the value of the work we put into writing it. So the finished article is more at risk of being stolen by someone else, than is the original idea, which they would have to work to turn into an article. And as a matter of fact, people do steal our articles, all the time. Our articles are frequently republished or reused without our knowledge. You can buy PDF copies of our books on line from sources that don't pay us for their use. That's the difference between an idea in draft stage and an idea that's been turned into something: between the two stages, you have worked, and thieves generally try to avoid that.

This small risk that someone might steal your unformed idea should not prevent you from approaching well-established customers. You can assume that if they have survived over the years and have earned a good reputation, it is probably because they have decent ethics. There's always a small risk this won't be the case. But the chances are that if an idea is interesting, they will buy it rather than steal it. If it's your idea, you are probably the best person to develop it.

However, it's smart to protect yourself anyway, if nothing else, to show clients that you're serious and to discourage less scrupulous customers. It can be hard to judge the honesty of someone until you've dealt with them a bit (although your instincts improve with experience). This is especially important in sectors where ideas are churned out incessantly and collectively, like in cinema, for instance, or in the computer science world.

All developed countries have had well-established intellectual property laws in place to protect ideas for over a century, in some cases almost two.

Jean-Benoît discovered a—literally—colourful story about protecting intellectual property when he was working on a story about the French-speaking minority in Ontario. The story demonstrates what a powerful tool intellectual property can be for protecting ideas when it is used intelligently. In the 1970s, a university professor at Laurentian University in Sudbury created a Franco-Ontarian flag with some of his students. The group wanted to find a way to protect their design while they pitched it to the provincial association of Franco-Ontarians. When they tried to register the design of the flag, an official at the Intellectual Property Office advised them to register a trademark for the expression "Franco-Ontarian flag," instead. He told them that could be done quickly for a few dollars. The flag designers followed his advice, then went to the *Association des Canadiens français de l'Ontario* (ACFO) and presented them with the *fait accompli*. They told the ACFO: "We have a Franco-Ontarian flag to offer you. If you don't take the flag, you won't ever be able to use the expression 'Franco-Ontarian flag' for another flag." It's what you call hard bargaining. A few months later, as expected, the ACFO adopted the flag itself along with the name.

Simple tips to protect your intellectual property

Before submitting their work to a client, graphic designers, illustrators and photographers use a handy trick to protect themselves: they put the original design and drafts of their project in an envelope and mail it to themselves by registered mail. When the envelope comes back, they archive it, unopened, in a drawer or safety deposit box. If a prospective client or a third party goes ahead and uses the work without paying the creator, the creator can just unseal the envelope in front of a judge to prove that the work was created before the date on the postmark.

You can also register your creation with the Copyright Office. If it is an important document, you can even place copies in the archive of the National Library, where your work will be assigned an ISBN number. The document issued proves prima facie (accepted as proof until proved otherwise) that you own the idea on a specific date. Unfortunately, this type of official registration is of limited use: the government is not required to verify that your work is authentic or original and that there has been no plagiarism, so in theory, a thief could also register your work in their name.

Courts recognize these methods, but they are limited since they only prove anteriority, i.e. the fact that you were the owner of your creation on the date of the stamp or seal. In the event of a dispute, your best recourse will be to use your own records. Always hang on to notes, drafts, plans and different drafts or versions of your creation. If the case goes to court, a paper trail will throw the opposing party's claims to ownership into doubt. Quebec illustrator Claude Robinson won a plagiarism case against the production company Cinar by using archival material this way. The case went on for almost twenty years until the company was forced to pay the creator $4 million for violating his copyright. That's why it is vital to hold onto—within reason, of course—all your documents, drafts and correspondence relating to the gestation and conception of a creation. It's the only way to prove your authorship of an original work beyond doubt. For each of our books, we save one or two filing boxes of paper. Over the years this has added up to a lot of paper, but it's a type of insurance policy.

On the web, with its universal culture of free-for-all and piracy, your creations obviously are highly exposed to theft, like our books are. We see pirated versions of them on the web all the time. Some protection technologies do exist (we'll talk about copyright notices further down). You can, of course, encrypt your data or limit access to your site to registered members. However, this can be counterproductive. It limits the number of people who can see what you're creating.

Another, more open solution is to use special software such as Adobe Acrobat or Flash that makes it hard to reproduce a work. Watermarking also shows the owner's name in the event of unauthorized copying. However, these techniques are not a panacea, since skilled programmers can circumvent them all. In short, Internet piracy is an endless battle and you have to evaluate the cost and likelihood of things being copied versus the cost and headache of trying to prevent this.

But what does the law say?

There are five common types of legal protection available for ideas: copyright, trademarks, patents, design registration and registration of integrated circuit topography. There is also a sixth, new form of protection, "plant variety protection," which applies to new plants created through genetic manipulation.

This chapter will explain the first three of these protections because they are the most relevant to self-employed people, particularly copyright (for tips on negotiating these rights, see Chapter 1).

Let's start with a number of general principles that apply to all categories of intellectual property.

Intellectual property should always be defined by territory, language, duration, medium and degree of exclusivity.

As a holder of intellectual property, all your rights are "reserved." This means that you own the totality of rights that apply to your property: you own your work for all possible territories, in all languages, and exclusively for the term of protection, which varies depending on whether it is a patent (twenty years) or copyright (in Canada, valid for up to fifty, soon to be extended to seventy years after the creator's death).

When the intellectual property expires, the creation or invention that was protected enters the "public domain." This means everyone is free to use it without asking permission from the inventor, creator or author (or their descendants).

All these rights have two essential characteristics:

- The rights are detached from the original. A painter who has sold their painting does not receive anything from the sales of the object if the subsequent owner later sells it, directly or at an auction. But in buying it, the collector does not (unless otherwise stated) gain the rights to reproduce, disseminate, distribute or adapt the work. These remain the painter's rights. The same applies to the person who buys your record: they can do what they want with the item itself (like destroy it or sell it to a second-hand record dealer), but they cannot reproduce it in part or in whole or authorize anyone else to do so.
- The rights are independent. Imagine a cupboard: just because you open one drawer, that doesn't mean the others automatically open as a result. An art gallery that has obtained the right to display your painting in Newfoundland doesn't get the right to make a T-shirt out of it and sell it in Ontario (or anywhere else), unless they explicitly acquire that right as well.

In other words, all the rights around a work belong to you, the creator, except those that you have explicitly sold in writing.

But in intellectual property, you actually don't sell anything. You either "license" or "assign." When you *assign* (also called transfer) this right you relinquish your ownership of this right permanently. It's the equivalent of selling your house. A *license* is the equivalent of a rental or lease; it's necessarily limited in duration. The property remains yours, but the other party acquires the right to use it for specific ends defined in the contract.

As the owner of intellectual property, you must establish the limit of your ownership. Otherwise, what would prevent anyone off the street from reproducing your mental arithmetic course book and selling it without paying you a penny? Anyone has the right to publish their own book on the subject (as long as they aren't plagiarizing your work), but they cannot copy and resell your book. Your clients and competitors will take you more seriously if you clearly establish the limits of the intellectual property you are assigning or licensing and stipulate the use they are allowed to make of it.

Bear in mind that intellectual property laws only protect ideas that are in an organized form. A raw idea in your mind—whether it's a three-dimensional puzzle or a movie script—cannot be protected. Your idea can only be protected when you've turned it into something concrete and tangible.

Intellectual property protection is a different matter in the services field. Offering the service of an "à la carte theatre company" might be a good idea, but there is nothing innovative or exclusive about the service itself. You are delivering something a lot of other people might offer in a different form. What you can protect is the script or the name of your service once they exist.

Understanding intellectual properly can give you formidable leverage: the Alliance of Canadian Cinema, Television and Radio Artists (ACTRA) has been able to establish itself as a national union for performers because it defends the intrinsic right performers hold over their performances.

Even if it's only "on paper," intellectual property can be worth a lot of money. Some publishers ask their authors to sign ten-year license even though they know that five years will probably be enough to earn whatever they plan on earning from published the work. So why do they buy extra years? It's because the bank views intellectual property contracts as "assets." Intellectual though it is, intellectual property is very real. Pharmaceutical companies, publishers, the audiovisual and recording industry, inventors and software developers rely heavily on intellectual property assets in order to finance themselves. If it's an asset for them, it is for you too.

How much is intellectual property worth? There are no strict rules on how to calculate it, but roughly speaking, the more interest a buyer has in an idea and the less they will have to invest themselves, to bring the idea to fruition, the more they will pay for it. A patent for a gizmo with no foreseeable use is worth next to nothing, but a patent for a kind of radio that would allow you to listen to music while walking (first a Walkman, then an iPod) was worth millions—or probably billions before mobile phones became universal mobile entertainment systems.

The legal protection of intellectual property has two flaws: it is territorially limited and it relies on the good faith of the parties. You don't get anything for your intellectual property if the buyer doesn't ask you for permission to use it. It can be hard to get people to pay up when they go ahead and use your intellectual property without asking. Basically, you're on your own, possibly against a big company with a legion of lawyers. But all too often, you're dealing with clueless consumers. The state has no special police to enforce intellectual property: it is up to the owner to take cheaters to civil court. The state rarely pursues criminal charges for intellectual property fraud except when entire industries are involved, like in the case of illegal downloading of music or film piracy. In Chapter 17, we explain what steps to follow to claim what you are owed.

Copyright

Copyright is the most common type of intellectual property. It applies to texts, songs and software, podcasts, films, paintings and sculptures, but not to titles, the name of the work (see the section on trademarks below) or the idea of a plot.

Copyright AUTOMATICALLY protects any work that is FINITE and ORIGINAL (which excludes say, a grocery list, or a note on a bulletin board). It does not apply to facts. "It snowed 93 cm this morning!" cannot be protected by copyright, although the wording, "My oh my, it snowed!" might if it was part of an original work. If Fido is really a green dog, then so be it. But if "Fido is green" constitutes a line in a poem, then that line belongs to the one who formulated it, especially if it is part of a creative ensemble that a creator can lay claim to as a "work." Then it is protected by copyright. Similarly, in a training course in mental arithmetic, no one can claim copyright on multiplication tables. Who owns 2×2 = 4? Everyone does. On the other hand, the wording of the course manual belongs to you, and you alone.

In Canada, copyright applies automatically from the moment of creation and lasts until the creator's death, at which point it can be passed on to his or her heirs for the next fifty years and soon seventy years. After that, the work enters the public domain where anyone can use it.

Finite means that your work must be organized and formulated. A shopping list cannot be protected under copyright. Your notes for a speech aren't either, but the speech itself, if recorded on some kind of medium, is protected under copyright law.

Original means that the creator created genuinely. It doesn't mean "unique." If you and your sister visit Toronto and each takes an identical picture of the CN Tower, both photos are "original" in copyright terms (even if they are not the slightest bit artistically original).

The copyright notice indicates your ownership, but you don't need to put it on your work in order for the Copyright Act to apply. Just as you don't have to fence off your land to actually own it, you don't need any government authority to put the famous little © on your writing, followed by the name of the right holder, the year and the mention, "All rights reserved." The copyright mention just makes explicit what is true anyway, that you are the creator and owner. It acts as a warning, but its mention is neither necessary nor mandatory. In other words, your document is protected by copyright, even if it does not say anywhere on it that you are the owner. That said, on the web in particular, the copyright mention can help ward off pirates.

Even if a client came up with the idea for a product, the finished and original work that was inspired by it belongs, in its entirety, to its creator, unless otherwise agreed. Copyright is very powerful.

Copyright is recognized internationally. However, in asserting it, you are subject to the regulations in force in any country. For a long time, the United States only protected works for twenty-eight years. In 1998, the United States increased the protection to seventy years, encouraged by Walt Disney whose copyright on Mickey Mouse was due to expire that year.

Not all countries adhere to international copyright treaties. For a long time, the USSR did not recognize any form of ownership. Another famous case is Taiwan, which is not even recognized as a country. And China is not clear on the issue either. This means that the risks of having one's work plagiarized there are greater.

The web and intellectual property

Everything on the web is subject to intellectual property, both in principle and in practice. However, Canadian law has limited the scope of the constraints imposed by copyright with the notion of Fair Dealing. The details of Fair Dealing are contained in Article 29 of the Canadian Copyright Act. This provision allows for a creation to be used without asking the author's permission within certain defined limitations. To determine whether your use is covered by the Fair Dealing principle, you must follow a two-step process. First, you need to determine if the material is being used in one of the following purposes: research, private study, criticism, review, news reporting, education, parody or satire.

Even if you are using the material for one of these purposes, you still have to evaluate your use according to six other categories.

Purpose. Is your use separate from that of the user? A commercial use might be seen as less fair.

Character. Is the plan to make a single copy? Multiple copies? Will the copy be destroyed when its use is completed?

Amount. Examine the amount of the work to be copied and the significance of the copied portion (will copies be made of a significant part of the work?)

Alternatives. Is a non-copyrighted equivalent available?

Nature. Is the work private, confidential? Unpublished? If unpublished, it could be seen as more "fair" since copyright has a goal of information dissemination.

Effect. Will your use compete with the market of the original work?

Any of these criteria can disqualify your use from the provisions of Fair Dealing. So, for example, if you quote a paragraph from this book, we don't have much recourse against you because the proportion is tiny and you can argue that it didn't have any economic impact for the author. On the other hand, if you quote one of the four stanzas in a poem we wrote, you've just quoted 25% of the work. That's too much.

If your objective is to talk about a work without selling it or defaming it, it is fair to show a part of it. However, if your act of dissemination has the effect of depriving the creator of the ability to sell the said work, that use is unfair.

If you have any questions about how you wish to use content found on the Internet, consult a lawyer.

There is a lot of creativity possible in what and how you apply copyright, but the types generally fall into one of four categories:

1. The right of first publication. As the name suggests, this authorizes a publisher or broadcaster to distribute your work exclusively for a defined period, territory or language. You can assign multiple rights of first publication simultaneously in multiple territories and languages that do not overlap. You can also assign multiple licenses in the same territory. However, not offering exclusivity means you will receive less for the use of your work.
2. Reproduction rights. These relate to photocopying, silkscreen or any other form of large-scale copying, including electronically.
3. Adaptation rights. These make it possible to make a film, a book, translations or audio books inspired by an original work.
4. Derivative rights. These relate to non-integral use, or use outside the proper framework of the work, like making T-shirts, toys, puzzles or films from the work.

There is only one right that you cannot assign unless you renounce it completely: moral rights. This ensures the integrity of your work. You cannot transfer your moral rights, you can only waive them, which means that you explicitly agree not to enforce them. But these cases are rare. No one should edit or otherwise alter your work without your prior consent, or remove your name from it if it is associated with the work, or change your pseudonym for your real name against your will. Anyone who decides to add a sepia tone to a Picasso painting should expect to hear from the artist's heirs.

Trademarks

People are always surprised to learn that the Star Wars films and books are protected by copyright, but not the title. The title is protected under trademark rules, which are a different story.

A trademark applies to a very specific wording that gives commercial value to the name and shape of a product but not the product itself. A trademark can apply to a word, a group of words, a design, a symbol, an abbreviation, a package, or even the shape of a product (say, butter-fly-shaped candy) or a combination of these elements.

Your name is Matthew and you are creating a new math course series called "Matt's Math" It's a nice brand name that you should probably protect. Coca-Cola Company is the only company that can market a soft drink or cola under the name Coca-Cola. Anyone else who put this trademark on a T-shirt without the authorization of Coca-Cola will be liable to a lawsuit for damages. The drink itself cannot be protected because it is a mixture. It's all about the name: that's the whole point.

After a process that lasts about eight months, the Canadian Intellectual Property Office will authorize a trademark that's valid for fifteen years and renewable indefinitely. This carries the symbol ® (registered trademark) or MD in French (*marque déposée*). The trademark applies only to the country that has authorized it. If you plan to sell your product elsewhere, you'll need to contact the embassy of the country concerned to find out how. It is possible to enforce a trademark without registering it by virtue of the fact that you own the product in question, its shape, and that you use it. Unlike copyright, the ® or MD symbol is only valid for duly regis-tered trademarks, but like copyright, registration is not mandatory—the abbreviation MC (for trademark) can also be used in Canada for marks that are not registered. However, the official registration of a trademark makes it easier to protect your rights because it reverses the burden of proof.

In Canada, the basic criterion for granting a trademark is originality. The name must not be a real one, nor easily confused with another brand, nor can it be a normal quality of the product. The government won't allow you to register the name Ice Cream for your ice cream. Brown Dog could not be registered, but Green Dog might. Your application will be denied if it is a family name (unless it has come to be known and identified with a product, such as Molson), or a description, whether real or misleading.

Self-employed service workers would benefit from knowing more about the scope of this form of intellectual property. If you offer a traditional cooking service, you could obtain a trademark for your menu. A Toronto consultant even obtained ownership of the term "New Economy," the subject of her book, which describes the changes in economic conditions that we have known about since the mid-1990s. Even the title of this book could be the subject of a trademark. We have a long-lasting disagreement with one of our US publishers because they misuse our books (by refusing to publish a new edition on the basis that customers will confuse it with the old one!) and we find their interpretation of the contract dishonest. Had we better understood the concept of branding when we chose the title of the book (a catchy one) we would have sold the book and its title separately to the publisher. In principle and according to the rules of both types of intellectual property, we could then have used our ownership of the title to force the publisher to renegotiate the copyright contract. That's exactly what George Lucas did with the title "Star Wars," which was distinct from the film itself.

Patents

Patents are the best-known type of intellectual property, but not the most common. This is because a patent applies only to an invention or a discovery. It provides a monopoly for a fixed period of time, e.g. twenty years from the date of application, but is non-renewable. You must apply for patent certificates, which are government-issued, unlike copyright, which is automatic, and a trademark, which you can obtain if you meet the conditions. Patents come with a number that must mandatorily appear on your product or in your documentation. To obtain a patent, you would benefit from using the services of a registered patent agent or an association of inventors, either of which may save you a considerable amount of money. The process of acquiring a patent is long (it takes almost two years) and very expensive (it can cost several thousand dollars). It is up to the inventor or discoverer to demonstrate that their creation meets the conditions of novelty, utility and inventiveness. A patent is granted only for the physical embodiment of an idea and only to the first person who applies for it, but you must not have disclosed information about it prior to filing for a patent.

There is no such thing as a secret patent: as soon as you obtain your patent, your invention becomes public. That is because patents were created for the purpose of the discovery or diffusion of technology. That's also why the patent number is mandatory. It is not always in your best interest to disclose your secret, and therefore it doesn't always make sense to patent your invention. Coca-Cola keeps its recipe secret. No one knows if its distinctive element is actually patentable, but one thing is certain: if the drink had been patented, Pepsi would be making Coke.

The drawback to the patent is that it only applies in the country where it was obtained. If you want to sell your new solution in every country in the world, you'll need to obtain 196 patents to cover the whole world. That might not make sense since not everyone is interested in the same product; snowmobiles are of no interest in the Sahara, and getting a patent for a personal watercraft is probably not useful in Mongolia. There is still no international convention that recognizes the patent as formally as copyright. Still, countries that are signatories to the Treaty of Paris grant a twelve-month privilege. If you file a patent application in any of the signatory countries within twelve months of your application in Canada, you will be given priority in examination over any competing applications.

The patent can be exploited by its owner, assigned in full or licensed to third parties in much more complex ways that involve territory and time. The patent can be valuable if your product has commercial value. With enough time on your hands, you may be able to obtain a patent for a belly-button viewer—a tool to look at other people's belly buttons—but really, who would buy that? The value of the patent depends on the commercial potential of the invention. Novelty is not synonymous with a good business idea. That's the drama of inventors.

And there's more

You can also protect the shape, the motif or the decoration of a mass-produced device or utility item. Unlike copyright, which is automatically granted as soon as the work is created, industrial design must be registered. The symbol for this is a D inside a circle.

The registration applies only to the visible, non-artistic aspect of a product. It is only valid for ten years and is non-renewable. There is even protection for an integrated circuit topography. This type of protection applies to the shape of miniature electronic circuit also known as a chip. The performance of a chip depends precisely on its shape and the links between the circuits. This protection of up to ten years only concerns the circuit, not the function. On the other hand, if a competitor produces a different circuit for the same function, that competitor is also protected if it is registered.

5

Put a price on it

Finding the right price for your product, for clients and for banks

Myth #5: "If I just get started, the money will follow."

For many people, the idea of meeting with a banker is about as appealing as a cold shower in January. That's mostly because money professionals know the difference between a bank account and a fairy tale, so they often have bad news. But you need to do a lot more than find a good idea and clients before you launch your business. You have to think about money. Basically, you need to be able to answer two questions: what's your price and how will you finance your business?

Let's start with the easiest question, price.

The price is right

After you have gotten a customer interested in your product or service, their first question will usually be: how much? Sometimes it can be difficult to provide a definitive answer. We know this, as writers, because there are a lot of factors to consider before naming our price for a job.

Your price will be based on two things. The first is objective data: your costs, the price of materials, equipment, office expenses. The second factor is more subjective: how much will the customer be willing to pay? When Jean-Benoît needs a haircut, he goes to the barber without an appointment and pays him $20. When Julie needs a haircut, she makes an appointment, sometimes weeks ahead of time, then pays three times what Jean-Benoît does—before tip. Of course, a hairdresser in a salon is not the same thing as a barber at the corner of the street, but even hairdressers in salons charge men less than women, simply because even the most image-conscious men won't shell out as much for a haircut.

Whatever the variables you factor into your price, the first thing you need to do is to establish your unit price, which is the basic cost of the service. Calculating your hourly or daily rate, or your unit cost, is fairly simple when you are offering a service, but a little more complicated when you are selling a product.

Calculating your hourly rate

To establish your rate, you first need to establish how much you want to earn (your personal income), calculate your start-up and operating costs, how many of the hours you work will be productive (billable) ones and your profit margin. Then put that in the number cruncher. Here's an example of how this can work:

X = your annual personal income: **$60,000**
Y = your start-up and operating costs: **$15,000**
Z = the annual number of productive hours (the number of worked hours in a year minus unproductive hours): **1,250**
P = profit: **10%**
Equation: (X + Y) / Z + P = Hourly Rate
($60,000 + $15,000) / 1,250 hours + 10% = $66/hour

To obtain the daily rate, multiply by 8.

There are three major errors you should be careful to avoid:

1. Don't underestimate your start-up and operating costs. Try to think of everything.

2. Also, never assume that you will work forty productive hours per week (i.e. 2,000 hours per year). By productive hours, we are referring to "billable" hours. Of the total hours worked, a portion will be devoted to "unproductive" jobs, including developing and managing your customer base, sales, contract negotiations and other things you need to do to develop your business, like shopping for supplies and furniture, taking care of bookkeeping, doing your taxes and more. This time is usually not billable to a third party. On average, your work will be productive for only five of the eight hours you work each day. The annual number of hours you work will therefore drop from 2,000 to 1,250.

3. Don't forget about profit. You have to earn enough money to live, but wouldn't you like to make a profit? That's your holidays, savings or emergency fund it you don't already have one. It's important even if you only use it to have more money to invest in developing your business. We put this tentatively at 10%, but if you want to charge enough to make a 100% profit, there's nothing stopping you, except the threshold people are willing to pay.

If you are selling a product, not a service, the calculation is a little more complicated because you have to establish the right price for each unit sold. This calculation must take into account the cost of your machines or tools, your labour, materials, inventory and so on. But it's basically the same calculation: the difference is that your divisor is no longer the number of productive hours, but the number of teddy bears, wheels or dishes you want to sell in a year—it's a little bit trickier, because some costs vary depending on the quantity you produce (materials, labour) and others are fixed (equipment, facilities). It's best to ask an accountant for advice.

Don't forget that your price has to be appropriate for the market in which you are working. Self-employed have a tendency to want to offer lower prices on the basis that they have lower overhead costs, but you shouldn't. Lawyers in Canada charge between $100 and $3,000 an hour, depending on the size of their firm, their experience and their field. As a freelance lawyer working from home, you should certainly not charge less than the minimum in your field, even if you do have lower overhead expenses. Image is important in law. Clients won't take you seriously if you are too cheap. Likewise, if you aim to be a hairdresser, no one will take you seriously if you charge the rate of a barber. And conversely, if you're a barber and you charge hairdressers rates, you will need to show the gents why they should pay more—and accept that many may take their business elsewhere as a result.

However, it's fair to charge less when you have less experience. When you are starting out, you may have to compromise on your price for a while at least until you are more established in your field. But you shouldn't do this for long. You can't work at a loss. You can't expect to survive if you end up paying to work instead of being paid.

Of course, you will have to prove the value of your work to justify what you charge. Graphic designers, for example, are facing strong competition now from countries like India and Morocco where you can hire a graphic designer for peanuts. However, you will probably be able to offer your clients a lot better customer service than these competitors can, since you are in the same time zone and easily accessible, for starters, but also because you probably understand the local market, their customers, their competitors, much better. Remember, it's not just about price, but what's included in the price.

You might also incur special expenses during the execution of a contract that will increase your unit cost. Julie had a ghostwriting client who required her to travel to do third-party interviews. The client paid Julie's travel expenses, but when Julie calculated her fee, she factored in all the extra time she would spend travelling. It is important to negotiate well and take all factors into consideration when establishing your price (see Chapters 11 and 12). If you have to travel, the expenses are not just the cost of gas and plane tickets, but also the hours you lose behind a wheel or sitting in an airport waiting for your flight to be rescheduled.

How to convert an hourly rate into a fee or unit price

When you are selling a service, one of the first things to figure out with potential customers is whether they want to pay a flat rate or an hourly rate. Flat rates can be advantageous when the work involved is fairly straightforward and predictable. To calculate the flat rate, all you need to do is multiply your hourly rate by the number of hours you expect to work. Make a schedule that lists all your work steps from order to final delivery. For each step, estimate the minimum and maximum number of hours required, then add them up for two totals of your estimated hours. Multiply these two estimates by your hourly rate. Then take an average between the maximum and minimum price and add 15% (for the unforeseeable). This should give you a realistic fee.

There is always a bit of a risk with charging a flat fee. Sometimes you come out ahead; other times you underestimate. And for those of you who are starting out, it can be hard to estimate out how long things will take before you've done them a few times. (With experience, we've generally increased our flat rates to compensate for the unknown factor.) The big variable for us is the time we'll spend on research: we know how long it takes us to write, but research depends on a lot of factors, like how hard it will be to reach people for interviews, whether a client can supply documents, whether these are organized or not, etc. So, we've learned to quickly suss these things out before we set a price for a project. Clients usually don't mind you asking questions to make your estimate. Being able to anticipate problems shows you are serious, experienced and professional.

For some services (such as a hairdresser or building inspector), your unit cost (per client) is based on your hourly rate. How many heads can you shave in an hour? How many hours will it take to visit a home with a client and produce a report?

In some other fields, the rate is associated with production: e.g. "per pound," or "per page" (of copy). To calculate it you need to figure out how many hours it takes to produce so many pounds or pages of copy.

If you sell a good or service that is subject to copyright, like artistic performances, you should first establish your unit cost (what it costs you for each seat) and add the copyright licensing price allocated to each ticket, keeping in mind that the value of the copyright will be what the customer is willing to pay (our chapters on negotiating discuss this in more detail).

How do I finance this?

Not having enough money to live on until they make their first sale is a classic problem many self-employed workers face. Before you strike out in your new endeavour, you'll need to take off your rose-coloured glasses and put on your banker's spectacles. You should think about this challenge before you start your business, not in the middle of a launch, when your energy and emotional stamina are being tested by the effort to get a project off the ground.

The question you need to ask is: how long can you survive without earning any money? It's the cruellest question (none of us wants to be living off our savings), but one of the most important ones to ask yourself when you are starting out. If you have a cash reserve of $10,000, but it costs you $4,000 to start your school of mental arithmetic, that means you will only have $6,000 left to live on until you start earning money. How long can you last on that? It depends on whether you have a house, children or a spouse with a stable income. If your family doesn't absolutely need your income to survive, then you might be able to sustain a much longer start period. If you are the sole breadwinner, your reserves will not last as long.

During Jean-Benoît's brief stint as a playwriting student at the National Theatre School in Montreal, the principal at the time, Michelle Rossignol, frequently told students: "There is no shame in doing jobs that just pay the bills." Her idea, of course, was to shake students out of their Prima Donna complexes and rid them of the delusion that they would start making money from "grand" acting roles the minute they graduated. Ninety percent of students who graduate from the National Theatre School remain self-employed during their careers and need to do the occasional "paying" job to put butter on their bread—or just buy bread.

The same wisdom applies to all self-employed workers: at the beginning and for a few years at least, you will probably have to support the most interesting part of your work with contracts doing less interesting, but more lucrative activities. Hopefully, the interesting part will become so profitable that you won't have any time left over to do jobs "for the money." That's the plan, anyway.

You should start by making a personal and family balance sheet that includes your personal finances and your provisional budget, so you can see what expenses you can avoid or delay. The balance sheet might show that you need a part-time job to finance your business until it gets rolling. So, you might want to keep your part-time job as a math teacher while your school of mental arithmetic takes off. There's no shame in that. The point is that it is a means to an end.

Here are the key concepts you need to master.

- **Balance sheet**. The balance sheet is like a snapshot of your finances at a given date. It shows the difference between the value of the net assets you have. It establishes the difference between what you own (car, house, cottage, furniture, investments) and what you owe (mortgage, personal loans, credit cards, miscellaneous debts). The result, your net worth, corresponds to the value that a banker can use as collateral. Don't count the leased car as an asset or a debt: it doesn't belong to you. The result of the balance sheet allows you (or your banker) to establish how much you can borrow without risk.
- **Personal finances**. Contrary to the balance sheet, which is a snapshot, your personal finances are like a documentary film. They give you a realistic picture of how much money you spend over the course of a year, or, if you have reserves, how long you can go without earning income or working at a deficit. This amount can then be used to

determine what a reasonable income would be for you. You determine your personal finances by calculating your monthly expenses, like rent or mortgage payments, heat, electricity, groceries; then adding your annual expenses like clothing, taxes, insurance, transport, recreation, home maintenance. And don't forget taxes. (There's a detailed income statement for calculating income tax in Chapter 20 and a list of deductible expenses in Chapter 18.) This data can be used to establish your projected budget. You'll notice that this data looks a lot like what you need to establish your hourly rate.

- **Budget forecast**. This is a bit like a science-fiction movie in the sense that you are imagining how you will live in an unknown future. It's about imagining your balance sheet and your personal finances for the next year as you start to see where this new endeavour is taking you.

The problem with banks

Though there are organizations that can provide financing for small businesses, the bulk of your start-up capital will likely come either from your first earnings, or from your loved ones. If you are starting a business, these parties usually invest in the form of a donation, loan or equity (a certain percentage of your profits). In business lingo, personal investments by you or your loved ones are called love money (capital in proximity or angel funds) and there are endless ways of setting them up.

Getting some love money is a good place to start. You will never convince strangers to back your project, let alone bankers, if you can't convince the people who love you, first.

Don't blame banks for not wanting to take a risk on you. That's not what banks are about. By definition, they take as few risks as possible. It's their duty. The law sets strict limits on how they loan money because, after all, any capital they invest is their depositors' money. The bank's primary responsibility is to preserve and protect those deposits and only secondarily to lend it. You and your investors are the ones who are supposed to take the risks.

Very few self-employed people who start a business will get a loan for that business, specifically. At best, they can hope for a credit line or a personal loan or an increased limit on their credit card. Most will have to work with the credit they already have. Whatever business you are starting, you have to make your project look viable in order to convince banks to back you, and this is hard to do.

But it can be done if you play your cards right with the capital you do have.

The basic rule of thumb for banks is that they never lend to those who have no money. They only lend to people who already have money or who can demonstrate that they definitely will have money. In 2003, we got our hands on $25,000 of capital and for a few months pondered how to use it. We wanted to both buy new computer equipment (two computers, a printer and a camera) and spend three months in France doing research to write a book proposal.

It was tempting to pay cash for the electronic equipment and be done with it, but we decided, instead, to borrow the money to pay for it. This was our thinking: the bank might give us a loan to buy equipment that they can seize if they need to, but they won't lend us money for a mini-sabbatical in Paris. Our reasoning turned out to be on the money. The bank gave us a nice little business loan for the equipment, repayable over twelve months and that allowed us to hang on to the cash to pay for our trip. And this is where it gets a bit crazy: they lent us $8,000 for computer equipment because we had $25,000 in the bank!

A lot, possibly the majority of self-employed workers, wait until they are running out of money before going to the bank to get financing. If you're going to visit your banker, even if it's only to negotiate for a credit line, you should do it early, when you still have cash reserves. Don't wait until you are dragging your tongue financially. If it turns out you don't need the loan, you can just pay it back. But when your assets have been liquidated and you have nothing left to put up as collateral, your application will be refused. This sounds flagrantly unjust. But ask yourself whether you would lend to a stranger who came knocking on your door looking for $10,000. If you did it, it would be a gift. Wouldn't you be more inclined to accept it if they promised to give you their BMW if they couldn't pay it back? Why would the criteria be any different for a bank? Remember, banks don't lend their money. They lend their depositors' money. So they should be careful with it.

If you need to finance a project, every financier will require a business plan written in due form. This plan (explained in Chapter 2) should include your market research, balance sheet, income statement, projected budgets for the next two years, alternative sources of income and your plan B in case of failure. Business school graduates (who work at banks) love numbers: short- and medium-term projections on prices, costs, sales, profits and cash flow. So give them numbers. What will your inventory be? How many customers will you have? Do you have samples? And remember, they're not looking for pretty numbers. They want real ones.

There are a few tricks you can use to show you're serious. One of them is to get a letter of intent or a written contract from a future customer. Find a customer who is credible: a letter with no letterhead signed by your brother-in-law won't impress anyone unless your brother-in-law is George Soros (in which case you probably wouldn't need to go to a bank anyway). Try to get the prospective customer to sign a "conditional order," i.e. subject to your business being in operation. For the record, in the huge file that we put together to ask for our computer loan back in 2003, we included photocopies of covers of our books to demonstrate to the lender we were legit as writers and could back our loan request up with copyright revenues. "Credit" comes from a Latin word meaning "believe"—so do whatever you need to do to make the lender believe in you.

When the banker agrees, they will then ask a silly question: "What resources do you have available if you have to refinance?" Typically, there are a lot of glitches in the first year of operations. The budget will be tight, and lack of cash flow will be your number one problem. You could even end up in a financial pinch because your business does too well: more orders will require more investment. Successful businesses all go through growth crises and many die when the entrepreneur has no other financing resources to get through them. Another favourite question bankers ask comes about when your business depends on machines: "Will you have the money to fix it if it breaks?"

It seems like another cruel paradox: bankers love borrowers who have resources to back up their project, professional assets they can fall back on if necessary, a financial cushion or a parallel source of income (an investment, or a spouse). In short, they want to see that you'll be able to bounce back from adversity and you won't collapse, and take their money with you on the way down.

Bankers always lend according to their rules, so don't imagine it will be any other way. You wanted $75,000? They'll make it an even $30,000. Maybe they'll decide that your application for a line of credit should be turned into an equipment loan. Bankers will likely require a guarantor and lend out at a higher rate for small businesses, even though small borrowers go bankrupt less often than large companies, and, when they do, it's for smaller amounts. Some bankers also discriminate by requiring a woman's husband to be the guarantor of the loan, but not the other way around. Grrrr. It still happens.

Fortunately, banks aren't the only ones who lend these days. Small businesses have the option of applying for grants or loans from provincial or even community business development funds. However, there's no point in approaching these if you're looking for less than half a million dollars. Self-employed workers are better off looking into organizations that provide microcredit loans from $1,000 to $10,000. Since their function is social, these types of loans often include support and counselling services in the package. These funds are generally less demanding than banks, but the criteria are basically the same: you have to be credible. Microcredit lending organizations are not banks, but they aren't charities, either.

Back when we were starting out in the 1990s, financial institutions were very unresponsive to the needs of self-employed workers. Things have changed a great deal since those days. We suspect the change in attitude is explained by the fact that so many of the new businesses that are being created, particularly in the high-tech sector, have the same basic characteristics as self-employed workers. New economy companies don't invest as much in bricks and mortar as they do in intellectual property. They rent spaces and buy electronic devices that quickly devalue. At one bank in Montreal's hip Plateau-Mont-Royal neighbourhood—where one in four households is self-employed—75% of loan applications are from self-employed workers. A quarter of these loans are for start-ups. This is certainly one of the financial institutions in Canada that best understand the needs of self-employed workers. It might be worth asking your bank how much they loan to small businesses and consider switching to another bank that is more familiar with the needs of the self-employed.

For banking institutions, the problems in dealing with self-employed people often boil down to determining their borrowing capacity. We discuss this in more detail in Chapter 18, but the challenge for self-employed workers is that they are entitled to deduct certain expenses related to their car and home office. Deducting these expenses reduces your taxes, which reduces your net income, which, in turn, reduces your ability to borrow. For example, if you earn $50,000 gross income, your overhead expenses are $20,000, and your rent and car expenses are $5,000, your net income will only be $25,000. Some bankers are willing to accept that the self-employed person's actual net income is higher than his or her declared net income because she or he deducts car and home office expenses. After all, you would have to pay for these things anyway, even if you were someone's employee. But other bankers are utterly intractable and refuse to take this into account. We recall some epic discussions with bankers who refused to budge in their fixed notions over this. Hence our advice to consider shopping around for a bank that gets it.

Crowdfunding: Does it work?

Internet has popularized financing formulas like crowdfunding (getting money from a group of people) and its close relative, crowdsourcing (getting information, skills of products from a group of people). These systems work by soliciting Internet users to invest or subscribe to your project for a few dollars (crowdfunding) or to contribute to your activity in some way (crowdsourcing).

Although Internet has undeniably made this much easier to do, there's actually nothing new about crowdfunding or crowdsourcing.

They are inspired by methods in philanthropic subscriptions that were developed over the last two centuries. But Internet has made them accessible fund-raising methods. The most spectacular use of crowdfunding was the 2008 presidential campaign, when Obama's team was able to quickly raise millions of dollars and organize "spontaneous" gatherings at the same time.

Active outsourcing essentially consists in outsourcing some of your activities so that the "crowd" participates in them. The best example of this is Wikipedia, an encyclopaedia built essentially through the effort and participation of a few thousand voluntary contributors (and now financed by a participatory funding system).

These activities, particularly crowdsourcing, are carried out through web platforms, mainly Americans, some of which have policies that guarantee the legitimacy of all projects on them. In general, calls for funding take two approaches. The first is financial and is similar to a share sale. Each individual, by subscribing, acquires a part of your property. In reality, you remain in control, but according to the letter of the law, this approach consists of sharing your property. The other approach, more common among creators, is similar to a gift system. You just donate money to a cause you want to support.

To be successful at crowdfunding, you have to be a very good communicator: the public has to buy into your project as if it were a cause near to their hearts.

Keep in mind that banks nowadays assess risks according to more esoteric criteria like research protocols, intellectual property or the quality of a company's management. The moral value of a company (e.g. its stance on environment, diversity, gender) is also becoming more and more important in assessing its overall potential. This is very, very subjective. The banker, whose ultimate dream is to get a promotion, is being asked to take a chance on a stranger by lending considerable sums of money based on the moral values of a project. It's understandable if they hesitate a bit before taking the plunge. Remember, the word "credit" comes from the Latin word for trust.

How you present yourself and your company is, therefore, of the highest importance. Bankers are sensitive to specific details. Your documents should be short and easy to read. Your banking history must be presented in a thorough and orderly manner. Don't send them a stack of receipts. Bankers also hate being kept in the dark about things like past personal bankruptcies. If you're the evasive type, or the kind of person who frequently creates misunderstandings, or you're hard to get hold of, or if you change auditors frequently, or have repeatedly been investigated for credit, you might as well forget about trying to get a business loan from a bank.

There are a few tricks you can use to make a good impression and figure out which institutions are more likely to buy your arguments. As we've said, shop around. Loan limits and rates may vary from bank to bank and even from branch to branch. A local commercial bank branch will be more familiar with business needs than one in a shopping mall. You should always talk to at least three or four banks or branches before making your choice. And remember, it's people who are lending, not machines. That's why you should always ask your accountant to give the bank manager a call to introduce you. This kind of detail will help you to put yourself in good standing with the banks.

However, be careful not to spread yourself too thin while you are shopping for a loan. Applying for a business loan is a time-consuming endeavour and if you try to meet the requirements of five or six institutions simultaneously, you won't be getting much sleep. Also, lenders are wary of people who shop too much, so don't tell them you're shopping.

Some conditions for financing are simply unacceptable so you should avoid like the plague any bank that proposes them. Watch out for loans at usurious rates. It still happens. The banks are not likely to ever go that far, but they could ask you to put up your house and all your belongings as collateral for even a tiny loan. It's a red flag, and if it happens, run. Just imagine what it will ask for when you apply for a larger loan.

The main thing is to give yourself some leeway. The bank wants you to be able to bounce back financially, and that's fair, but it also needs to give you some room to breathe. If the bank offers a home equity line of credit (HELOC) before it offers you a line of credit, look elsewhere. Otherwise, you may risk depleting all the money saved in your mortgage, at which point you might not be able to get a line of credit because you'll have no collateral.

Sometimes the problem at the bank is a small one: for instance, what you are offering is not clear to them, or your business plan is a little too optimistic. Don't be afraid to take the time you need to explore and discuss whatever is creating friction with the bank. It might turn out the bank is refusing you a loan because of a problem that doesn't exist. You might have made some faulty calculations. The only way to get to the bottom of these problems is to be willing to discuss them, then possibly revise your plan and go back to the drawing board. It doesn't always work, but the long days you spend obtaining financing can turn out to be the most important part of your preparations.

6

To Inc. or not to Inc.

What you need to know about legal structures

Myth #6: "I'll have to incorporate."

Just about everyone who considers becoming self-employed asks the same question: do I need to be incorporated? The short answer is, probably not.

The only thing you need to get started running your own business is, literally, you. There is no law that prevents you from carrying out an economic activity of your choice. What could be more natural than someone paying you to do, or make something for them? You don't need to ask anyone's permission to do it, certainly not the government's. No license is required to do business unless you are planning to work in a regulated sector (if you're not sure whether this is the case, then check).

Otherwise, just go ahead and do the work and bill your clients.

And, no, you don't need to incorporate. The only reason you might need to register a company is if you want work under a name other than your own, but as we will see, there are ways around incorporating. Some people might want to have a business name to project a certain image.

You should ask yourself if image matters in your area of business. Do large companies in your sector only deal with other companies? It sounds silly, but that's how it works in some fields.

That said, you absolutely should register to collect HST or GST and provincial sales tax as the case may be (see Chapter 19) as soon as you start out. But again, your name is the only thing you need to supply for that. You certainly don't have to be a company.

Self-employed workers get to enjoy almost all the advantages of being a business without any of the administrative inconveniences or legal obligations that, say, Esso or Apple or IBM has to contend with. On the other hand, you might feel the need to expand beyond yourself at some point. You might want to have a partner or hire someone, either to escape the solitude of working alone, or to cut expenses, or to increase your revenues.

Your business can have many legal structures. You can always consult a chartered accountant, lawyer or tax professional to choose the best one for you. However, the first thing you have to do is to think carefully about what your goals are.

Here's what you need to know about business structures, starting with working alone (sole proprietorship or a company), then for making the organization leap to having employees or working with other self-employed people (general partnership, cooperative).

Sole proprietorship

The business structure that the authentic self-employed worker adopts is called "sole proprietorship." It's the basic model for someone who is doing business on their own. This type of self-employed business exists the minute a person carries out an organized economic activity that results in them offering a product or service on the market. This business (you) can hire outside help: you don't need to obtain any particular legal status to fulfil your legal obligations as an employer. If the business is you, that means you are personally liable for lawsuits and for debts. This type of business entity rarely survives its owner in the event of death. In terms of deductions for business expenses, a business of sole proprietorship is entitled to the same tax benefits as any corporation (see Chapter 18 about deductions). You can even register for and collect GST/HST/PST on your own behalf (see Chapter 19).

The only thing that will complicate this paradise of simplicity is if you decide to do business under a name other than the one your parents gave you. There are good reasons you might opt for a different business name. Maybe you're not comfortable using your own name to sell sheep manure. In that case, you may opt for another one, such as My Friend's Manure.

But in such cases, you won't be able to deposit cheques issued to "My Friend's Manure." To do that, you need a "business name." In such a case, all you have to do is go to the business registrar of your provincial government and register your business name. You will then be given a registration number, which will allow you to open a business account and deposit cheques made out to My Friend's Manure. Even if you use your name for your business but add another word to it, like say, "Julie Barlow's Manure," you'll need to register it.

The person who registers a business name—in Ontario, it costs $80 in person, $60 online—must file a declaration every year to renew their registration number. This number does nothing more than authorize you to operate as a company: it is not a company registration number and does not make your business a legally incorporated business, or even a company, legally speaking.

Registering for sole proprietorship is really simple. The income tax declaration is made in your name and so are all the legal responsibilities.

The joint stock company or company

A company or corporation is a legal entity that is considered to be a legal person, i.e. it has some of the rights and obligations that are specific to individuals. For example, the company pays its own taxes and borrows on its own behalf, although it cannot vote, receive a pension or go to jail. It must produce financial statements. In the event of a lawsuit, proceedings can be brought against the company and its representatives but not against the shareholders, except in exceptional cases. So, operating a company reduces individual risks. However, the division of responsibilities between executives, shareholders and directors becomes theoretical if you are all three.

Registering a company does have certain advantages, particularly from a tax standpoint (see box below). A company handles money very differently from sole proprietorship. As a company owner, you can pay yourself with a salary (taxable as personal income) or a dividend, which will be added to your income. But a company allows you also to accumulate capital on which you will only pay corporate income tax, but no personal income tax, at least until you withdraw it (see The famous tax advantage box on the next page). On the other hand, the company must pay tax on the capital. To finance the company, you can use your RRSP up to $25,000, but only under very restrictive conditions—the main one being that you can't be the sole shareholder. Being incorporated facilitates deductions for the home office, because it allows you to rent space in your home rather than just counting the financial and maintenance costs. If you have only one client, an incorporation protects you from having your self-employment privilege challenged by the tax authorities—for more information on this point, refer to the last section of this chapter on how self-employment is defined by tax laws.

Filing the request federally costs $200. At the provincial level, it goes up to $450 in Alberta. But there are other consulting fees with lawyers, not counting fees for the annual renewal of your registration and to produce an annual incomes tax declaration.

Once you are incorporated, you have to file a separate income tax return for your company, financial audits and pay salaries. The process is lighter if the company has a single shareholder who is also chairperson of the board and sole administrator. But these three functions must exist.

Administratively, it's a lot more complicated than sole proprietorship. You have to choose a federal or provincial charter according to certain criteria, get authorization for your company name, issue shares, keep a share register and minutes of meetings, operate according to regulations. In principle, you can do almost everything yourself, but you'll have to put in the hours. Most people pay a professional to do at least part of the work.

The famous tax advantage

The choice between sole proprietorship and incorporation depends entirely on your goals and your situation. Before deciding, you need to understand the tax advantages of each model. To illustrate these differences, let's take the case of two self-employed workers, Mr Me and Ms Inc, who produce the same service, with the same expenses and generate the same income.

Ms Inc is incorporated, and Mr Me is the sole proprietor of his business.

For his first year of business, Mr Me has sales of $50,000, with expenses of $15,000, for a net profit of $35,000. This net profit then becomes his personal salary, on which he is taxed—in Ontario, he will pay about $8,750 in personal income tax (about 25%). But if Mr Me is so successful that his sales climb to $200,000 in the first year (and miraculously, he has the same expenses), he will then write a cheque of $68,450 (or about 37% of $185,000) to the government for taxes.

Ms Inc, meanwhile, saw the money train coming and got incorporated. Her company earned $200,000, but pays her a salary of $35,000 a year, on which she will pay the $8,750 in personal income tax. However, her salary becomes a new expense to the company, which now nets $150,000 ($200,000 – $15,000 in expenses – $35,000 in salary). Since company profits are taxed at about 9% in this revenue bracket, the company also writes the government a cheque for $13,500. The total of Ms Inc's personal income tax and the company's tax for that year then, is $22,250 ($8,750 + $13,500). So, Ms Inc has paid $46,200 less tax than Mr Me—*that year*.

It sounds like a no-brainer, but there is a caveat. This scenario is only true if Ms Inc *leaves* her after-tax profit of $136,500 *in the company*. If she transfers the profits straight into her personal bank account by paying herself a dividend, she will then be taxed on these additional sums *in her personal income tax declaration*.

And if she does the transfer the same year, she will pay at least as much tax overall as Mr Me.

Why does it work out that way? Because Canada practises the doctrine of "tax integration." According to this framework, Mr Me and Ms Inc will pay the same amount of tax whether they are incorporated or not, if they cash in all the profits. The logic of the system is precisely to encourage company owners to leave money in their companies so they can invest and grow. It may well be a different story in other countries, or in tax havens, but that's the rule in Canada. The only things that can thwart the principle of tax integration are special incentives offered on specific years by different jurisdictions, but these are always short-lived and limited to economic sectors considered of great value at a given time.

So, now you might be wondering, what exactly will I gain from incorporating? There could be advantages, depending on your goals. One might be if you want your business to serve, first and foremost, as a capital reserve for your retirement, or for your investment projects. It will also be in your interest to incorporate if your business requires large investments: the slightly different accounting rules will ensure that you end up with more liquid assets. Incorporation also has the benefit of limiting your personal liability.

In any case, it may be worthwhile to run as a sole proprietor for a while before making a move to incorporate, just to give yourself enough time to figure out the "fiscal landscape" you are working in. For instance, if you are a creator, there are cases when incorporating actually works against you, like, for instance, if royalties on intellectual property are subject to special juicy special tax incentives at the personal level, and companies do not qualify for them—we, for instance benefit from a $15,000 tax credit on royalties for copyright offered by the Quebec government to encourage creation. Check with your professional association or with a tax specialist before deciding.

Because of the administrative and legal costs associated with being incorporated, most accountants and tax specialists agree that there is no point in incorporating if your revenues don't regularly exceed $100,000, which is quite high, but also because the tax advantages of incorporation are not as obvious as generally believed. A lot depends on your specific situation. There is nothing that prevents you from figuring things out as you go, so start as a sole proprietor and see what you need. If running your business will require significant investment in equipment, incorporation may work to your advantage even if your sales are less than $100,000.

For creators like us, incorporation poses serious tax problems because the generous tax credits we get for our copyright royalties only apply to us personally and wouldn't apply to our company. In short, before you choose to incorporate or not, you have to think of your goals and do your homework. It's always a good idea to talk to other people in your field. If you're working on major contracts abroad or dealing with very large foreign companies, they may require you to be incorporated. They may also require a lot of other things from your organization, including insurance (about insurance, see Chapter 22).

Coworking: "Roommates" who share expenses

Rather than a defined legal status, coworking resembles an agreement between roommates in an apartment. Roommates pool their activities to share expenses, not profits. The only goal is to reduce their overall costs.

This type of grouping is very popular among young professionals who are starting out, because they generally have limited means at their disposal. They share an office, equipment and sometimes other office expenses like accounting or secretarial services. They also help each other out, advise each other, correct each other's mistakes and share contacts. Clients appreciate this kind of grouping because they can call one place and get hold of two or three people who can potentially carry out different aspects of one project. Beginners love it because it's a great way to find new clients and get advice or even mentoring from colleagues, and they get access to moral support in the package. And best of all, no one has to make promises about their respective performance. As long as each member pays their share of office space and services, everyone should be happy.

The main drawback of this type of informal association is that it has a high turnover rate. What usually happens is that one member finds a job or a long-term contract and leaves. The lack of capital outlay means that no one is tied down. So, if the other members want to keep their expenses down, then have to quickly replace the associate who leaves (find a new roommate!).

After all, it's the numbers that make this type of group useful. One solution to the turnover problem is to tie your "roommates" together with a lease that lays out the rules for withdrawal. Having this kind of agreement is a good idea: even the most impulsive people will think twice before signing up.

Before finding roommates, you should carefully consider the pros and cons of this type of arrangement. The emphasis on reducing cost and offering mutual support is primarily of interest to people starting out in their field. If your business is doing well and you are happy working from home, why would you pay an extra $500 a month to share an office with someone? The distractions might outweigh the benefits. Will it bring you enough extra business to be worth the added expense? Unless, of course, you have to get out of the house because you just can't work there anymore, because of the isolation or the distractions there, for instance.

Making the leap to an organization

Are you better off owning 10% of a bakery, with all the organization involved in running it, or do you want to own 100% of a bun? During your preparations, you may realize that you don't have the capacity or skills necessary to run your business alone and do everything yourself. You might need a partner or an ally. Sometimes ideas turn out to be more promising than you originally think. In short, there is no particular virtue in working alone unless you have to. Circumstances, the nature of your idea and the amount of ambition you have will all influence the path you follow.

Take the case of engineers: it is rare for a single engineer to carry out a major project alone. Engineering projects generally require the

TO INC. OR NOT TO INC. **93**
contribution of civil, electrical, mechanical, industrial and other types of

contribution of civil, electrical, mechanical, industrial and other types of engineers. Teamwork is inherent to the profession. Engineers who work at home or alone are often looked at by their peers—wrongly, in our opinion—as outliers who lack teamwork skills. The market limits self-employed solo engineers to small projects and feasibility studies. Group work is natural in any field that requires a combination of several skills.

Technically speaking, if you start hiring staff or if you partner formally with other self-employed people, you are not on your own anymore. But in reality, the nuances are so murky that it is worth considering alternative structures for working in groups. We, for instance, have been working in joint partnership for thirty years but we have no employees, so in practice, we remain self-employed.

Before making any organizational leap, remember that every structure of business brings obligations and responsibilities. For self-employed workers, it can be harder to start working with a partner than it is for an organization of two employees to expand to ten. Craftspeople face this difficulty when demand for their product outpaces their ability to produce. Craftspeople thrive on the cathartic pleasure of producing. If they want their business to grow, they have to hire, manage and fire people. But it's hard to keep being a craftsperson when you have to manage fifteen and keep them working.

You also have to consider your means. Every organization needs to generate enough money to pay for its overhead: a decent office space, a meeting room and employees. If three individuals earning $50,000 each team up, the total revenue of their new company should exceed $150,000 unless their overall expenses decrease significantly, or because being associates allows them to benefit from new tax advantages. One thing is certain: the overall net profit should be greater than the sum of the parts. Otherwise, what's the point of joining forces in the first place?

Simply put, you have to sell more to afford to expand. A self-employed worker who works alone in the service industry generally makes a net profit of 65%. A business, with employees and administration and representation costs, will be less profitable proportionately. So, the larger operation necessarily must do much more business to generate more profit. Large consulting firms make a net profit of 5% at the most (although partners usually pay themselves a good salary). That should give you an idea of how much more efficient you have to be when you expand.

A self-employed person starting a business will have to spend a lot of time selling their ideas and finding clients just to get the machine going. Running a partnership with others can potentially generate bigger profits if things go well, but doing so will require more organizational work—not less. You might find yourself saying, "I didn't give up my job and work my butt off starting my own business just so I would end up back working for a company again!" And you won't be wrong. The difference is that whether you are a partner, shareholder or owner, you are now the boss. Instead of growing bonsai trees, you will be growing big trees, or even a whole garden, or an entire forest of them.

General partnerships

No, a general partnership is not a company or a cooperative. The "GP" is simply the grouping of several individual owners under the same banner. Registration is mandatory for this. You should also draw up a partnership agreement with a lawyer. This agreement sets out the obligations of each individual, their financial contribution and the share it represents, the rules that apply if and when the company is dissolved, and what happens if a partner leaves the partnership or dies. The fact that the members of a GP share responsibility might make it easier to obtain financing, but the tax benefits are limited to those of individual members. A profit of $100,000 must be divided among the partners according to each partner's agreed share, and each member will pay tax at their personal tax rate.

The GP works pretty much like a company, except that it has no legal or fiscal personality. It doesn't produce an income tax report. Every partner files their own according to their share and legal responsibility belongs entirely to the partners.

The GP consists of employers (the partners) who share common resources in order to pay each other salaries, receive social benefits (vacation, insurance, etc.) and generate a profit. The partners, each of whom has provided a down payment, won't have any incentive to look for another job or contract: they are working for the good of the group and to make their investment grow. If a partner leaves the general partnership, they must sell their shares to the other partners according to a pre-established formula.

There are infinite ways the partners can divide their shares, depending on the capital outlay of each one but also on what they will contribute to the partnership. A single partner who finds work for all the others, manages the office and builds the reputation of the partnership should have some special prerogatives. A former solo worker who becomes a partner should have performance benchmarks: the other partners won't be happy letting the new partner share their profits unless they produce and contribute to generating them. If the new partner does not meet the benchmarks, the original partners can then buy this person out and keep them as an employee.

The cooperative

This entity is similar to a company, but operates according to different principles. Each member has only one vote, regardless of their capital outlay, whereas in a company the vote is proportional to the capital each member contributes. If the coop makes a profit, the members can put these in a reserve for future investments or distribute them to members. The disadvantage of the co-op is that even if you work more than others, your share doesn't increase. The co-operative works towards a common goal: to provide a service and to supply work to members. A group of self-employed people could very well form a purchasing or collection cooperative where everyone benefits in proportion to the amount of business they do. Some very large companies started out as small cooperatives. One of the best known is the Desjardins Group, founded in Quebec in 1900, which now has almost $400 billion in assets. But there are also many cooperatives in finance, housing, farming, fishing, retail and for consumers. The cooperative is, however, a cumbersome formula that does not necessarily make sense for a small group of self-employed workers looking for a way to reduce their expenses. In such a case, it would be better to stick to being "roommates."

But if you want to pursue a great goal, or give yourself a common purpose, the cooperative is certainly a good alternative.

Becoming an employer

In principle, a self-employed person must want and be able to do everything on their own. But in practice you may need other people to get everything done.

Even if you are an individual, self-employed worker doing business under your own name, you can take on one or more employees who will perform specific tasks. These employees may be full-time or part-time, or simply contract workers.

In our case, within the framework of a General Partnership, we hired an assistant and web editor, Veronica, who worked about twelve hours a week for us, about half of the time at our office for a year and a half. At the time, we were having a particularly hard time juggling different kinds of writing work (journalism, book writing, book promotion and speaking) while trying to develop our web presence. Veronica did a lot of things we would never have had the time to do. However, we had to get used to the fact that part of our job was now staying on top of and checking up on what she was doing. That meant supervising her and paying her, but also keeping her busy. All this took time too.

You'll notice when we talk about Veronica, we don't use the term "employee," because she was, in fact, a self-employed person herself, whom we hired on contract. She worked for an hourly fee, and we guaranteed her twelve to twenty hours of work per week. She had her own computer, her own clients and her own business card. For the work she did on our behalf, she had her own email address on our server, but it wasn't her primary address.

Sometimes there is a fine line between being a contract worker and an employee. The difference is that employment is associated with certain payroll expenses assumed by the employer, including deductions for employment insurance (EI) premiums and contributions to the Canada Pension Plan (CPP). That creates a great temptation to disguise employees as self-employed contract workers, as we mentioned in Chapter 3.

So, you need to ask, is the person who works for you really self-employed or are they an employee disguised as a self-employed worker? This question could have serious implications if tax authorities take a look at your contract worker and decide this person is actually your employee.

If that happens, you will have to pay CPP and EI contributions for the current and previous year as well as a penalty.

You should know what the tax authorities' criteria are for determining if someone is self-employed or an employee (see box below). If you are wondering about your own status as a self-employed worker, you should apply the same criteria. You could be hired by someone on a contract basis for a position that is, or ends up being a quasi-job. Sometimes the line between the two is fuzzy, but you need to be aware that there is one.

How self-employment is defined according to tax law

According to the criteria established by tax authorities, the term "self-employed worker" refers to any person who receives fees or sells property for personal profit. The full criteria are available on the Canada Revenue Agency website. Here is a summary of the main criteria the RCA uses to distinguishing the self-employed worker from the teleworker (i.e. the employee who works from home) or the false contract worker (i.e. the employee disguised as a contract worker):

1. **Control.** A self-employed worker works independently and does not have anyone overseeing their activities. They can refuse or accept work from the payer.
2. **Tools and equipment.** The self-employed worker owns their own tools.
3. **Subcontracting or hiring assistants.** The worker does not have to carry out the services they are hired for, personally. They can hire another party to either do the work or help do the work, and pay the costs for doing so.
4. **Financial risks.** The self-employed worker is liable financially if they do not fulfil the obligations of the contract. They may

lose money. They are responsible for their own debts and expenses incurred as a result of errors and pays for their own sick leave and vacation time.

5. **Investment.** A self-employed person is expected to make investments in order to produce a good or provide a service, including costs for equipment, raw material, accounting services or other.

6. **Opportunity for profit.** The self-employed worker negotiates their fees, so they have the chance of making a profit as well as the risk of suffering losses.

7. **Contracts.** A self-employed worker should have a paper trail showing what they sold and to whom. These could include refusal letters.

The rules are slightly different in Quebec, which has a Civil Code legal system. To determine if someone is self-employed or an employee, Revenu Quebec considers the agreement between service provider and payer and asks: what was the intent of the payer when the worker is hired and when they are working? Was the contract one of employment or business? For details consult the Revenu Quebec website.

The self-employed duo or trio: How to work as an effective team

Doing business as a team is like doing home renovations with your spouse: it can make or break you.

Whatever legal status you've chosen for your business, working as a team means you have to be able to accommodate another person and live with your—and their—limitations.

The key to a establishing a successful collaboration is reciprocity, not equality. You don't have a business partner because they are similar to you. They have different abilities and inclinations than you do. That makes you complementary.

We team up with someone because it allows us to focus on what we do best. For instance, we have an agent who represents us for book sales. He gets 15% of the contracts he negotiates for us. He doesn't produce anything—although the result of his work is publishing contracts—or even manage anything. He represents us to our publishers or prospective publishers, negotiates our contracts and collects our royalties. This suits us, because honestly, neither of us is particularly interested in that side of the business and our time is better spent doing what we do well: writing. It suits our agent as well because we bring water to his mill.

On the other hand, it would be totally inconsistent of us to complain that our agent doesn't help us write better. That's not the goal of our union. He's there to help us sell books. It looks simple in the example above, but reciprocity becomes more complicated when partnerships become closer, more complex and touch more facets of your business.

It is possible that the right partnership formula may not be a 50/50 one, but another ratio based on the respective contribution each partner makes. Our agent, who takes 15% of our royalties, is able to go out and get contracts we wouldn't otherwise be able to dream of getting. But all he does is represent us. We talk to him once a month, at the most, except for when we are negotiating contracts. Of course, you can imagine a situation where his role would become more important in our business. In that case, he might expect 25% or maybe even 50% of our royalties. This would be justified if he brought us either a fantastic network or if he took on almost every facet of our business and let us concentrate entirely on writing.

While having a good understanding of everyone's contribution is essential to any partnership, it's also important to nail the details down in a contract. Even a good agreement won't last long without a solid contract (the basics are not that different from what we discuss in Chapter 14).

The contract stipulates how revenues and expenses are to be shared, but also what each partner's obligations are and the limits of what you can both do outside the alliance. A good contract should also include agreement about how to resolve conflicts and an eventual separation. Thinking about the way things might end is not pleasant, but it's safe. You are better off clarifying the rules of the game from the outset, rather than attempting to negotiate them when a problem arises.

Complicity is key. Being married to our main business partner, we make the transition from the bedroom to our office quite effortlessly. The challenge is that our two lives—as a couple and as business partners—tend to overlap. In practice, this means that during our little candlelight dinners, conversations often veer to work. We've agreed that sometimes we need to get the worrisome work issues out of the way so we can have more personal discussions. Neither of us can simply hang up the phone and ignore the problem: we are always together. When one of us has a problem, it quickly becomes the other's problem too.

Of course, it shouldn't get this personal if your partner is not your spouse—in theory. However, in practice, bear in mind that you'll most likely spend more time with your partner than with your significant other and you'll spend a lot of time talking about your partner with your spouse. Not everyone likes this, especially jealous lovers.

Like lovers, business partners may break up. But while the dissolution of a marriage is partially managed by the state through laws on matrimony and family, business partners have to agree on and set out the rules to follow in disputes or breakups.

You don't necessarily need to hire a lawyer to do this, but it is an excellent idea to consult one about the conditions for a separation or buy-out and on the different mediation or arbitration mechanisms available for this. There are certainly a lot of choices out there. Take the famous "shot gun" clause, where, if you offer to buy back your partner's, they can only refuse if they buy back your share under the same conditions. Obviously, this forces you to make a reasonable offer, because if you try to buy them back at a discount you could really lose out. In business, like in love, breaking up can be hard to do.

Mentor to the rescue

You may not actually need an employee or a partner. Depending on your needs, a mentor might do the trick. For the past twenty years, business magazines have devoted huge chunks of copy to the question of mentoring, and a mentor can be a very useful tool for a self-employed worker.

Everyone who goes into business feels lonely at some point, usually when they are in the middle of trying to solve a dilemma or overcome a hurdle. Mentors are particularly helpful in these moments.

The mentor is a master counsellor. They agree to give you regular input on your business decisions and help you solve problems as they pop up. They can help you design and write your business plan, give you advice about convincing a banker to lend you money or even open doors for you with future clients. You can see them once a month or once a week to discuss problems. But you should count on doing some homework as your part of the deal, including research and setting a clear agenda to follow together with objectives and goals.

Mentors are most often business veterans, sometimes retired, but friends or relatives with experience or just good common sense can also do the job. Mentors are generally not paid for their advice. A good mentor has to be someone you trust and who will be willing to devote a fair bit of time to helping you. But a mother, a friend or an uncle can also play this role very well if they have good judgment, good listening skills and know how to ask the right questions.

To find a mentor, you mostly need skills at convincing. You shouldn't consider that an obstacle. It's the self-employed worker's version of a teachable moment. Convincing someone to help you out is good practice before starting out as a self-employed worker: you will need these skills for the rest of your career. Organizations like the Business Development Bank of Canada or Ontario's Young Entrepreneurs (and similar organizations certainly exist in other provinces) have networks of mentors, most of whom are experienced business people.

Selling and Financing 2

7

The message

The ABCs of selling

Myth #7: "I'm no good at sales."

No matter how much market research you do and no matter how thorough your business plan is, you won't really know how good your idea until you start selling it. That's the real test.

When it comes to selling, there is good news and bad news. The good news is that your best sales tool will be "being good at what you do" or make. The bad news is that just being good will probably *not be enough*, in itself, for you to get yourself known, where it counts, and sell what you make or do.

Selling ideas is so important in the work of the self-employed that we decided to devote eight of the chapters in this guide to the topic: four on selling and advertising (Chapters 7–10) and four on negotiating (Chapters 11–14), which is really the second stage of a sale.

Most people who say they are bad in sales really aren't. They just lack experience selling. Back in his 20s, Jean-Benoît was an aficionado of an unusual sport called spelunking (cave exploration). Much of the physical activity in spelunking involves squeezing your body through wet, narrow passageways in total darkness. Let's say it has a certain charm that you may understand after you've done it a couple of times and literally seen the light at the end of the tunnel (Jean-Benoît saw people who had claimed to be claustrophobic try out spelunking and come out of it feeling invincible). All of which is to say that the fear of exploring dark caves can be overcome by actually doing it and doing it with the right equipment and preparation. In our experience, the same is true of sales. As writers, we are sort of conditioned that we aren't the sales "types." Yet with time, each of us has developed quite a knack for it. In fact, when it comes to negotiating our intellectual property rights, we're pretty fierce.

While some people are certainly born with a natural *talent* for sales, the *skill* is not innate. You can learn to sell. And the learning becomes easier when you understand there are different ways to sell. When we talk about selling, people imagine mobile phone peddlers or car sellers, but selling comes in many different forms. It can be done with a carefully crafted message, through face-to-face interaction, through classic advertising in newspapers and magazines, via social media outlets, or through plain old one-on-one negotiations. Actually, you are likely to combine various methods in your sales efforts.

Sure, you are bound to be more at ease using some of these skills than others. People with verbal flair will be inclined towards in-person sales. Shy and introverted people will want to keep their distance and use the Internet and advertisements. The truly flamboyant extroverts will gravitate towards the kind of sales that allows them to be seen and heard, like on radio, TV or in town hall meetings. A good place to start is wherever you are the most comfortable and effective.

One thing's for sure: the best salespeople are selling something good. Since, as a self-employed worker, you are the president-designer-salesperson-accountant of your business, the quality and relevance of what you are selling depends entirely on you. The better you target the needs and desires of your potential buyers, the easier it will be to convince people to buy what you are selling.

Selling is like love: people think it should come naturally, but you actually get better at it with practice. Of course, if you really hate sales, you can always delegate it to someone else. But in practice, few self-employed workers can afford to do this, especially when they are starting out. And everyone really *should* make the effort to sell, especially in the early stages of a business. Having this direct contact with your customers helps you understand them and their needs better. Sometimes it even teaches you things about what you are selling. This is essential to building a successful project in the first place. But if you try to sell and still think you stink at it and still hate it, that's not the end of the world. There are all kinds of representatives, from salespeople to agents, who will happily sell your product for a fee. And they are very likely to be self-employed themselves.

That said, keep in mind that the sales effort is very different depending on the degree of novelty of your business. If you are a hairdresser, setting up shop and putting a sign out is already a good step and may be enough. If you want to do consultations or sell a transport service, you will have to find a way to get the word out to the people who buy that kind of service. However, you will be working in a market that is already structured, so the path is already beaten. But if you are aiming to sell a totally novel type of service or product, you will be looking at a much heftier effort to identify your target clients and how to reach them.

The three psychological hurdles to selling

To learn to sell, every self-employed person has to face and overcome three psychological hurdles:

1. **The "small potatoes" hurdle.** Being small is not a barrier to success. Some 59% of US exports are done by companies with nineteen employees or less. That's almost two thirds of all exports.
2. **The "too far away" hurdle.** Running a business outside a major urban centre is not an obstacle and you shouldn't look at it that way. Your idea may actually be of interest to the entire country, maybe even the whole planet. Self-employed workers fight the same battle wherever they live. Cities just might make it easier to network and find customers. However, as remote working continues to gain in popularity, distance will be even less of a factor. But it's always more of an effort to sell in a location you're not familiar with.

3. **The "hard work" hurdle.** The only problem with big ideas is, you have to live up to them. We had a very ambitious idea of writing a book on the history of the Spanish language. We knew we would have to become fluent in Spanish to pull it off. So we learned Spanish while we were doing our research, well enough to give TV interviews at the end. Not every challenge is that extreme, but if you are willing to work hard, you will be able to turn problems into challenges and find ways to overcome them. (And it makes a great story in your sales pitch . . .)

In short, trust yourself and don't be afraid to put yourself out there to promote your business, your product or your service. If you don't make a sale right off the bat, consider it a learning experience, not a failure. Try to figure out what went wrong, then adjust your product or service (or your message) according to the needs your target customers are expressing. If nothing else, after striking out a few times, you will have a better handle on how to improve your pitch or reconsider your idea.

Before learning to make full use of Internet, carry out promotional campaigns and do face-to-face canvassing—all topics we tackle in the following chapters—you have two main tasks to complete: develop your message and prepare the basic documents you'll need.

Developing your message: The five ingredients

When you've made your business plan, you're off to a good start in formulating the message you want to get across in sales. This is the message that you will convey on your website, in your brochures, in your emails and in all your meetings.

However, it's not as simple as photocopying two or three pages of your business plan. The message is not always easy to articulate concisely, especially in the early stages of a business or product development.

So what makes your message good? It lets you introduce yourself in a favourable light, in the most interesting way possible. The message needs to do much more than relay information: it has to demonstrate the context you are working in and compare your product to that of your competitors and not always in a way those competitors will like.

Hiring advertisers costs a fortune, and the best advertisers will start by spending quite a bit of time talking to you. Most of the content they end up using will come from you, whether that's what you've already written or what you said about your industry and product while talking to them. Bearing this in mind, even if you want to hire someone to help you formulate your message, you should put some effort into developing your message *before* you seek outside help from a professional.

There's nothing truly magical about advertising. It involves identifying the ingredients of good communication and formulating them. What are these ingredients? People often think advertising works because it is "sexy." But sex has little to do with it. Regardless of the age, socio-economic status or gender of your target audience, when you are trying to get their attention they will react to the same five ingredients: story, timeliness, originality, personality and "signature."

We'll break these down for you.

1. **The story.** This is probably the most difficult ingredient for most people to grasp, but it's the most important. Telling your story well will have a direct impact on the form your message will take and on your ability to sell. The story is often about the genesis of your idea or product. A typical story is one of discovery. It has built-in suspense that holds people's attention. For example, you tore a ligament in your knee while playing hockey with your kids and went on to discover a collagen that rebuilds the knee cartilage on its own. Another story along those same lines (but true, this time): the son of a garage owner in Valcourt Quebec died of appendicitis because a blizzard prevented him from getting to the hospital. The garage owner was a certain J.A. Bombardier who went on to invent the snowmobile.

    Once you understand what story is and why it's important, it's not usually hard to find your own story: it's what you instinctively want to tell people about how and why you created your product or service.

    Why are stories so effective at catching people's attention? There are university scholars out there who can explain the psychological appeal of storytelling in great detail, but basically it boils down to the fact that stories reflect how people already think. Stories supply information in a way that is engaging, sparks our curiosity and satisfies us with a conclusion. We always want to find out what happens. In spite of all the random information life throws at us daily (or maybe because of it), our brains have a preference for stories, which tell us how the facts fit into the big picture and why they matter in our daily lives. Again, it would appear that the human brain recognizes a story because we think that way in the first place. We are always trying to make sense of things that don't make sense.

For stories to "do their job," they need to answer what journalists call the five W's: who, what, where, when and why. And we would add a sixth W, except that it's an H: how. Stories naturally organize these bits of information in a way that makes us want to learn. They do it so well and so naturally that when we read them, we don't feel like we're learning, we feel like we're discovering and figuring something out that we were already wondering about. You don't need to write a 500-page biography. Effective stories can be very simple, sometimes just a few lines.

2. **Timeliness.** There is a cliché that "timing is everything." The truth is, when you are selling something, good timing might not be absolutely essential, but it sure helps. If you're launching a new window-washing service that uses climbing ropes instead of cranes, and suddenly there's a tragic accident involving window washers on cranes, say, in downtown Toronto, your timing could be good. Your product may offer a safer way to do business. And cynical as it may sound, accidents do raise awareness about problems and open the door to good solutions.

Naturally, you don't need to wait around for accidents or natural disasters to happen—and you really shouldn't. (*That* would be cynical!) Awareness-raising moments are always out there: a lot of timing is cyclical and therefore, predictable. If you stay up to date on current events, you'll know when the next Earth Summit is scheduled and can launch your new recycling consultation service around the same time. Or say you have created a brand-new hurricane detection process. Hurricane season comes back every year around the same time too. There are always cycles in the news: events and anniversaries that are foreseeable well in advance. Plan around them to optimize your timing.

Of course, if your product sheds light on a current affairs issue, you're in business. Is there some controversy brewing over students using calculators for their eighth-grade math exams? A report on the effectiveness of training in mental arithmetic will be timely and of great interest to journalists covering the story—and great publicity if you happen to be offering training in mental arithmetic. The same effect can happen if your product contradicts the news. For example, we launched a book in the United States called "Sixty Million Frenchmen Can't Be Wrong" at the outset of the war in Iraq in 2003. You may recall that, around the same time, the United States invaded Iraq with the pretext of disarming the country of weapons of mass destruction and that a lot of countries joined the coalition, but that the French famously refused. So the title of our book became quite controversial thanks to current events. Naturally, that got the attention of many different media. We ended up doing some sixty radio interviews about our book in a matter of weeks at stations all over the United States. The book had *nothing* to do with the war, but journalists didn't care. The title resonated with everyone on earth (*Who* were these crazy authors defending the French at such at time and *why?*)

3. **Originality.** No one has talked about your idea, or at least no one has done it the way you're going to do it. When you are creating your message, it's important to point this out, and to be as specific as possible about what the originality is, exactly. For instance, every day, roughly a million commuters take one of the twenty-four bridges that lead onto the island of Montreal. Yet Jean-Benoît was the first person to propose a magazine article about travelling around the island of Montreal in a canoe—it was a 120 km voyage that took him four days.

4. **Personality.** This is not the same as the story we described above, but the two can overlap. If you're a guidance counsellor and you had a difficult youth, your personal story adds credibility to what you do. If you are an architect inventing a new kind of building structure, the fact that you are Mohawk and your father was a New York structure

builder (many of whom were Mohawk) adds strength to your message. However, be careful because your personal story can also play against you. A marriage counsellor who's on his fifth divorce or an obese dietician will not help their business by playing up their personal story in their advertising.

5. **Your "signature."** We're not talking about how you sign your name, but the distinctive traits that are associated with you. For example, people in Paris refer to a bright royal blue as, "Michou" blue. Most of us would call it electric blue; it's almost neon. But in France, the colour was the trademark hue of cabaret performer and famous transvestite Michel Georges Alfred Catty, who went by the stage name Michou during his career. Michou's nickname and colour were both part of his "signature."

It can be hard to distinguish a person's "signature" from their personal story. The difference is subtle but important. The signature is instantly recognizable. You don't have to listen to a story about it. It's an identifiable name, slogan, a logo an attitude or even a gesture—like Churchill's "V" for victory—or quality. Some people also call it "your brand." Unlike your personal story, you can invent a signature out of thin air. For example, if you are starting up a pet shop, you might paint your car—or better yet, your house—in zebra or leopard stripes. If you are opening a barbershop, maybe you'll want to shave your head, billiard-ball style. Think about Elton John's glasses. A "signature" could even be a gesture: the actor Leonard Nimoy will forever be associated with the Vulcan salute. The logo is the visual equivalent of the slogan. Think of the M in McDonald's pizzas or the lettering of Coca-Cola.

One of the most famous signatures in the science-fiction world is author Isaac Asimov's name. Yes, his name. When he started writing science fiction in the late 1930s, he was one of the first successful American authors to write under a name that sounded "foreign." By the 1950s, in the middle of the Communist witch hunt, it took guts to market books signed with a Russian name. But gradually the name became part of the universe Asimov created and then became indissociable from it. Another author, Allan Stewart Konigsberg, faced the same challenge so he changed his name to Woody Allen.

And sometimes signatures are accidental, or the result of an error. The most spectacular example is the name Google, which should have been Googol (a mathematical concept representing ten to the power of 100) but someone made a spelling mistake and the founders liked the mistake and registered it that way. It stuck. Another famous case is the name Ski-Doo. Its inventor, Joseph-Armand Bombardier, thought his first snowmobile would replace dog sleds, so he called it "Ski-Dog." But the printer miscopied the name in the first catalogue Bombardier produced and called it a Ski-Doo.

The eternal "branding" question

The word branding has been bandied around a lot in the last decade, but you shouldn't let it become an obsession. We're talking from experience. We desperately tried to "brand" ourselves when we were making a new website in 2014. The previous versions of the website had all been specifically designed to promote a single book (whatever was the latest release at the time). But as the books started to pile up, we had to find a more practical way to carry the message about our careers.

Basically, it was time for us to be a brand of our own. But how? After some failed attempts to come up with a flashy concept, we just decided to start with the content of the site and work back. With the help of our web designer, we put together a site that showcases all our books as well as other ongoing projects whether radio shows, interviews, presentations or the odd blog posting.

This obviously posed the problem of coming up with a new name. After months of brainstorming, we realized the best solution was just to use our own names, Nadeau & Barlow (which is the name of our general partnership and appears on all our invoices). Then we realized we already sort of had a "signature": it's rare for authors to work as a team and both publish in two languages. Our visual signature (i.e. logo) is a "&" sign between our names. Now it's part of our brand. So the brand kind of grew from the site. Five years later, people refer to our unique partnership like a brand name—there are certain kinds of projects only we can do.

Plain old names can become brands. Heinz was the last name of a certain Henry J. for many years before it became ketchup and the same was true for Ford, Kellogg, Perrier and Vuitton.

Speaking of names, during research on a story about Celine Dion, Jean-Benoît discovered that years before the Quebec singer launched her American singing career, one of her older sisters, also a very talented singer, had considered doing the same. The sister had even changed her last name, believing that no one could make it in the United States if they used a French-Canadian name like Dion. In the end, it was Celine who finally made the breakthrough, using her very own name.

When you are creating your message, you can combine these five ingredients (story, timeliness, originality, personality and signature) in many ways. But remember: you don't need to apply them all in equal measure, or even at same time. A good story will pretty much always work, but if it's not recent, or not at all original or if there isn't any real personality to it, it might not end up being as effective. Likewise, you might come up with very successful message by relying mostly on the originality of your product. However, generally speaking, if your message combines each of the five ingredients in the right dosage, it will spark word of mouth because people will want to share it—with their friends, or on social media. This is the ultimate goal of communications: going viral, in whatever form. If you create a strong message, it will get out there and reproduce itself.

Sales materials

Creating your message first will help you prepare your other basic promotion material: you may need a website, Facebook or Instagram, Twitter, Tik Tok or other social media account; a dossier of documents you use to present your product or service and flyers and business cards and a portfolio and images you will use in all the above. All of these should be designed to convey the content and essence of your message but you can only choose and create these things when you know what you are trying to say.

In general, your promotion material has to say:

- what you do
- why you're good at it
- who you are
- where to find you

Clever readers will notice that this list looks a lot like the basic contents of a website. That's because good web sites follow the basic structure of all effective communications by providing essential information in the most engaging manner possible. That said, you will, of course, need more than a website for your communications effort. The website and the Internet are the subjects of the next chapter, so let's look at how the four communication points work.

What you do. It sounds simple, but describing what you do can be the hardest thing of all when you are crafting your message. Sometimes it's a good idea to start with the other points and come back to this later. This text has to state, in a short and clear manner, what you do and give a hint of the other main points (why you are good, who you are and where to find you).

Why you're good at it. This is your sales argument and includes supporting documents like photos, video, customer reviews, endorsements and press clippings that praise you. If it's your first sale, you won't yet have much positive feedback from customers to include. An influential person who helped you get started might be willing to say a few good words about your work instead.

Who you are. While a resumé/CV is an essential tool when you are searching for a job, in the self-employed worker's sales material it is usually backup material, especially when you are selling a product. In the service sector, the resume/CV is more important. Just be careful not to include *everything* in it. The content has to be concise and relevant. There's no need to explain how you came into this world or mention your first job washing dishes at The Keg (unless it's relevant!). A short, well-written biography is a much more useful tool in communications. We each have at least ten different biographies of different lengths on hand for different purposes, from our Amazon profile to book jacket covers to bios for the different associations we to which we belong.

Where to find you. There is no question nowadays that most inter-action is done online, or facilitated by online connections, but you will certainly still need at least some basic handout material, such as business cards, pamphlets, leaflets or packages. These must carry your message and tell customers where to find you.

Whatever documents you decide to produce, they all must be concise and convincing and carry at least some of the above information. Don't beat around the bush. You need to be clear in your message and interesting in the way you communicate it so people can quickly see who you are and what you are proposing.

Although clarity is a very relative notion, if you intend to sell to a small circle of specialists, using some jargon in your material is okay. But if the decision to use what you are selling is going to be made by non-specialists, or if you are addressing the general public as well, your message must be conveyed in plain language. Take the time to check how your message is interpreted and be ready to adjust it if it is not getting through.

We all have a little computer inside our heads that quickly assesses offers and decides whether they are interesting. But the circuits in this little computer overheat when the incoming message is too detailed or confusing. The savvy calculators in our brains make decisions about what's interesting in just seconds, so your message has to be clear and concise or it will be quickly passed over for something more attention-grabbing.

You should also keep in mind that many different types of people will be reading your material and making their decision based on it.

Even if you meet with the President of McDonald's face-to-face, his or her decision about you will be made after consulting with colleagues. Whether your material is on the web, in a folder, a brochure or a letter, the simple fact of it being written guarantees that all these people hear the same message communicated the same way—unlike delivering a spoken presentation, which is tailored to specific listeners.

A word of caution: although it's not hard to design your own brochure these days using free online graphic design tools, it still might be worth asking a professional, or hiring a graphics student to do it. The student will be inexpensive and happy to add some professional experience to their portfolio. To find a good one, call the graphic arts department of your nearest college and ask for a recommendation. Teachers will tell you.

Another important point: make sure you correct the language and remove grammar, spelling and formatting mistakes in all your documentation. It won't cost you much to hire a freelance copy editor. Check the website of the Canadian Association of Editors or for freelance writers, the CFG. If you're thinking of cutting corners and saving a few bucks, remember: the highest quality people in their field, the ones you most want to reach, are likely to be the pickiest ones about details. Even people who aren't "literary" will spot spelling and grammar mistakes. Presenting writing with mistakes makes you look sloppy and instantly casts doubt on your professionalism. You should always have someone else proofread your copy. In a pile of proposals, even the best one will sink to the bottom if it has spelling and grammar mistakes. The same goes for everything you publish on the web.

The video

With the web, YouTube and editing software like iMovie, almost anyone can easily and affordably make a promotional video. Some of these videos end up snowballing on YouTube or Instagram, but you should be realistic. Your video will probably not make YouTube's Top Viral Videos of the Week.

The best video you can have, by far—the one that will give you the most exposure but also cost you the least—is one with you being interviewed by a journalist on TV interview. However, it is always hard to get a media outlet interested in your work when you are starting out and have little to show for your efforts (being journalists, we're on the selection end of the process so we can assure you, this is a fact).

But don't lose hope. You can produce your own promotional video for a few dollars, or a few thousand if you want. But before you invest any time or money, ask yourself if it will really help you reach your customers, or if you are doing it for the prestige factor. Videos matter a lot for self-employed workers who are selling a performance—an actor or musician or inspirational speaker, for example—or to promote mass-market items. For our last book, we invested a few hundred dollars in a thirty second trailer. Our film editor spent thirty minutes filming it, one hour editing it and got it on line in less than two hours total.

As audiovisual material has crept further into our lives in the form of online videos, we've noticed people have become more tolerant of casual, amateur-looking productions. This was definitely not the case twenty years ago. This trend has pros and cons. You can come across as being more "yourself," more "natural," less produced, in your video these days. But bear in mind that the "casual" look is often very "fabricated," meaning a lot of testing and editing work has gone into it to make it effective. Whatever the style you opt for, your video's sound quality has to be impeccable. If your listeners have to strain to hear you, they'll tune out no matter how great or engaging you are onscreen. Make sure your sound is good.

You can make a video inexpensively by renting equipment and hiring a communications or film student (or, honestly, almost any teenager these days) to do the editing. Just don't make the mistake of diving into the project without a plan, what's called scriptwriting. Scriptwriting allows you to plan ahead, clarify what you want to say and determine the sequences and shots you'll need to say it. A good script will serve as a guide to both the filmmaker and the editor.

Your video should be no longer than two or three minutes. There are longer videos out there—we've all seen them—but if your goal is to attract maximum interest from a large number of people, keep it short.

As for choosing a format or style, a documentary or interview format works very well. If you have nothing to show but an office, forget it; the same goes for a "talk show" style video, with people sitting around pontificating. It's boring. No one cares.

A final, important word: it's a good idea to get familiar with the large quantity of free online dictionaries and thesauruses out there. Since we are professional writers, we run everything we write, including emails, through Antidote, which is an excellent (though not free) correction software that works in both English and French. In our business, we definitely can't afford to be sloppy about spelling.

You probably can't, either.

8

Using the web

Getting the most out of Internet

Myth #8: "I need an expensive website."

"Have you seen my new website?" We are old enough to remember when people actually started conversations like that—it was only twenty years ago. Websites are ubiquitous today, so obviously no longer conversation starters. Internet has revolutionized global communications, and although social media have to some extent replaced websites as communications and promotional tools, few self-employed workers can afford to go without an actual website. Almost anyone who runs a business needs a web presence.

Yet even today, websites are more important for some businesses than for others. As writers, having a website is absolutely vital. We have published some fifteen books in Canada, Quebec, the United States, France and the United Kingdom. Our books have been translated into French, Japanese, Mandarin, Dutch Vietnamese and Turkish. Since we can't be everywhere at once, our website serves as a tool for our customers (readers), to get basic information about us and our books. We use the website to post our latest reviews (good or bad), interviews and appearances and to share news. We also have a Facebook feed on the home page where our latest social media posts appear.

The present version of our website is actually the fifth "edition." The site has evolved enormously over time, mostly because we continue to publish books, but also because the role of websites itself has changed. In its present form, the site is really a slick blog that we try to keep active with news and movement. Our friend and web strategist (that's the label he goes by) Sam Benahmed recently informed us that we get forty visitors on the site per day, on average. But that number fluctuates from five to 100 visits per day. We are certain most of the traffic is driven by activities that happen elsewhere: posts on social media, sending out emails to our mailing list, speaking at conferences, teaching courses, publishing articles in magazines or newspapers, writing columns, doing interviews for radio or newspapers or getting mentioned in the press.

We've come a long way in the world of the World Wide Web. Our first website, created in 2003, was as static as a stone sculpture. We designed it exclusively to promote our first book, *Sixty Million Frenchmen Can't Be Wrong* and recall panicking when translations and foreign editions of the book came out and we didn't know how to update the site ourselves (it wasn't easy at the time and involved actual coding). This was before sites had built in blog features. Today websites can showcase new information as it unfolds and can have built-in cash registers if you want one.

The biggest mistake people make when they are designing a web site is to only think about the website itself. You have to distinguish between your website and your visibility in cyberspace (with all of its web pages, blogs, discussion groups, images, videos and social networking formats). You can become very visible online without spending a penny on a website, namely by maximizing your social media presence or simpler things like getting a Wikipedia article written about you or your business. Websites can cost a fortune and not end up giving you value, in the form of exposure. For that matter, it might be wiser to spend more money on an effective webmaster than on a knockout website loaded with all the plugins (the bits of software that make your website do stuff). In any case, before you dive in, take the time to think about your goals and about how much time you want to devote to your online presence (e.g. Plugins require constant updates, as does security software, which is absolutely essential as hackers find new ways to mess up sites). It's very, very easy to get lost in the details of a website. If you're not careful, you can easily end up spending gobs of time and wads of cash on tools you don't really need.

The other thing to consider is that even if your YouTube tutorial or commercial video goes viral, it may not end up bringing you much real business—that is to say, direct material gain. Take the case of that Korean rapper, Park Jae-sang (stage name: Psy). His song Gangnam Style became a global phenomenon in 2012 when it got almost three billion page views on YouTube. By the end of 2012, the song had earned Psy some $7.9 million in rights—or $0.001 (one tenth of a penny) per page view. That sure sounds like a lot of money, but think about it for a second: if your tutorial or video ad gets 1.3 million page views (which you could call a huge hit), YouTube will pay you exactly $1,300. You will have probably spent more than that just making it.

So you need to ask yourself, what impact do you want to have online? And how this will translate into sales? Psy's online success sure brought him listeners and sponsorship deals, and he probably went on to make more money through those than he ever did from the original video. In other words, the usefulness of the web depends on what you are selling. If your product or service is for a local clientele, it's probably not worth going to the trouble of trying to create a video that will go viral—except maybe just for the fun of it. You can reach your customers more effectively through much more humble means like local advertising and good old networking. In that case, your web site just needs to make you findable. You need to let people see what you are selling in more detail. On the other hand, if you are like us and you sell goods or services to a distant clientele, much of your success will depend on spreading the word about your work far and wide. Internet does allow us to reach members of a very distinct club (people who love French and France) who are literally spread across the planet. Before we had a website, it would have been almost impossible to reach them directly and tell them we had a new book coming out.

We quickly abandoned the idea of trying to make videos in the hopes they would go viral. We have more luck getting interviewed on radio and getting publications, whether online or on paper, to write about us. We use our web presence mainly to advertise what we are doing and what people are saying about us. We keep our social media accounts warm by posting semi-regularly, but we're not obsessive about it.

One of the paradoxes of the web is that, despite all the hype over it, it can be hard to evaluate what it actually produces, concretely. Developing and maintaining your presence on the web demands work and may bring you nothing directly unless your site is transactional (i.e. actually sells things). Most of us have to turn exposure into money on our own. A lot of the time it's even hard to judge the results of an effort to get exposure. To do that you need pretty sophisticated technological skills (skills we don't have) or you have to pay someone who does. One tool, Google Analytics, allows you to analyse the traffic on your site. But for most people, even that doesn't directly translate into higher sales. For most small businesses, clicks don't necessarily translate directly into dollars. They are a form of advertising and there are others.

In other words, the web does have limitations, like any other type of advertising. You can get pretty excited about it. There are a lot of people out there who will help you get excited and take your money to build a sophisticated website or web strategy for you. But unless you are actually using it to sell something, it's best to build with caution.

The bottom line of developing a web presence is: you do need it, but unless web presence is a concrete objective, don't squander all your energy (or money) on it. Don't lose sight of the fact that it's your achievements that sell you, first and foremost. The main purpose of the site, for most of us, is to help spread the word about those achievements. Advertising, on the web or elsewhere, is important, but the most important thing is to do a good job at whatever you do.

Before the website

There are a number of things that you should do before getting a website. These will have a direct impact on your business and might even turn out to be sufficient until you have time to really think about you want your website to achieve.

Investing in a website before you tackle these preliminary steps is putting the cart ahead of the horse.

First, you should get a good email address. Email has come to seem a little old-fashioned these days, but it remains a very effective sales tool in many industries. In ours, for instance, where most of our sales actually involve convincing a handful of publishers and editors of the value and interest of what we want to write, "sales" are done with custom-made communications. We approach individuals one at a time. We would have done this work by mail twenty-five years ago. Now it's carried out almost exclusively by email. Since neither of us is a web information junky or compulsive iPhone user, it's fair to say that about 90% of the time we spend communicating online is through email. We send our emails with signatures that might include links to our website or social media coordinates so the people we communicate with can find us with a click and easily see examples of our work, or our bios, or see what we are doing elsewhere on the web. We post and converse with readers on Facebook but we don't use it to reach out to, or communicate with people unless it happens to be their tool of preference, in which case we don't have much choice. Even then, we quickly ask them to switch to email, which is just better suited to our needs (for sending texts as attachments, for example).

We strongly encourage you to get a domain name for your website and use that to generate your email address. Annie@hotmail.com or bob@me.com is fine for emailing friends or managing your online subscriptions. But in the professional world, email accounts that use the name of your Internet service provider sound amateur, especially among communications professionals. Addresses provided by your Internet company are also more likely to end up in junk boxes. A better address would be management@jackandjill.com or julie@oldfashionedmanure.ca. Everyone with whom we communicate gets a nadeaubarlow.com email address (which is the domain name for our website). Emails make us look serious and strengthen our brand, in one shot.

It's not hard to make a "custom" email. You don't need a website. All you have to do is buy the domain name (oldfashionedmanure.com or jackandjill.com) and then create an email address associated with it. There are all kinds of domain name registration businesses, such as www.register.com, where you can reserve a domain name for as little as $50 a year, depending on the services you need. Once you have your domain name, all you need to do is find a company that does web hosting services and they'll use your domain name to create email addresses you can use. These companies are not hard to find, but they are different from telephone or cable companies like Bell or Rogers who provide your Internet connection (who use their own name in the email address they provide with your subscription).

Is it better to have a ".com," ".ca" or ".org" after your domain name? It was an important problem fifteen years ago when fewer people were familiar with the system. But today it's just a question of what market you want to reach and what image you want to project—and sometimes, what domain names are available. It might be important, to some foreign customers. We've noticed Americans prefer American addresses (.com, .edu, .org) over "foreign" addresses that end in ".ca" or ".fr." But if your business is selling French courses in Latin America, the ".fr" address might give you some cachet that a ".com" address doesn't.

Finding domain names can be a bit of a treasure hunt. When you are starting a business, one of the first things you should do is check if the name you want for your website is available. Someone else may already be using it or have purchased it for future use. But there is usually a creative way around this issue. For example, say you offer a math course that you want to call Mathis. It would be nice if you discover that mathis.com or math.com is free. If they're not, you can try mathismath.com, or mathis-math.ca. We've also reserved domain names for some future book projects years before writing them. It's like an insurance policy. It doesn't cost much and gives you options for later.

The question of domain names will come up if you decide to launch a new service separately from the original one advertised on your site. For example, say you want to diversify your dog grooming service, Clean Rover, and enter the cat grooming market. You might call your new line of services Tidy Kitty or you expand into the animal transportation business and create something called the Port-a-Doggy. In that a case, it may be worth having a separate domain names for each service that link to one central website: your hosting service can give you the addresses www. tidykitty.com and www.portadoggy.ca and they'll both take you to the central site, which might be www.cleanrover.com or something else. Products look better advertised with a website that matches them. We still own our original domain www.sixtymillionfrenchmen.com, but if you type that address into your web browser, you'll be automatically directed to our homepage, www.nadeaubarlow.com.

Get a good database

Reaching out to people directly is important for many businesses, whether it's through newsletters or plain old emails. It's definitely worth going to the trouble of organizing your contacts in a storage system. What kind of system you use depends on what your precise needs are. Thirty years ago, people used a thing called a Rolodex to store business cards. Today, we have databases, which are basically electronic versions of the same thing: they're an organized contact list (but way better, since you can search them to come up with a targeted list). The difference is that that a well-designed database will allow you to quickly build mailing and contact lists so you can easily communicate your different achievements and/or offers to exactly the people you know will be most interested in them.

Creating a contacts database is not as hard as it sounds. It mostly requires discipline and keeping up the habit, like making your bed. When you sit down to think about it, you'll be amazed how many people you come to know, and how many people know you. You can easily collect a few hundred names with a few months of regular work. Jean-Benoît is very systematic about this, Julie a little less so, but in the last five years we have collected about 3,000 contacts between us. Don't forget friends and relatives, who have their own contacts as well. The database is useful for almost all your activities: sending emails or targeted messages about events, distributing a newsletter or simply sharing the occasional bit of really good news—for us that could be winning a book prize or being quoted in the *New York Times*. You can also inform your contacts about significant milestones, though this is done more and more with social media these days.

The most important thing to remember is that investing a lot of money in a website without creating a good database of your contacts might be a waste of time. The database is the best leverage you have to get people to visit the site. They are not likely to discover it by accident.

There are, of course, tools out there to help you, like the specialized database management software FileMaker. There are even websites like MailChimp that offer free email sending services. We tried a few of these but ultimately went back to something more basic: a good old-fashioned Excel spreadsheet. It's a simple spreadsheet, functional and easy to use. We enter each contact's name, coordinates and relevant information like their relation to us (e.g. friend, press), the language(s) they use and any personal information (e.g. their spouse's name, subjects of interest). You should never set up a database using Word format. Transferring it into another system is difficult, especially if you have entered the data in text mode rather than in table mode. The advantage of Excel, which is part of the basic Office software, is that you can adjust it as you go along, adding new columns when you need them. The other advantage of Excel is you can easily transfer your contacts to a more powerful system or email service. Basically, nothing you do in Excel is ever lost (unless you neglect to back up your computer).

One point to remember about Excel: only put one piece of information in each column. For example, "city," "province," "country" and "postal code" each requires separate columns. If you make the mistake of jamming all the information into a single column, none of your information can be separated for search purposes. This is because Excel allows you to make sub-lists. Our list includes 3,000 contacts, but if we search our own database using the words "Canada" + "French" + "Montreal" as selection criteria, we will come up with 1,000 contacts. But if we then search those 1,000 contacts using the word "Press" + "friend," we come up with forty-seven names of journalist friends. Sometimes we need to contact our journalist friends. Sometimes we just need to reach colleagues in Quebec. In that case we search with the words, "Press" + "Quebec" and come up with 377 contacts. If we had made the mistake of putting "Montreal," "Quebec" and "Canada" in a single column, we wouldn't have been able to narrow down the search. Sometimes we want to reach out strictly to local contacts in Montreal. The important thing here is to be able to use your criteria to put your contact database to good use.

You also have to be very systematic in the way you enter data. If, for your American customers, you sometimes write USA, sometimes US and sometimes United States, the computer will only find a third of the contacts you are searching for at a time.

Using social media (without losing your mind)

Even ten years ago, few of us would have imagined how much businesses would come to rely on social media to ensure their online presence and visibility.

To be precise, Facebook, LinkedIn, Twitter and Instagram are platforms used to publish content. They are a pre-established format through which you can do the equivalent of blogging. Twitter allows for messages in 280 characters. LinkedIn is used mainly for professional communications. Facebook can handle images and longer posts and can be used to create virtual word of mouth, conversations and debates between "friends."

Jean-Benoît has about 1,200 Facebook friends; Julie has double that and together, we have about 5,000 connections on LinkedIn. We also have a professional page together (that can't have friends, just followers). We don't spend hours a day posting and commenting on any of these networks but we are often surprised how useful they are for getting the word out about our work. We really do "meet" a lot of people and refresh acquaintances by posting news on the pages and we are surprised by the number of people we don't really know personally, who turn out to be regular followers.

Of course, Facebook does have rules you have to follow when you are using it: if you are too aggressive in "friending" people to build your network, the mother company will notice and you can end up being penalized or even removed from the system—it almost happened to Jean-Benoît a couple of times. The rules also change on a regular basis. At the time of writing, Facebook was making it harder to share posts with links to news from traditional news sources. This was taking a toll on our communications, since much of what we do is share our recent publications and articles about topics our followers are interested in. But we found ways around this, like not mentioning the name of the media in the post itself.

USING THE WEB   129

By the time you are reading this, Facebook's practices will have certainly changed again. If nothing else, this instability is a good reason to diversify your social media outreach on a few different platforms.

The main problem we have with social networks is that outside of work hours, we don't love spending time on computers. Social media can be such a time suck: to make to strong impact with social media, you really need to be part of ongoing public or group conversations. As we mentioned above, we use social media mainly to make announcements and inform our networks about a new book or article, interview or appearance. In other words, we advertise and take questions. We very rarely post anything that involves our private lives or especially our children: they are busy enough with their own social media activity and don't need to be dragged into ours. Nor do we post pictures of our holidays, which are not that exciting (but whose are, really). Setting boundaries like this probably doesn't help our social media effort, but it does keep us sane and limit the exposure our kids get as the offspring of two journalists.

With Facebook, you can choose between two kinds of pages: a "personal page" or a "fan page." The personal page allows you to exchange with people whom you have "friended" or vice versa. The fan page is visible to everyone on the Internet and can be used to publicize promotional activities like contests. Business, organizations, celebrities and political figures use fan pages. You should also make an effort to appear on other open sites like YouTube if you have something to show, or Wikipedia, which is the authority for supplying accurate content in cyberspace.

Measure your online discoverability

When we type "graphic design" into Google, the first entry that pops up after the advertisements is Montreal's Dawson College. The second entry is a definition of graphic design on the page of a school called the Interactive Design Foundation. After that there are a few other school sites, then a YouTube video explaining what graphic design is. What determines the order of these results? Three words: algorithms, search engine optimization and discoverability.

To create an effective website, you need to understand how the web works and what works best. Dawson College and the Interactive Design Foundation figured it out. Websites are made up of multiple "pages," including a "home" page, an "about" page and "contact" page, all of which can be subdivided into other pages as required by the quantity and detail of information on the site. Each news release, for example, is a separate web page. Each page has its own URL (Uniform Resource Locator), which is the web address of each page, presented as a line of code, sometimes too long to be recognizable at eye shot.

The sites of Dawson College and the Interactive Design Foundation have what's called high "discoverability." That's because their designers and webmasters understand what search engine "robots" are looking for. Robots are algorithms created by search engines like Google or Bing. Yes, Google is a robot. It weighs the interest of all web sites according to a list of approximately 200 criteria and puts them in order of importance. The criteria that the robots use to judge the relative interest of pages is actually a trade secret, but web designers have been able to figure out what the robots like: clear titles, subtitles, photos, certain words and hyperlinks. Google's robot is gregarious. It likes to see that there are a lot of people milling around a particular site. It also likes to see that a site is referenced on sites elsewhere and in social media. These links are like official endorsements from big players: the more "reliable" and highly frequented the sites that reference your site are, the more they will increase your ranking in search engines. Sites that meet those criteria come out on the top of your page during a search. Wikipedia is excellent in referencing and this is why Wiki articles pop up on the first page of search engines.

Over the past decade, a whole industry of consultants specialized in "referencing" has sprung up to help people win in the discoverability game. In the industry jargon, the trade is called Search Engine Optimization, usually referred to with the acronym SEO. There are lots of SEO consultants out there. Some are good, but many make ridiculous claims about the amount of traffic they'll bring to your site. We suggest you familiarize yourself with the mechanics of SEO before hiring anyone to help you. We rely on advice of our trusted web designer, Sam, to whom we pay a monthly fee for site maintenance.

You can make your site more "discoverable" on your own by paying attention to key words. Google's robot searches for keywords. Keywords are just particular words that are frequently used by people when they are doing searches. If you want your content to be discovered, it's a good idea to include the very words on your site that people are using to search. Search engines are very literal when it comes down to it.

You can find lists of key words by searching "AdWords" on Google's site. You can then use popular terms in your field in the content you write for your site. Some crafty folks add highly used (though often completely irrelevant) popular keywords like "your" "free" and "get" to the content on their site just to attract traffic. But the robots are smarter than that. They can tell when you are pushing it and will penalize you (by lowering your site's ranking) for using keywords that don't actually belong in the text.

In essence, SEO makes sense because search engines like Google or Bing have just figured out how to perform mental processes that we all share, but they do it on an industrial scale. After all, who doesn't pay attention to a friend's insightful comments about a product? Again, Google understood how to write algorithms that would replicate and industrialize something we all do spontaneously and naturally. The algorithm itself is secret. Whatever they say, SEO specialists guess how the criteria work. They get a rough idea by looking at search engine results and working backwards. Having a social media strategy has come to feel essential these days, and there are lots of people who will take your money to help you create such a strategy. However, you have to remember that the strategy is only good if it allows you to actually sell more and generate revenue. A basic "strategy" like ours may be all you need.

Think Wiki

One very effective way of making yourself discoverable is by using Wikipedia. It's one of the most used websites in the word and if you have a Wikipedia article it's almost guaranteed to appear very high in search engines. Having a Wikipedia page about you also increases your credibility. The spirit of Wikipedia is that of an open and collaborative encyclopaedia. Unpaid contributors work together through a process of posting, checking and criticizing each other's contributions, to produce articles of varying lengths about topics. Studies have shown that the content on Wikipedia is roughly as accurate as that of traditional encyclopaedias.

If you are a true pioneer developing something entirely new, you don't need to wait around for someone to spontaneously decide to write a Wiki article about you. You can ask (or pay) a contributor to create a page about you or your company or industry. This practice does not exactly reflect the spirit of Wikipedia, but it's being done more and more and is tolerated as long as contributors are transparent about it. But beware: you don't own or control the content about you on Wikipedia. External contributors will always be able to correct and update content. One way you can use Wikipedia to boost your visibility in your field is to become a Wikipedia contributor yourself and either write new pages or collaborate on existing Wiki pages about your topic.

However, if you decide to set up a page on Wikipedia with your name or your company's name on it, be careful about the style you use. Wikipedia texts are meant to be encyclopaedic. As a result, their tone is neutral. Secondary sources must be quoted. You cannot publish anything that sounds promotional on Wikipedia: other contributors will sniff it out and correct or remove your entry, then very likely push you out of the community—the atmosphere among elite Wiki contributors is actually quite warlike. Your text should cite credible sources and it should also include external links. If there is some controversy about you or your activity, a good Wikipedia article will say so. If this makes you uncomfortable, just stay away from Wikipedia.

What you want is for people to find you: you want to be "discoverable." This buzzword in the small world of SEO describes "the quality of being easy to find via a search engine, within an application, or on a website" (Oxford Dictionary). Although it can be difficult to figure out how to boost your discoverability, you can do a simple test to see if your efforts are bearing fruit. Just type your name or business name into a search engine and see what comes up. If it's your website or your own Facebook or LinkedIn page, you're off to a good start. If it's someone else, you're in trouble. Another test is to check where you come out when you type your industry in the search field. When we type "Julie Barlow" into Google, our own website comes up in second place. First is the Wikipedia article about her. Third place is her page on *L'actualité*, the public affairs magazine she has been writing for since 1996, which reaches about a million readers online.

Ideally, you should make a constant effort to improve your discoverability with SEO. But again, that requires time and effort. The criteria used by Google's algorithms and other search engines constantly change so it's important to stay up to date. Paying a consultant to help you might be a good investment. After all, what's the point of having the best-looking website on earth if it's buried in 20th or 30th position on Google? If a search engine can't find you, or it finds your competitors first, how will customers find you?

Designing a website that meets your goals

A showcase website is not designed the same way as a transactional website that you use to actually sell your service or product. Before you start thinking about website design, carefully consider what goal you want it to achieve. Do you want a web site that acts as a showcase, or one that's a commercial tool? This might take you back to your business plan and thinking about your business strategy.

For instance, we found ourselves at a crossroad the last time we did a major redesign of our website. We thought it might be a good idea to create a transactional site and sell our books directly. We also thought about allowing advertisements on the site (we get the occasional offer to do so from different businesses, especially in the language learning field). We probably could have made a bit of extra cash doing this.

There are lots of different tools and platforms you can use to create a shopping site. For payments, there is, of course, the classic PayPal, but there are other more elaborate tools available too. However, running a transaction website is complicated. You need a reliable and easy-to-use interface. Then you have to manage stock and inventory and the logistics of shipments and returns. It is possible to do business via third-party companies that manage this aspect for you (e.g. Amazon), for a fee. But you don't get anything for free so this, again, will add to your expenses.

We decided against turning our website into an online shop. First, we have no expertise selling books and didn't particularly want to learn. Indigo, Amazon.ca and a host of independent booksellers do the job just fine. Our site directs readers to those sites. Also, our professional circle includes publishers and agents whose job it is to sell and promote our books. Each member of the team takes care of a part of our business, but no one is entirely responsible for Nadeau & Barlow except us. And no one (in that group) can write as well as we can. So that's where we decided to put our energy. We opted for a website that would be a showcase, in several languages, of all our books and all our activities (conferences, training and so on).

One big obstacle we encountered when we were designing the new site was language. The two of us write in both English and French and we need to communicate to our community in both languages. We also publish in four distinct markets (English Canada, Quebec, the United States and France), in two languages. We also have a wide variety of "products": the self-employment guide you are reading was originally written in French; Jean-Benoît wrote a book on making a living as a writer; we wrote four books about the French, two books on the French language and a book on Spanish. We've also published or co-authored books on hydroelectricity and how to use online resources in medical diagnoses (in collaboration with a university professor). In addition to that we both do translations and are developing our skills in scriptwriting. We wanted a website that would allow visitors to easily find the same content in French and in

English. That's easier said than done. This time we found a web consultant who had experience dealing with this kind of "challenge" and he came up with an inexpensive and effective solution. But it took us many years of experimenting to get there.

For the last twenty years web communication has been organized in a standard way: websites have an "About" page, one for "Frequently Asked Questions," a "Contact" button. The content and services on the site are organized in menus or tabs. Not too many blogs or websites operate outside this basic framework. But the number and variety of gadgets you can add to your sites is constantly increasingly: there are thousands of features available, from scrollbars to videos interfaces to a huge assortment of flashing spinning images, each more exciting than the last. These new features, called plugins or widgets, will make your website look very in-the-moment. However, going the route of flashy gadget has two disadvantages. They add to the work of running and maintaining a site, which is already considerable. Also, the more gadgets you have on your website, the more vulnerable it will be to hacking. While no one denies the appeal of gadgets, they should be used judiciously. If nothing else, remember that web users are notoriously impatient and won't wait for information that doesn't pop up right away because their system is too slow loading your very slick website.

At the moment of writing, the fashion for websites is long pages organized in a linear fashion that you scroll down. They feel a bit like scrolling on a smartphone. That's probably not coincidental. People use phones more than computers now to search the web. The shift to smartphones has also simplified and streamlined websites, which today are less cluttered and easier to navigate than previous generations. You should bear this in mind when you are designing your site. The other thing you should do is look at your competitors and see what kind of sites they use. There's no use and no real wisdom in reinventing the wheel: these sites probably work well. Also, bear in mind the size and shape of the screen on which your site will be read. Computer screens are large horizontal rectangles; phone screens are small vertical rectangles. As a result, content that looks good on a wide computer screen might turn out to be unreadable on a phone. You can format your website to fit any screen by using a "responsive screen" function, but it should be added at the time of design and not as an afterthought.

The good old-fashioned blog

The other thing to decide about the format of your website is whether it will be static or dynamic (interactive). A static website doesn't move or change much. If your goal is to have a site that is basically a glorified business card with information about you and answers to basic questions about your product or service, then a static website will do the trick. It costs a lot less to design and manage a site like this. Updates on a site like this might be difficult to make.

Most websites these days are interactive and that's what we opted for. Technically speaking, our site, built on a platform supplied with WordPress, is a blog. The term blog is short for "web log" (say it out loud and you'll understand). Invented in the 1990s, the blog platform was designed to be constantly modified and updated with new content. Visitors can register and respond to the host's posts. Blog sites have built-in content management software that makes it possible to modify content quickly and simply. The blog format is essential if you want to post new entries on your site or add new images on a regular basis. Blog platforms are also ideal if you want to put out a press release once a month. It's very easy to do. You don't have to call your web consultant for help (unless there's a glitch in the site: it occasionally happens). The blog interface is literally built so you can do it on your own. Using it is about as simple as changing the settings in an email account.

That said, the layout of a blog site is about the same as that of a static website: a menu with "About," "What We Do," "Frequently Asked Questions," "News" and "Contact" buttons, or some variation on the theme. You can add video, scrolling banners and any other gadget you want but you'll probably need professional help for that.

The main difference with a blog format is that you can change the images or text on your home page whenever you post a new item, whether it's a press release, a new article, a photo or other. And visitors to the site can leave comments if they want (though most people communicate feedback via social media these days). Taking feedback on a blog and answering questions has pros and cons. Answering comments takes work and comments are not always nice. On the other hand, the more you post, the more likely you will be to attract greater numbers of visitors to your site—if that's your goal.

The most user-friendly and universally recognized blog platform is WordPress: it's a gigantic blog publishing and hosting platform with a powerful content management system. In 2022, WordPress estimated that there were 455 million websites in the world using their system. WordPress is free and open source, meaning anyone can use it. You can create and get a basic WordPress blog online in a few minutes. You don't even need a separate web hosting service for it. The advantage of this formula is obviously that it's simple: WordPress offers hundreds of preset templates you can choose from. The disadvantage of using WordPress is that you're not on your own website, so you don't have complete control over the format or the content, which is stored by WordPress.

You can also hire a professional to make your own custom blog/website using the WordPress platform. This is what we did because we needed to introduce some features that aren't standard. Notably, we needed a multilingual environment. The online WordPress templates do not accommodate multilingual sites easily, so for $3,000, our web designer Sam Benahmed created a functional, rather sophisticated website for us using WordPress technology. It's hosted by a hosting service. It's a bit more complicated and a bit more expensive solution than a standard WordPress site, but we have our own address (which looks more professional) and full control over our content. The site does exactly what we want it to do and we can manage the content updates easily by ourselves, without calling poor Sam day and night for help.

As we said, having your own blog means you have to manage the interactive part of it. But unlike with social media platforms, you have full control over what comments appear on your blog. You can accept or reject them as they come in. It's a good idea to filter them because sometimes comments are unnecessarily cruel or simply irrelevant (though again, most of that behaviour happens on social media these days). If you filter, you have to read everything and broadcast only what you deem acceptable. In our case, we tolerate criticism as long as it is documented and polite. Free, overly personal or insulting criticism goes to the trash.

The hidden costs of the web

At $3,000, our custom website was quite inexpensive, but we put a lot of time into organizing and planning it with our web designer. Generally speaking, the more websites do, the more they cost. We were happy we didn't go overboard building the site because in the end, running a blog with regular posts was more work than we anticipated. At some point we stopped trying to reach readers by posting fresh, related content on a weekly basis. We just couldn't keep it up.

In fact, barely a week after we got our blog up, we realized that we would need help running it. For us, the math was simple: it was fairly easy to generate content for the blog, but the rest of work managing it was a mountain. So we hired a webmaster.

There are all sorts of webmasters. Some are journalists and editors wrapped into one. But since journalism is our day job, we didn't need someone who could write so much as an editor who could do graphics (neither of us can) and had good technical mastery of online tools. The young woman we hired, Veronica, had a knack for web monitoring and enough initiative to help us come up with ideas for content. What we failed to anticipate was that after two years, our website would be hacked—three times. This recurring problem became so acute and so costly that we had to hire a consultant and redo the whole site. In the end, what we needed (and could afford) was not an editor but a consultant who would supervise the site and do regular security updates—which still costs us $1,500 a year.

The great advantage of the blog is that it can make you a credible information source for people in your field who are interested in your views and willing to share them with others. The disadvantage is that to create and maintain an information source, you have to publish regularly—which, by the way, is also true of using social media. You really have to stay in the loop about your subject and constantly update the information you provide. In addition to coming up with new content, you have to: spread it through social networks; manage and react to comments; keep an eye on the site and do repairs when it gets hacked; manage the relationship with the service provider that hosts your website; and analyse all the website traffic statistics to see what's working and what's not. Even when you have a relatively static website there's a lot of regular upkeep work to do.

This is the hidden cost of the web that people don't talk about much.

Whatever approach you take, whether it's using social media or a blog/web site (more on this in the next chapter), you shouldn't expect to see convincing results for your efforts for at least six months, probably a year. You have to be willing and able to stick to it. Building a reputation online is only part of your larger promotional effort, but it requires patience, perseverance, good judgment and takes a lot of elbow grease. And you will still need to make your first sales.

9

Creating buzz

What you need to know about self-promotion

Myth #9: "It's expensive to do marketing."

"Going viral," "selling like hot cakes," "making a splash." There are a lot of catch phrases out there to describe the advertiser's great dream: generating so much buzz and word-of-mouth that their product sells itself.

The problem is, nothing sells itself until you help sell it, first.

So, here's how you do it.

The first thing to do is make sure you understand what you are doing. Let's start with "promotion." It is about selling, but it's not sales and it's not advertising. Promotion is what draws attention to you, or to your service or your product, so there will be demand for it. If promotion is well done, a portion of the people who react to your message will go on to bind themselves to you in a contract of sale. Only then can you, your agent, your representative or the salespeople selling your wares at Wal-Mart or Staples call it "a sale." It's important to understand the distinction between promotion and sales so your promotion efforts will be effective and bear fruit. Not every dollar or hour you spend on promotion will necessarily bring about a sale.

Advertising is different than promotion. The philosopher Archimedes said, "Give me a place to stand and with a lever long enough, and I will move the world." Advertising is Archimedes' lever. It amplifies your strength. But you have to know how to use this new strength. Not everyone can afford to run a TV ad in the middle of the seventh game of the Stanley Cup finals. And what good is spending a ton of money to get your message out if hockey fans won't want to buy what you are selling anyway (the newest electric SUV, probably, but an innovative anti-aging cream? Probably not).

The art of promotion consists of two things: controlling the message, which we discussed in Chapter 7, and selecting the right medium with which to transmit it. The web, which was the subject of Chapter 8, is pretty much a mandatory medium for advertising and promotion today, but it is not the only place to get your message and your information out there. For example, we have seen over the years that our website helps us reach people, but its effects are multiplied tenfold when we use it to retransmit the message of a traditional media of high stature, like the *New York Times* or CBC. So the traditional ways for doing promotion do matter a lot. Which means that, for us, publishing *is* promotion.

Your promotional activity must be targeted and include several points of support. It must also be realistic and have short-, medium- and long-term objectives. When it is well done, promotion doesn't need to cost much. For example, it costs less to be a guest on CBC's The Sunday Edition (it won't cost you anything, besides your time and bus fare or parking) than it does to take out advertising time on the CBC.ca website. But to get an interview on The Sunday Edition, you will have to be interesting enough to be invited as an on-air guest and be able to convince the hosts to invite you. A more realistic objective might be to get an interview at your local paper, or even writing an op-ed for that same paper or online media. These relatively small efforts can get you some interesting visibility without costing more than a couple of hours of labour. We'll talk more about this later.

If you are selling a highly specialized service, your promotional activity might be best done individually, person-to-person. We'll look at this issue in more detail in the next chapter. Even when your promotional activities succeed in generating demand, each buyer will probably have to be won over one at a time.

Niches and influencers: Finding your "everyone"

The best advertising "media" to transmit your message depends entirely on what your activity is. "Media" is a big word. It really means any method of communication used to get a message out. "Media" is often understood as mass media: the traditional press, either online or paper, radio and TV—now divided between digital media and legacy (traditional) media. But there are other, targeted media that can be very effective in helping you get exposure.

Who wouldn't want "everyone" to talk about what they want to sell? But "everyone" is a very broad category: if you are selling an ultra-specialized service like communications for the pharmaceutical industry, then "everyone" is actually a few hundred key people. It's not worth going to the trouble getting an interview on a major news show on CBC for something so specialized. The key to successful promotion is to locate the right channel through which to reach your "everyone." To do that, you first need to target your market. For example, we sell our books in the United States and France (as well as Quebec and Canada). But long before the actual books are sold to customers, we have to "sell" our book projects to publishers. And to do that, we need to figure out who their end customers—the readers—are. There are thousands of small categories of customers in each of the countries where we sell, and some are more likely to be interested in our books than others. One of the keys of our success has been the ability to demonstrate to publishers that we know who our readers are and that we know where and how to reach them. We are not trying to reach 325 million Americans or 67 million French people.

For example, for our book on the Spanish language, we figured out that there are not only 50 million Hispanics living in the United States, but also about 20 million Americans who speak Spanish as a second language, as well as 6 million students learning Spanish in schools. This constituted our core market. Then we figured out what kind of associations they belong to (Language Meetup Groups, teachers' organizations), what media they listen to (Rick Steves' travel shows, but also NPR and CBC radio) and who the credible spokespeople were that could help us get the word out (Hispanic journalists, leading academics in Spanish language and literature, the American Association of Teacher of Spanish and Portuguese).

To be clear, you need to identify your niche, then figure out how to reach it by identifying the influencers within it. The term "influencers" is automatically associated with online figures with a lot of followers, but all it means is "opinion makers," and you can find those off-line as well as online. Despite what those born after the Internet tend to believe, influencers existed before the Internet. Depending on your niche, your influencers could be a person, a particular media outlet or a well-known company. The better you identify your niche and its opinion makers, the faster you will be able to get your message out to the people you want to reach.

Paul Gallant, the inventor of the three-dimensional puzzle whom we discussed in Chapter 3, was very good at finding his "everyone." Gallant made his mark in the toy industry remarkably quickly by identifying and reaching out to influencers. In his case, it was one huge influencer: the New York toy store, F.A.O. Schwarz. When Gallant was ready to market his puzzles, he took his Puzz-3D prototype to New York City and set up a meeting with buyers at this iconic toy store, which is the reference (and therefore, "influencer") in the toy business. F.A.O. Schwarz bought 200 boxes of Gallant's puzzles on the spot and quickly assembled them for all to view, right in the store's window. The stamp of approval from F.A.O. Schwarz gave Gallant's subsequent promotion efforts enormous clout. He put that to use in the next stages of his promotion campaign: hitting trade fairs, doing media outreach and creating infomercials.

There are three lessons to be learned from Gallant's approach. First, he didn't make the (common) mistake of underestimating the value of his idea. Beginners often think that because they are small, they necessarily have to start by winning over small fish first, then work their way up. But why do big clients become big? Because they had a big idea and were not afraid to show it. An industry leader like F.A.O. Schwarz will recognize other people's great ideas.

Secondly, Gallant correctly assessed the scope of his idea. You need both knowledge and instinct to be able to do this. Some ideas really are local, like hairdressing or other personal care services. A home foot care service will necessarily start out locally: it won't make sense to offer that kind of service in Toronto if you live in Windsor because it won't be cost-efficient to drive to Toronto when you can reach clients close to home. Other ideas are ultra-specialized, like "public relations for the pharmaceutical business." In both cases, say, if you develop a PR franchise or if you expand from foot care into designing cases for travelling nurses, your idea might grow and cross borders—municipal, provincial or even national. But you should still start by thinking locally.

Thirdly, Gallant carefully selected the right medium to transmit his message (the F.A.O. Schwarz showcase) with a specific, measurable goal (to gain visibility in the toy industry). In other words, he didn't try to get his toys into F.A.O. Schwarz just for the ego boost, but because this was the most effective place where he could gain notoriety. TV commercials might be suitable for launching an astrological consultation service or a new potato peeler (potentially anyone could be interested), but they probably aren't the best choice for advertising a new web-based atlas. Newspapers would not be not the best place to promote or advertise a "colour therapy" consultation service because they are generally black and white; radio would also have obvious limits for this concept.

Lawyers take on pro bono cases—i.e. for free—ostensibly for the public good, but also for the visibility they get. That's not to draw from the merit of offering free legal advice: there are certainly cases with important principles at stake where clients can't afford lawyers. But lawyers' "altruistic" gestures are generally calculated. They will find a case interesting if it ensures visibility in the media or in legal circles. Every self-employed person should follow this example and make sure they are visible when and where it matters.

Whatever medium you choose, tailor your efforts to the size and location of the audience you want to reach. And if you are opening a barbershop service in Kitchener, Ontario, people in Brantford don't really need to hear about it, so choose a local media outlet.

Once you identify your niche, it will become much easier to design effective advertising and decide on the right vehicle to carry your message. Do not skip this stage of thinking. Never assume that "everyone will be interested" in what you want to sell. They won't. And you'll waste a lot of time and effort if you don't think of whom you want to reach, ahead of time.

I network, you network, we all network!

The power of networks should never be underestimated. A Hungarian author, Frigyes Karinthy, was the first to formulate (in 1929!) the theory that we are all connected in chains of acquaintances that have six people or fewer. In a short story called "Chains," Karinthy articulated the idea that would be later known as, "six degrees of separation." His theory turned out to be remarkably accurate: using a database of a few billion Facebook exchanges, specialists from Microsoft calculated that the actual degree of separation between individuals is between 4.74 and 6.6 people (if you could divide people into fractions).

In 2003, we discovered we were one or two phone calls away from President George W. Bush. Really. One of our American friends, a photographer by the name of Susan Sterner was hired as Laura Bush's official photographer that year. Depending on how you count the degrees, we were one or two from George W. Of course, in our case, the distance was highly theoretical: to reach the president, we would have had to convince at least seventeen people to get him to take our call. However, thanks to our friend Susan, we knew where to start (and she actually did discretely place a copy of one of our books in the First Lady's line of vision).

For most self-employed people, who offer a niche service, their most effective promotional effort will be networking.

Have you ever wondered how lawyers and chartered accountants reach new clients? In Canada, like members of all professional orders, they have to abide by strict rules of conduct that limit their ability to make wild claims. (You don't see anything in Canada like the US lawyer's ad: "With McClutcheon and McClutcheon, you'll get a BEAUTIFUL DIVORCE!") Because of these restrictions on "advertising," the members of professional orders use indirect methods instead to get their message out and reach potential customers. The bulk of their promotional activity involves making sure they are seen where it matters. They distribute business cards and get visibility by attending community activities (see box on next page) and networking.

There is an element of luck in the effectiveness of networking, but it definitely increases your likelihood of being lucky.

The strangest thing about networks is that you never know who will end up opening doors for you. That's why you should always enter them with an open mind, not a specific strategy. It could turn out that So-and-So is married to Another Person who happens to sit on the Board of Directors of a Big Foundation, and she spoke about you to the CEO of the XYZ Enterprises who sits on the same board. It sounds a little random and circuitous when you describe it like this, but these kinds of connections actually happen and they can work wonders. When people connected to you hear that you have something really interesting to offer, they get a lot of satisfaction from telling other folks about you. It's just human nature.

In your case, this may mean signing up for networking events at your local Chamber of Commerce or getting on a plane a couple times a year to attend conferences or conventions or the annual general meeting of your professional association. One thing that savvy journalists do, especially early in their careers, is to submit articles to contests. There are a lot of contests out there: writing associations hold these contests primarily to promote their members and increase their own visibility. Winning awards always brings recognition and respect from colleagues (the wider public doesn't pay attention to most awards but they are an excellent excuse to send out a message or newsletter to your community). And even if you don't win, entering contests can help you gain visibility in your field. Juries are usually populated by experienced and influential members of a profession. And whatever the result, you are showing you have confidence in your work.

Aside from contests, all professional associations have activities designed to foster relationships among their members. Most associations have their own online newsletters where members can publicize their achievements. Associations often offer training seminars by members or leaders in their field and sometimes organize mentoring services for junior members. Getting involved in these associations helps break the solitude of your work and keeps you abreast of news and developments in your field. It also helps you get promotion ideas from your colleagues and or competitors. To get the broader picture of your industry, it's a good idea to become a member of at least one association outside your local area. Everyone gets ideas, inspiration and motivation through learning about what other members in their field are doing.

Some networking activity is more "directed." As we mentioned, lawyers and accountants are known for getting involved in local politics, or in philanthropic or cultural work. There's no doubt they believe in the good causes they support, but they also get involved for less altruistic reasons, namely, to become better known and more visible in their communities.

Also, when it comes to "networking," be careful not to spread yourself too thin. Your goal is to sell a service or product, not to build a huge database with contact information of people you hardly know. If networking is taking up all your time, maybe you might want to consider a career as a lobbyist.

The following checklist will help you decide what activities are most likely to produce the desired results:

1. **Know what you want.** Which suppliers or customers are you targeting? Who could be your partner? Do you want local, regional, provincial, national or international visibility?
2. **Be effective.** How much time can you really spend each month writing and building relationships?
3. **Invest a little.** Find out which conferences, luncheons or seminars would really benefit you.
4. **Establish a timeline with goals.** Plan milestones and try to estimate when exactly you should be reaping what you sow.
5. **Re-evaluate.** If nothing works as planned, be ready to go back to the drawing board and change or adapt your approach.

Sign up and sign on

Getting involved in organizations—through committees or by being on a board of directors—can be a powerful way to build relationships with well-connected decision makers in your field. These people can help you develop your ideas and even open doors for you.

If you are going to play the game this way, just be careful not to juggle too many causes all at once because you will come off as insincere. And you will never sleep.

The other thing is that you have to want to get involved in a cause for the sake of it, not just to push your professional agenda. If you get involved for the wrong reasons, people in your field will quickly see it. If your involvement is entirely self-interested, it will end up being superficial and have an opportunistic air that everyone will sense. And this will reflect poorly on you in the long term. Volunteers are quick to spot those who are "strictly in it for themselves." If you don't work genuinely towards the common interest of whatever group you join and demonstrate a minimum of altruism, or if you have a tendency to keep track of all the moral debts people owe you for your good deeds, your effort will backfire and you will eventually be pushed out.

If you are going to play the game this way, just be careful not to juggle too many causes all at once because you will come off as insincere. And you will never sleep.

Ten ways to showcase your business

When you have a message, here are the promotional tools you can use to get it to your targeted audience. Some of these tools are very simple; others involve more time and investment.

(The web, Internet and social media are powerful tools we discussed in the previous chapter.)

1. **The storefront sign.** This is a tool for local promotion. Before you put one up, ask yourself: how many passers-by might cross your threshold because they saw a sign outside telling them you exist?

2. **Direct mail marketing.** Mailing promotional brochures will cost more than sending emails, but they give you a better chance of getting your message into the hands of your target customers (and avoid ending up in their email spam filter). The more targeted, personal and relevant your message is, the more likely it will end up reaching the right person. There are many tricks for making mail-outs effective, like personalizing the message and using the envelope itself as the ad. Whatever the form, the entire document should be as detailed as possible. The message should be clear and concise. Use numbers to support your argument whenever possible. Be specific. Make sure your potential consumer can translate the message into action (buy, rent, subscribe, etc.).

3. **Internal corporate communications.** People often overlook corporate newsletter, but they shouldn't. Employees of large companies are large groups of well-paid consumers share important information among themselves and they pay attention to their colleagues' recommendations. If you want to convince managers to buy your product or service, start by getting employees (whom they are likely to consult) on board. You can network with them at conferences, Christmas parties and sports events. Consider contributing to their internal newsletter, helping with employee onboarding kits or posting on the office bulletin board.

4. **Internal publications of associations.** This is different than targeting company newsletters. Associations tend to have fewer employees but a larger number of members who consider themselves part of a community. For that reason, many associations are geared to communicating to members and sympathizers: they have websites, usually a newsletter, their own conference(s) and local chapters. If an association endorses you, or if it shows interest in your product, service or just you (especially if you are a member), it will become a powerful ally. We have gotten a lot of well-paid writing work and valuable information about our markets from the associations we joined.

5. **The good old window case display.** This tool has fallen out of fashion mostly because it is misunderstood. Window showcases don't work when you just pile up products hoping to catch the eye of passers-by. They can be a work of art and a destination. A leader in the art of window displays, like the F.A.O. Schwarz toy store, is a great example of how effective window displays can be.

6. **Trade shows.** There are two ways to make these work for you: as an exhibitor or as an attendee. Being an attendee is obviously the cheapest way. We've discovered that just visiting international trade shows can also be useful: we try to attend book fairs whenever we can to shake hands with publishers and see what's going on in the market. Some government subsidies might be available to help cover the costs of attending these events. Being an exhibitor at a trade show is an expensive way to do promotion: you need to rent a stand, fill it, transport staff to a location to take care of it and then spend whole days at your own expense tending to it. But it may pay off. The interest of trade shows depends on what you are selling, but it's important to know how to present yourself. You should definitely hire a professional to help you. There is also a difference between public shows, like craft fairs and trade shows reserved for specialists in a particular business or industry. You could start by testing your idea in a less expensive way.

7. **Telemarketing.** This is a hybrid between mass advertising and personal solicitation. But be careful: it can play tricks on you. Since telemarketing often feels like harassment, the public's tolerance for this type of solicitation has dropped to the point where legislators have created no-call lists that people can get themselves on to avoid it altogether. The success rates of telemarketing are also very low: if you get one sale for every 100 calls, you're considered a genius. To succeed in this game, prepare a dialogue plan and choose telemarketers who know how to answer hard questions. The telephone is an intimate medium: an interested customer will quickly go to the heart of the matter and may ask you unexpected questions. That means an inept, unskilled or untrained telemarketer (we've all encountered them) can burn your campaign to the ground. For instance, if you are

selling orchestra subscriptions and your telemarketer can't pronounce Rimsky-Korsakov or Dvořák, the music lover on the other end of the phone will very likely hang up before you have time to make your pitch.

8. **Lectures and workshops.** Public speaking and teaching are very effective ways to get your message out to a targeted audience. The dream, of course, is to be invited to make the keynote speech at the conference or annual general meeting of a big association that all your potential clients will be attending. For this to happen, you first need a proven track record as a speaker or authority. You can acquire this by participating in roundtable discussions or being on panels. The only drawback of this formula is that you won't be reaching out to specific individuals. You'll be speaking to groups. On the other hand, you will often be paid to speak and therefore, to sell your own product. The best people in the field don't try to "sell" themselves when they are giving lectures. They strive to set themselves apart and make an impression on their listeners. They do this by saying something intelligent and memorable. If you end up speaking frequently at conferences, be careful not to make the mistake of giving the same speech over and over. If you have a good joke, switch it up for the next presentation or at least gracefully acknowledge that your listeners may have already heard it. Remember: many people in your field will attend more than one conference.

9. **Become an opinion-maker.** Sharing your experience and wisdom is another well-proven technique for promoting a business or project. You can do this by writing opinion articles or commenting on other people's articles whether in traditional newspapers or on blogs. For that matter, why not start your own newsletter or blog? You just have to make sure you're conveying an opinion from an informed vantage point and not just advertising yourself. Newspaper editors will instantly know the difference as soon as they read your material. You can also get yourself recognized as an "expert" on a particular issue by approaching writers in the printed press or researchers who find and develop stories for radio or TV. Once you are recognized by other opinion makers, you will be frequently invited to comment on current

events or to share your own experience. Don't neglect community newspapers or/and specialized papers of different cultural communities as forums for your opinions. Consultants often manage to carve out a place for themselves as a columnist in a local paper or web-based newspaper, slyly "mentioning" their services in the process.

10. **Use cyberspace.** We devoted all of chapter 8 to this topic, but we're taking the opportunity here anyway to repeat the message: the web is not just websites. Websites can be powerful vectors for your message: in their best form they can be a storefront sign (home page), a media outlet (blog) and a conference (links to videos of you speaking or being interviewed) all wrapped into one. The drawback is that websites are relatively passive. In addition to a website, you should make as much use of social media networks as you can. Use them to share your opinions (on Twitter, Facebook, Instagram, TikTok), start conversations (easier on Facebook but also possible on the other media) or catch the attention of influencers (Instagram is probably best for that). Social media tools are constantly evolving. (Just ask a teenager you know!) Using social media gives you the potential to create "buzz" about your product or service. Don't forget to use keywords. And pay attention to what age-group uses which platform (older folks will be on Facebook and Twitter; younger ones on Instagram and TikTok). If your work is more visual, a fun or informative video on YouTube might be an effective way to reach your audience. Also, don't overlook the potential of your Internet contact database, not to mention purchasing advertising in association directories or on specialized websites.

Whatever you do, remember that it can distract you completely from your objective, which it to make sales and work on your product or services. The challenge of using cyberspace is to convert all the visibility it offers into revenue. You have to keep your eye on the ball.

Using traditional media to "advertise"

When it comes to promotion, there is still nothing as powerful as the major media for drawing attention to your product, whether that's newspapers, weekly papers, magazines, radio, TV or established online media like *HuffPost* of *Buzzfeed*. Social media, by the way, largely feed off what the professional media publish first. There are two gateways for getting your message out in the traditional media: the advertising department (expensive, but fast) or the editorial department (free, but a gamble).

Let's start with the media from the point of view of the advertising department. Generally speaking, even if you pay for your advertising, you must comply with the publication's advertising guidelines: an ad in *The Toronto Sun* isn't the same style as an ad in *The Globe and Mail* or the *Halifax Chronicle Herald*. You have to tailor your advertising to the style and standards of the publication. The same goes for advertorials, or fake articles, which are paid for by advertisers and are designed to be barely distinguishable from the rest of the news publication.

Some points to consider:

1. The advertisements in newspapers and weeklies are less elaborate from a graphic standpoint than the ones in magazines, where the price and the exact address of the services offered do not stand out. Advertorials, or advertisements disguised as newspaper articles, are quite in vogue these days, both in online and in paper media. You can even get them into glossy magazines. Make sure the media source you choose is the one most likely to reach your audience. If you offer home care, community newspapers are probably the best choice for you.
2. Advertising in magazines and journals stands out because of the images. Magazine ads have text, but advertisers use high-quality photos or graphics to create a strong visual impression. A mainstream magazine like *Maclean's* may not be the ideal place to advertise your foot care service for the elderly, but magazines for seniors like *Good Times* or *Zoomer* would be. If you are selling a new folding seat for home care, consider a specialized nursing publication. You can find out about specialized publications on the websites of related associations.

3. Radio is the electronic equivalent of daily and weekly newspapers. It is local in nature. A radio ad costs less than a TV ad. Radio is generally considered a better medium for selling than for creating buzz (or for advertising, as opposed to promotion). The message has to be short and clear: you can't rely on images to help make your point. Radio advertising, of course, requires strong language and verbal expression skills. Think about it like one-way telemarketing. Your audience is a captive one: since radios, unlike televisions, don't have a remote control, listeners aren't as likely to "zap" you. However, a radio audience is more likely to be distracted while listening—for example, by traffic when they are driving, or by a boiling pot while they are cooking.

4. Everyone dreams of being on television. However, TV advertising is a costly and time-consuming endeavour, and the "zapper" significantly reduces viewers' patience for sitting through ads by improving their ability to skip them. If you want to go the TV route, don't neglect the small, inexpensive local or community TV stations. If you have something noteworthy to offer, you might even be able to get the news channel of a smaller station to do a report on you (more on this later).

5. The web and the Internet. There are various advertising techniques on the web, and we are not experts on this. The field of web advertising is evolving very quickly. In the beginning, web advertising was much like TV or magazine ads, geared towards large audiences. Today, thanks to Google's profiling of Internet users, advertisers can sell advertising space targeted to the profile of individual Internet users. If nothing else, Facebook ads are a good way to learn if your buyers are on Facebook. In other words, two Internet users reading the same article at the same time are likely to see a different ad selected for them based on their tastes (which is based on analysis of the other pages they visit). You'll need to hire a professional to do this type of advertising.

The journalist: A complicated "publicist"

Our fellow journalists are going to hate us for writing this, but from an advertising point of view, there is nothing better for gaining visibility and legitimacy than getting someone to write a whole article about you, or interview you on air. A good interview can seal your credibility and build your reputation in one shot. The impact of this kind of media coverage is potentially much greater than that of conventional advertising and comes at a tiny fraction of the cost of buying advertising. The biggest expense is usually the time you spend preparing for the interview. In case you think traditional media have gone the way of CDs in the face of music streaming, think again. Social media rely on the "traditional" press for stories, which they then post and share. We discussed the Gangnam Style phenomenon earlier: the video by the Korean singer Psy ended up getting some 3 billion views on YouTube. But things really took off for Psy in the summer of 2012 when US media like the *Huffington Post*, the *New York Times* and *Time* magazine picked the story up and gave it wings. It doesn't have to happen like this anymore, but it still can and it still does.

But from an advertising point of view, journalists have a major flaw: they can't be bought. There are publications where unscrupulous editors or reporters will accept money to do a story that's not really interesting or a TV interview with someone who really doesn't have much to say. But everyone else in the mainstream media can spot those kinds of rags and the fake stories they publish, so ultimately, you are more likely to lose credibility than gain any with this approach. Good journalists and good newspapers—the ones with the best reputations and therefore the best advertising potential—are good because they defend and maintain their editorial independence.

Also, journalists are picky. They are constantly being bombarded with a litany of press releases and advertisements and people trying to get their attention. Journalists don't ignore these messages: they are just one among many sources of information and they will evaluate their interest alongside other sources. In other words, journalists aren't likely to be interested in an advertisement unless it is a story in itself. If the message you send them is, "I have a client who is a very successful consultant," or "We're celebrating our tenth anniversary," don't bother, they won't care. There's nothing of interest to them.

Big communications companies that hire advertisers and public relations specialists at a premium and give them large promotional budgets do manage to carve out spots for their clients in the top media. They even manage to do this when the message is pretty dull. That's because it's the highly paid professionals' job to transform something dull into something that sounds exciting. But our personal experience is that you can get media attention with modest promotional efforts if you have the right stuff.

What's the "right stuff"? Journalists, like the general public, look for the basic ingredients of a good story, which we discussed at length in Chapter 7: Story, timeliness, originality, personality and signature. Good journalists are masters in the art of sniffing out the ingredients of a good story or a good idea. They will be interested in you and what you are doing if it has a story, relates to the news, shows originality and has a strong element of personality in it. If you want to interest a reporter, you must demonstrate that your story has those ingredients. Journalists are busy people and they are rarely specialists of anything in particular. It's up to you to barge in and show them what they need to know.

Journalists are particularly sensitive to the ingredient of "newsiness," or what's already on people's minds. Another important thing to understand: since daily journalists are looking for "news," they are drawn to what's sensational or exciting. Don't blame them, excitement is what we all want when we watch news. We often say "No news is good news," but in the media, the opposite is true: good news is not news. No one talks about the planes taking off and landing on time. If you want people to talk about your good news, find a way to relate it to the (probably bad) news. Your company's 3-D simulation software helped engineers figure out how to free the Ever Given freight ship after it got blocked the Suez Canal for a week in 2021.

Journalists despise being treated like advertisers; so, when you are dealing with them, be careful to respect their independence. Don't utter the word "promote" when you are dealing with them. If you say "publicity," they'll get suspicious. *Never* tell journalists you want to "reread" or (worse) "edit" their story before publication. And *never* offer to pay them in any way for their work. We mean, NEVER.

Good journalists also question things. Contrary to advertisers, they will look into details and want to verify what you are saying. For fairness and balance in their story, they may include outside opinions about you. You should be prepared to provide an estimate of your sales figures, explain who your competitors are or supply names of people who can support what you are saying (and then hope that they really will). The journalist's goal is not to ruin you: their job is to publish accurate and credible information about something interesting. If you beat around the bush or are evasive or prickly, a reporter might get suspicious about you and sink the story—or sink you. Reporters are used to people trying to win them over. They see right through exaggeration and have a sixth sense for factual misrepresentation. And if they don't, their editors will.

It is also important to understand the nature and purpose of different media outlets. Radio shows often announce current events; TVs show them; daily papers explain what's going on; and magazines explain why events are important (and often what the next news will be). The different goals of each media are the product of logistical constraints (or advantages). Radio is light and fast to produce; TV is heavy; the daily press is fairly fast. Magazines are the slowest of all. They can take months to write, edit and publish. That's why their content has to go beyond the immediate news and explain the big picture behind things.

Think about the obvious. Your story is not a good one for radio if you can't understand it without seeing it (e.g. a celebrity diver in your aquatic club performs a brand new feat). On the other hand, it probably won't interest TV if there's no visual aspect to it (this was a big challenge to TV channels when they were trying to cover the COVID-19 pandemic: there were no images. Journalists weren't even allowed to enter hospitals. Lucky for TV there were anti-mask protests to provide some interesting footage). Your story won't interest the daily press if no one has anything to say about it because newspaper articles need outside quotes. And it won't make it into a magazine if it doesn't relate to a longer-term trend of some sort, a "bigger" issue because the magazine will come weeks or months after an event happens.

Making your message go viral

The ultimate goal of all promotion is to make your message go viral. This term has gained some unexpectedly negative connotations since the COVID-19 pandemic, but people still talk about "going viral." All it means is that word-of-mouth is working so well that your message starts transmitting itself, all on its own.

If you keep working away at it, you may get to a stage where each piece of information you communicate starts to feed the others. The content of your website will be passed on by journalists reporting on you or your product. Then it will come back to you in the form of emails from friends, colleagues, clients or relatives who saw and liked the "well-written article" about you. The thing is, the piece was well written because you produced and provided information that was good enough to be passed on through someone else's mouth (or keyboard). Then it got a life of its own. You may be the only person who is really aware that "objective information" about your product or service was provided by you (in your own promotional effort). But you don't owe anyone any explanations once it's out there—unless, of course, the information is false or somehow harmful.

As you "fight the good war" in promoting your product or service, it's wise to recall that one of the best examples of infectious messages in history was about Iraq's supposed "weapons of mass destruction." We're not suggesting you model your campaign on this approach, but it is a good illustration of how toxic information can intoxicate all coverage of a story. It was in 2003, before the United States invaded Iraq. The justification for the invasion was that Iraq supposedly had these WMD. Originally, no one really believed Iraq had them. But then a reporter, Judith Miller, claimed to have discovered a pile of pipes that were being shipped to Iraq to make atomic bombs. Quickly, before anyone had the time to figure it out, the White House dangled the idea in front of the press and it started circulating. Other reporters then took the bait and gave the rumour legs. By the time anyone figured out the story was false, it was too late: the White House had already used the story to convince other journalists that Iraq was building bombs and the public was already fixated on WMD, which justified the case for an invasion. It took a war and years of occupation to understand what really happened.

In the case of the WMD, information that was biased and misleading ultimately did great harm to millions of people. Yet it does demonstrate an important point: if you want to get your message out and get people to believe it and pass it on, start by creating the message yourself and passing it on to the right people.

10

Getting your foot in the door

How to be effective in sales

Myth #10: "Selling is a natural talent."

Promoting your product or service well will boost your credibility and create demand for what you are selling at the same time. But as a self-employed worker, you are still basically selling yourself. Even if you hire agents or other types of sales representatives, those reps will be doing much the same thing as you would without them: try to win over customers, one by one, and try to get their foot in the door.

Selling is never an exact science. Customers always have their own personalities and individual concerns. The key is approaching each potential client with a problem-solving frame of mind. Whether you are selling to companies or individuals, your customers will be interested in what you have to offer for three reasons: it solves a problem for them; it answers a well-defined need; or, it helps them make more money. If you promise solutions to these challenges, customers will listen.

Customers have different needs and concerns, and some are better informed than others, but they all share some basic characteristics: they are regular people with busy schedules and lots of things on their mind. They don't have time to weed through a poorly explained or incomprehensible pitch to figure out what problem you are going to solve and how. Your future customers work in the closed universe of their own company or profession. When they are done work, most of them just want to go home (or leave their screen behind if they work from home) and see their spouse or their kids, their pets or their large screen TV. Your challenge is to figure out quickly what they need and offer them a solution so they sign on to your offer during business hours.

Who are you talking to?

A friend of ours who sells cars for a living says the first thing he does when a customer enters his showroom is to look at their shoes. He can figure out everything he needs to know about who they are from the brand of their shoes and how worn they are. Those two things tell him what their tastes are and what kind of shopper they are—either the kind who's going to buy, or the kind who's going to think about it. Our friend wouldn't explain exactly how he does this because it's very intuitive. But the point is, everyone in sales needs to hone their techniques for assessing clients and their needs. You need this information to be able to gauge your chances of success and figure out how to land the sale.

Good salespeople can figure out what the deciding factors are in order to make a sale. Many car salespeople have watched a potential sale slip through their fingers because they mistakenly thought Mr Buyer was making the purchase when actually Mrs Buyer was deciding. Though somewhat stereotypical, it's a classic example of an important point: a buyer rarely decides alone. Even when the car is fine for the man, there is a good chance that the sale will fall through if the seller fails to identify the needs of the spouse buying it with him (and vice-versa, of course).

There is an additional obstacle when you are selling a product to companies: you need to figure out exactly to whom you should be talking. For instance, you won't get anywhere if you accidentally offer your services to an employee or manager who does the same thing you are proposing to do for them. A procurement manager will not be keen on hearing about your external procurement management service. Hiring you could eliminate their job or three quarters of their staff. On the other hand, the vice-president of purchasing might see your offer as an interesting way to reduce costs, so they might want to give it a shot.

You can usually find the right person to speak to by asking the secretary or assistant of the company's president. They are usually very well informed about the general operations of the company. Generally speaking, it's a good idea to get these secretaries and assistants on your side from the start: they filter information before it gets to the boss, so they play a huge role in determining what offers make it into their boss's inbox. Never, ever be dismissive towards secretaries and assistants.

How should you present your idea? When it comes to form and style, remember that clients always have their own preferences. So, start by asking them. Call your potential customer to see if they want you to present your idea in a specific way: by email, over the phone, by videoconference with a colleague or in an in-person meeting. This might sound like a lot of extra work, but if it's effective, it will be worth it. Also, if you don't go about things the proper way, you may always end up starting over from scratch, which is a real waste of time. You are not looking for a lesson in how to make a sale. You just want to agree from the outset on the best method to use for presenting, so you won't waste anyone's time. Your professionalism about this will be noted.

It's never a good idea to send a resumé unless a customer specifically asks you to. The resumé reflex is common among new self-employed workers who aren't yet used "looking for work" as opposed to "looking for a job." For the self-employed worker, sending potential clients a resumé is about as useful as sending them an advertising leaflet from a grocery store. How is a potential client supposed to guess what you are offering them from among all the things you have done over the course of your professional life? And how exactly does your resumé solve their problems? There is only one case we know of where the resumé produces results: start-up companies looking for cheap labour to help them get off the ground. Showing that you have an education and a minimum of relevant experience will be enough to get them interested in you. But this is no place for a self-employed worker, who should be spending their energy getting their own business off the ground, not someone else's.

Three ways to approach clients

There are three ways to approach potential clients: by telephone, in person/by videoconference and in writing. You will probably use them all with the same customers, at different points.

1. On the telephone

The great advantage of the phone is the following: when you get the right number, the right person answers when it rings. The drawback is, the telephone is an intimate, unforgiving medium. A lot of things can go wrong on the phone and there is a lot of potential for misunderstandings. The customer may find fault with you in ways they wouldn't notice if you were physically present: your voice might come off as shrill, your speaking style might be too hesitant or you might be too insistent or clear your throat too much. If you want to use the phone anyway, make a tape of yourself and listen to it so you can work out the ticks before you go live. Make a plan of what you want to say with arguments you might want bring up. Unexpected questions can throw you off.

Make sure you can answer the most important questions on the spot. For all you know, a secretary might put you right through to the boss before you even have a chance to rehearse what you want to say. Things sometimes go faster than you think they will, too, especially when you have a good idea and the timing is right. However, sales are rarely concluded over the telephone, especially for large contracts. Your goal on the phone should be to get an in-person or videoconference meeting. Keep some information as a backup for that meeting, like your price. The point of approaching clients by phone is to get them interested in meeting you face-to-face. On the other hand, if your customer is in a hurry and wants to come to an agreement and settle the details on the spot, don't hedge. You should have your offer ready, and whatever other information you need ready just in case things go more quickly than you anticipate.

2. In person/by videoconference

Meetings, either in person or by videoconferencing, are effective, but harder to pull off because before they happen, both parties need to agree to meet and set up an appointment. If a client asks to meet you, whether in person or by Zoom or Teams, prepare for the meeting as if it's a job interview. Be meticulous. Anticipate questions and have your answers ready. The purpose of the meeting will be to create a strong first impression. Make sure that the meeting takes place in a controlled atmosphere (like an office or board room, not in a café or the company cafeteria where there are too many distractions). You want your client to listen to you without being distracted or interrupted by others. If you are videoconferencing from home, make sure you won't have unexpected interruptions from roommates or children or spouses, or pets. You need your client's full attention.

Welcome to the age of videoconferencing

As we all know, Internet has spawned a fourth way of doing direct sales: the videoconference. Inaccessible twenty years ago, this technology gradually became democratized and affordable thanks to compression technology, miniature cameras and built-in microphones. The Skype platform was the forerunner in taking face-to-face meetings online, but a litany of new platforms has since entered the market: Zoom, GoToMeeting, Teams, WhatsApp and more. Apple users also have the option of using FaceTime, which is probably the easiest-to-use videoconferencing platform of all since the platform is integrated into all of Apple's devices.

Then, of course, videoconferencing went mainstream during the COVID-19 pandemic, setting off what promises to be the

Golden Age of videoconferencing. There are few if any business that can do without it now. Videoconferencing combines the advantages of telephones and in-person communication. It's practical and inexpensive and gives you more than just your voice to work with when you are communicating. (It also supplies a good option for recording a conversation while wearing earbuds, which has long proved challenging.)

However, as we all know, videoconferencing does have its pitfalls. For starters, it is a strangely intrusive medium that forces you to control all aspects of your environment (see Chapter 1). A bad Internet connection, bad lighting, kids crying in the background, dogs barking, toilets flushing and many more common day-to-day noises can quickly turn a Zoom meeting into a circus. Mute buttons for microphones must be used whenever you are not speaking. In short, videoconferencing must be carried out with care.

Always follow the basic interview rules: be courteous, firm and clear. The difference is that you are not asking for a job. You are offering a service. So, even if the client requested the meeting, you must control the interview. You need to simultaneously probe your customer's needs and convince them that you can meet those needs.

A journalist's tip: before the meeting, try to get your hands on some biographical information about your potential client. Their website might have a short bio, but we find that LinkedIn profiles are an excellent source for background information. You can find out where a potential client went to school, what associations they belong to. You might find some prize tidbits of information that can help you break the ice and make you look well informed, like:

- "So, I saw on your LinkedIn profile that you were an army captain. Which unit? I was 48th Highlander."
- "Hey, by the way, we went to the same university."

- "I see you are an Amnesty International supporter. I've been a donor for years."

You get the idea. That kind of personal connection works miracles.

3. In writing

The customer may be unreachable or may ask you to send written material by email before they agree to a meeting. It's another good reason to make sure your promotional material is ready. You need to be able to strike while the iron is hot and send your pitch before the client has had time to forget about you. Turning an idea into a good written presentation is a demanding exercise. It might be worth spending some money to get a professional writer to help you with it. The document has to be clear, convincing and concise. You can attach detailed documents to your letter, especially ones that relate specifically to the client's company or field. But it's the cover letter that opens doors. Your arguments should fit onto one, or one and a half pages (500 to 750 words).

In the audiovisual or print media field, this short presentation document is called either a synopsis, query letter or pitch (different names for the same thing). It is an overview of your project that explains in two or three paragraphs what you are proposing, why you are the one offering it and what problems it solves for your customers.

The importance of the written word

Whether you are reaching out to potential clients in person or over the phone, you should *always* have a written document on hand to send to them. It should be a letter outlining your idea or the main points of your proposal (it can be straight from your promotional material, adapted for the individual case if necessary). You can include brochures and your business card—or better yet, articles that quote you—but the letter itself has to stand on its own. The purpose of the letter can either be to open doors, or to get you through a door you opened with a phone call or face-to-face meeting.

The written document also works as a reminder. Even if your face-to-face meeting seems to have worked like a charm, your efforts may fall flat if you don't have a written letter to leave behind. Why? Because the person you talk to is busy, has other responsibilities and is therefore likely to forget your name an hour after your visit. It all depends on what's going on with the person in question, which is out of your control. The written document helps you get a bit of control back. Sure, a business card is good for jogging the memory, but what good will it do if the person you met isn't able to recall the details of your conversation? Your best visiting card is always a short, well-formulated written proposal with your name and contact details at the end of it.

There is another reason the written document is essential. In almost all companies, decisions are made by groups. Even if the first person you spoke to miraculously recalls details of your idea from your meeting or phone conversation, they will need to pass the message on. Unless it's written down, it will end up getting deformed, even twisted out of shape, in the process. Human memory is not very reliable. Your idea could well end up being distorted and transformed beyond recognition as it gets passed around. Business communication is often a game of broken telephone. It's no one's fault, but you can avoid the problem with a strong written document.

If your brilliant proposal is written, your contact person can pass the document on to his or her colleagues so they can read the idea exactly as you presented it. And just writing it down will help you in face-to-face meetings, since it will help you make your points clearly and concisely.

Finally, if you don't write your idea down, you will be completely reliant on the good faith, memory and reliability of people who don't know a thing about you. In other words, you're taking a big chance.

Five ways to stay out of people's junk folders

Email costs less than regular mail, but it's not one hundred percent reliable. Spam filters are sometimes so tight that nothing gets through. There are also restrictions on soliciting by email in Canada. According to Canada's Anti-Spam Law (CASL) senders of commercial electronic messages (CEMs) are required to have "express consent from recipients, either orally or in writing." For all the details on rules about doing e-marketing, visit the website of the Office of the Privacy Commissioner of Canada.

Even when your email campaign is very targeted, emails can end up in the trash before they even reach your correspondent's inbox because the recipient doesn't know you and your name is not on their contact list.

There are several tricks to prevent your emails from ending up in spam filters:

1. **Don't send any attachments with your email.** Many spam filters reject strangers' that have attachments. The body of the text should be limited to a few paragraphs and contain links to your website. You can send attachments with larger files once when your contact responds and you have exchanged emails with them.

2. **Avoid using trigger terms.** Many spam filters are very sensitive to the presence of certain words: if they detect the word "Viagra," "penis" or "breast," your email will immediately be considered spam. That's going to obviously be a problem if you are selling Viagra or maybe women's lingerie but you can probably find a way around this. Spam filters may also reject emails with words like "money" in the subject line because the word is so frequently used by spam scammers (whose objective is generally to lure you into giving up passwords).

3. **Use Facebook or LinkedIn.** When we write to people we don't know, we always check if they have a Facebook or LinkedIn account. If a person accepts you as "a friend" or "colleague," there's a good change they will read your subsequent email. If your mail doesn't get through, you can always send it directly through the social network itself: Facebook and LinkedIn both have internal messaging service for members. It's quite convenient and surprisingly effective.

4. **Check out a company's corporate structure.** You can see this on most websites. The email addresses of the CEO or VP Finance are rarely advertised on companies' sites, but those of their secretaries, assistants and press secretaries usually are. You want to reach these people. They are the ones who read the executives' correspondence in the first place and decide whether to pass on a particular letter or email. It's a good strategic move to know who reads the mail first.

5. **Be interesting.** Emails get caught in spam filters for the simple reason that they use commonplace vocabulary in the subject lines. If you use extremely common terms and exaggerated marketing language ("amazing") you'll sound like the most predictable spammers on earth and go straight to the junk folder.

Etiquette: Good manners for different cultures

If your project is not aimed at a local market, there's a good chance you'll be doing business with people who speak different languages or live in different cultures than your own. Finding your bearings in an unfamiliar universe could turn out to be even more challenging than coming up with sales arguments.

After decades of being brushed aside, etiquette, protocol and decorum are making a comeback in the international business world. Etiquette, long considered the equivalent of "being uptight," is, in reality, exactly the opposite. It's the art of recognizing cultural codes—our own and others'—so as to avoid offending people. Burping at the table is rude in Western cultures; elsewhere it can be a considered a sign of appreciation.

It's no coincidence. The more global business gets, the more people have to strive to understand how other cultures think and communicate. The purpose of etiquette is to avoid accidentally offending people and losing a sale in the process.

For example, when Jean-Benoît visited Japan in 2008 and again in 2015, he discovered you can't get by without a business card there. Japanese airports even have quick printing services for travellers to whip up a quality business card on arrival. When Canadians exchange business cards they generally glance briefly at them, then stuff them into a pocket or purse. Not in Japan. The Japanese exchange business cards with both hands stretched out in front of them like they are offering a precious gift. The recipient of the card is expected to receive it accordingly and read it carefully on the spot. If you are at a table, you should put the card down in front of you so you can refer to it from time to time during a meeting. If you are standing when you receive a card, you should hold it carefully without creasing it for as long as possible. It took Jean-Benoît a few days to get the hang of Japan's business card ritual. Decorum does not come naturally to him. But he understood that it was an essential part of meeting and interacting with people in Japan. All cultures have their own mysterious rituals, even Canadian. Think about it for a second: we smile to be polite. The French and many other Europeans think that's insane (we know from experience!). They think smiling for no good reason makes you look naïve, even kind of stupid or hypocritical. You have to know these things when you are doing business with people.

Respecting the basic rules of etiquette is as important as writing a proposal with proper spelling and grammar. Table manners, for instance, are more important than you probably realize. When a client asks you to dinner, make sure you don't hold your fork like a pitchfork.

If you work with French speakers and you want to show a little respect by using a few French words, make sure you address people with the formal subject pronoun "vous" and not the informal one, "tu." The informal "tu" is for children or personal friends.

Even among English speakers, there are important cultural differences, so you should always err of the side of formality. English speakers also have ways of conveying respect and avoiding sounding too familiar, like choosing the right title, whether it's Dr, Mr or Ms. You should never say "Miss" to a woman over eighteen; it's condescending. The key is to be thoughtful and unassuming. In short, mind your Ps and Qs.

The best language for doing business

What's the best language for doing business? Many would say English, but the best language for doing business is actually the language your client speaks. Of course, since English is so widely used, it is often a good bet. But even if you are far from mastering the mother tongue of a prospective client, making some effort to express yourself in their language is a gesture of good faith, courtesy and respect—up to a certain point. (By which we mean, don't unwittingly force them into being your language teacher.) Neither of us speaks or writes Spanish well enough to conduct our business entirely in Spanish, but when we write to Spanish speakers, whether we are writing in French or English, we take the trouble to start letters with the salutation "Estimado señor or señora" ("dear Sir or Madam") and conclude with an "Atentamente" ("kind regards") or "Un saludo muy cordial" ("warm greetings").

You might ask why English speakers should bother to try to speak other languages when everyone speaks ours? Well, for starters, there are 6,000 languages spoken on Earth including, 137 that are spoken by more than five million people. Some fifteen of these languages are spoken by more than 100 million people. The French language, fifth for number of speakers, shares the distinction with English of being among the most widely taught languages in the world, more than Spanish, Portuguese or even Mandarin, which has a greater number of speakers for whom it is the mother tongue.

The point is that 80% of the global population *doesn't* speak English. And there is no such thing as a small language when you are doing business. There are far fewer Inuktitut speakers (the language spoken by Inuit peoples) in the world than Portuguese or Hungarian speakers, but if you want to do business in Nunavut, Nunavik or Greenland, learning some Inuktitut will give you an advantage over the competition.

Six ways to do a follow-up

Follow-up is key to direct sales. But it can be tricky. You don't want to miss a sale by being too low profile, but you don't want to pester a potential customer to the point where they block your number. So where is the sweet spot just between firm and pushy? It can be hard to find it, especially since the game of calling and waiting for decisions can go on for months.

We have found that one good way to remind customers you're there, without seeming like a pest, is to send them "news." This could be an article that just came out about your company, or a prize or some other kind of recognition you recently got. Showing you got an endorsement from other clients or source helps convince new customers of your merits and can even answer some of their questions (e.g. what kind of track record does she have?) Don't feel shy about posting or sending links with news about your recent accomplishments. Invite them to become a connection on LinkedIn. We do this systematically with book and journalism prizes, but also with opinion articles we publish in major media outlets like *The Globe and Mail* or *The New York Times*. Also, if you have just landed a big contract, it's a good idea to let potential clients know you're sought after. You might just have to reassure them you'll still have time for them if they want your services. Sometimes all they need is a nudge. Remember, they are busy and thinking about other things.

Any excuse (used moderately) for reminding customers is fair, even, in some cases notifying potential clients that you are taking holidays. People always appreciate clear, fair, pertinent thoughtful communications.

Remember, your first sale can take a long time to finalize, especially if you are offering a service that doesn't exist in a market that you are creating from scratch. It is up to you to show your customers the value of your offer. A self-employed worker we know in Quebec City spent two years getting his first client interested in his innovative air quality test. He had to develop it first. Then, when the product was ready, he got a few local newspapers to write articles about it. The process took many months of preparation but it worked. He got interest from buyers.

Here are the six classic steps of a follow-up:

- First call: "Just calling to make sure you got all the documents I sent."
- Second call: "Is there anything missing from what I sent?"
- Third call: "Did your team have a chance to think about my offer?"
- Fourth call: "Have you decided? If not, what stage are the discussions at?"
- Fifth Call: "Would it help if I adjusted my pitch for your colleagues?"
- Sixth call: "Is there some kind of issue I don't understand?"

How to handle "no"

What do you do if the final answer is, "no"? When you are advertising, the only really negative answer is silence. If the person bothers to actually say no, keep probing to figure out what the problem is. Bad timing? Something wrong with the idea? The wrong approach? Something else?

If the answer really is "no," then there are two things you can do. You can give in and lick your wounds. Or you can take a good hard look at what you did and try to understand where the "no" came from. When someone turns you down, it's always a good idea to get as much information as you can about what went wrong.

Your potential customer just may not have had time to fully consider your offer. Maybe they're juggling two or three issues at the same time and your offer just wasn't a top priority. Or maybe you were talking to the wrong person.

Ask your client what went wrong. Maybe they found your proposal interesting, but hesitated because they thought that your presentation didn't include solid arguments that they could use to convince their colleagues. Whatever answers you get will help you refine your approach for the next customer you approach. A failed customer can actually become an ally if they are willing to spend some time helping you improve your next offer. People can spot potential even if the product is not right for them.

Some "no's" actually turn out to be pivotal. When we were starting out as freelance writers in the early 1990s, we submitted eight story ideas to *Saturday Night Magazine*, the most prestigious general interest magazine in the country at the time. After two months of waiting, we received a postcard-sized card (this was before email!) from the editor-in-chief. He didn't want any of the stories, but he wanted us to call him back because he liked our writing style. We had pitched a story idea during the run-up to Quebec's second referendum on sovereignty. Quebec was a hot news item and the editor was looking for strong writers who could tackle topics on the issue. He saw the advantage of having a pair of bilingual writers (balanced perspective and the ability to do interviews directly in French) and ended up assigning both of us a number of stories in the years that followed.

Besides, nothing prevents you from going back to the drawing board and taking another shot. If a potential client turns down your offer, it might be because you didn't present the product or service accurately, or in a convincing manner. We've had hundreds of rejections for story and book ideas over the course of our careers. In a few cases, we were so convinced of our idea, we went back to the drawing board and wrote a second, better pitch for the same idea. Most often, customers didn't even remember they had seen (and rejected) the first pitch. This frequently happens. People in decision-making positions are busy and have to juggle a lot of responsibilities. Keeping this in mind makes you better at selling, helps you avoid taking rejection personally and allows to you get back in the saddle and take another shot.

The eternal agent question

We have several agents. One of them, Patrick Leimgruber, lives on a horse farm in Sutton, an hour east of Montreal. He represents our work in French to publishers and producers. For the books we do in English, we have an agent in Toronto, Evan Brown, who is part of a large literary agency with other agents. He represents our book for the English-language market. For book translations, both of our agents hook up with local agents in different countries who represent us there and then split the commission with them. The same thing goes for audiovisual rights: our agents use the services of more specialized agents for the production of documentaries and split the commissions. In the United States, yet another agent, MacMillan Speakers, represents us for conference tours.

You might want to hand part of your sales effort to one or more representatives like we do. It depends on the industry in which you work. Agents are common in the publishing world. Writers sign long-term contracts with agents, and agents represent them for a percentage of the fees or royalty payments they receive from publishers (which vary according to the size of network to which they have access). However they work, the purpose of agents is to make it possible for you to multiply your sales potential.

The primary advantage of agents is that they should secure much better conditions for you to work on your project than you can get on your own. The person should have connections and a proven talent for sales. This person will take the steps required to sell your project to potential customers; they will lead the sales effort and negotiate terms and contracts on your behalf. People are often worried about an agent taking a chunk of their fee, but the agent will get you more money than you would have gotten on your own, so you'll probably still be ahead. A good agent can also help you improve your project and your pitch, since they know your market. We have had periods when we were writing a book and talked to our book agent (our English-language literary agent previous to Evan was based in the New Jersey) every month. He even told us which of our ideas would work best in the market at specific times, and which ones he would have a harder time selling to publishers.

However, it's important to understand agents' limits. They can help you refine ideas to enter a specific market and give you their opinion on what is most likely to work, but they don't help you actually create your project. That's your responsibility. Another thing agents don't do is marketing, advertising or promotion. Their work is to represent your business interests to people who will pay you. The agent won't give you instructions of any sort or set deadlines for you. You know where you want to go. You'll have to figure out what to do and how much time it will take to get there on your own.

One more thing the agent won't do for you is to evaluate their own performance. That's up to you, and it's important not to forget to do it. You need to have frequent conversations with your representative, to keep abreast of projects and evaluate how well they are representing you. An agent, even the best one, must be monitored. Even if they know the market inside out, they will never know your product as well as you do. To do their job well, agents need your feedback too. A good agent also has other clients. So, it's a good idea to communicate regularly with them, in a productive and constructive manner, to make sure you stay at the top of their list of priorities.

How do you go about finding a representative? It depends on your industry. You will need to do some research. If there are established networks and directories in your industry, there should be a list of specialized agents somewhere, too. Once you get your hands on it, contact them, let them know who you are and what your goals are and try to find out if they are a good fit for you. To convince an agent to represent you, you must sell yourself in the same way as you would to convince a client.

Not all the agents in a given industry are good. So it's important to do your homework. Check an agent's client list. You can even contact their clients and ask them what they think about working with them. You will probably get useful information in the process.

When we set out to get our first American literary agent, we read a directory that had detailed profiles of about 250 literary agencies in North America. The first thing we did was rate them all from zero to five points, according to how interested we thought they would be in our work (given their client list and stated interests). Of the original 250, we narrowed our choice down to about fifty and then sent each of them a letter that described who we were and the book project we wanted to sell. Eight of these agents wrote back to us and asked to see a detailed description of our project. In book industry lingo, this is called a book proposal. It's quite an elaborate document; ours was about sixty pages long and we had already prepared it before we reached out to the fifty agents in our first cut. Of the eight agents who wrote back to us expressing interest and asked to see the proposal, three offered to take us on as clients. So we met them one by one and signed with the one who seemed to understand us and our goals the best. He wasn't the agent who promised the biggest book advance, but he was experienced, showed good judgment and had a long-term vision of how our careers might evolve. (He also had a rare quality the others didn't: he was a US agent who had experience in and a good grasp of the Canadian book market.) We made the right call. He made it possible for us to develop our writing careers in ways we had never imagined when we started our careers as magazine journalists.

An agent always represents you on a contractual basis. However, they can also represent you on an ad hoc basis for a specific project or for your entire production. In the latter case, this means in principle that you must first submit all your projects to them. They may offer you a contract that gives them exclusivity over representing your work for a specific territory and/or duration. When signing with US agents, we usually ask for our work in French to be excluded from the contract. The agents usually agree. They're not kidding themselves. They know we'll get better service being represented directly in French for our work in French.

There are two ways to pay an agent: by percentage or for a fixed rate. The percentage they ask for can vary greatly: 10%, 15%, 25%, 50% (for syndication). In the writing business, you never pay more than 15%, although speakers' bureaus will charge around 30% if you use them. Find out what the norm is in your business. Also beware of an agent who asks for too much exclusivity. Every one of our agents has worldwide rights to what we do, but we know they will use co-agents to sell rights for our books in territories outside their immediate jurisdiction. It's written in our contract with each agent.

Personally, we have always favoured percentage-based remuneration because we know the agents' interest will always be aligned with our own: the bigger the book advance, the more money everyone makes. Also, if we don't get paid, neither do our agents, so they have a built-in incentive to chase down publishers for what they owe to us.

You absolutely must trust your agent, because, in practice, they are the first person to receive payment from your clients and, subsequently, pay you your share. An agent is not your boss or your employee. They're your partner. They advise you, but they can't see the future and can't know everything—like what you have in mind for future projects. Also, they'll make mistakes as well as good moves, and it will be up to you to judge whether they're doing their job or not. The bottom line is: it's not your agent who decides, it's you.

Service offers: The first step of negotiations

If you sell well, a prospect is very likely to ask you for a service offer. If they don't, but you sense they are interested, you can also propose presenting one to them. What is a service offer? It's the ultimate sales pitch, which details prices and conditions. Some self-employed workers use a service offer as a sales tool, even their primary one. Our friend, Sam Benahmed Ahmad, was working as a consultant in search engine optimization when we met him. He used service offers systematically as a sales tool. Sam targeted companies whose websites left something to be desired. He studied the company and its site in detail and put together a document to explain to his client exactly what he could do to improve their SEO. It took him a week to do the study, but he was selling a high-end, hyper-specialized service in a sector where customers are highly motivated to have good SEO.

In general, you will have had preliminary discussions with your prospective client and their team before you make the service offer. Those talks should give you an idea of what their needs are, how much they are willing to pay and what kind of information you need to include in order to convince them.

Producing a detailed service offer can take several hours, if not several days, particularly if it's for a large contract. This is normal. Service offers are a halfway zone between sales tools and contracts—you could think of them as a first draft of the eventual contract you will write, or a "memorandum of understanding." If your service offer is good, it can become the contract.

Whatever you do, don't dash off your service offer. It shouldn't just rehash your promotion material: it's more complex, detailed and concrete than any of your promotional materials (though it can include some elements of this material). The service offer has to describe what you are going to sell (or the service you are going to provide), as well as what you are *not* going to sell; it includes the price, the terms and the conditions of production and delivery. The amount of detail in it should be close to what a contract would include. It has to be targeted to the specific customer.

That's because the service offer is often the first stage of negotiations with your potential client, the subject of the next four chapters.

The four steps for writing a service offer

It is difficult to generalize about what a good service offer should look like, since it is always a "tailor-made" job adapted to a particular situation. Still, there are four basic steps in producing a service offer: writing a letter of intent, having exploratory discussions, making a quote and, finally, negotiating the terms/readjusting the quote. It is sometimes possible to skip the first step, the letter of intent, if the other party has made the first move and asked you to apply. But most of the time you will still be expected to produce a letter of intent that outlines your vision of the project. And in all cases, it's a good idea to make as many things clear as possible from the outset.

1. The letter of intent

This can also be an email, but generally it's quite long. The letter of intent explains:

- Your idea
- Who you are
- The context of your proposal
- The value of what you are proposing
- Why you are interested

Writing a good letter is about making a direct mental connection with the recipient. It is a special exercise that is not everyone's forte, but it can be learned. The best letters, while not necessarily personal, are always personalized. If your letter follows a meeting at a cocktail party or convention, you should remind your correspondent of the event. If someone has recommended you to reach out to this client you, you should say so. If you have completed relevant or prestigious projects that make you particularly qualified, state it as clearly as possible. That said, unless we know the person very well, we are careful not to be too familiar, among other things because the document will probably be circulated to others.

This is not the place to make quotes or provide contractual information. The letter of intent is similar to a cover letter for a job, except that it often proposes a service that the recipient may never have thought of. Even if you were able to discuss the matter verbally beforehand, the letter of intent will provide more details about the nature of the project. If several people have a say, your letter of intent should summarize the steps involved, who proposed the idea, etc. (this is what we call the "context" of the proposal). This is especially useful because a letter of intent supplies the same information to everyone.

Sometimes it can take a while to move from that letter to the next steps. For some book projects, for example, we have waited fourteen months before getting an answer. During that time, we checked in several times with the prospective client to see if they had forgotten about us. They told us they were thinking about it, so we let them keep thinking. There's no point in forcing a client to talk about a project if they are not ready to. Insisting rarely makes things move more quickly. In this case, when the client called us back, they were ready to go, and the whole project—a $70,000 writing job—was tied together in two weeks.

2. The discussion

The discussion phase is critical. Its purpose is to see if you will develop enough chemistry to start an ongoing relationship. Obviously, it will be very different depending on who made the first solicitation, you or your prospective client. This discussion should be as thorough as possible and may even involve a series of meetings. Normally, your discussion with your interlocutors must clarify the following points:

- Who they are
- Their vision, what they have in mind
- Why they want to do this, what problem they want to solve
- Why they are interested in you and their level of interest
- Who is decisional in the project (it might not be the person with whom you are speaking)
- What they know about your business and who told them about you, etc.

And that's not counting the points your interlocutors will want to clarify on their own! The key word in this list is probably "et cetera," because you want to learn as much as possible. The more you know, the more you will be able to assess whether you can work with them and then prepare a good quote. You need to know if the person you're talking to is authorized to do so, whether they have done their homework, if they have a budget and if they have an idea of what the project will cost.

The more homework you do ahead of time, the more productive the discussion will be. Find a few articles or read their website. A biographical note can tell you a lot about a person. But it might also be helpful to talk to someone who knows the organization or even the person you are targeting personally. The discussion meeting will go better if you understand what they do, what their problem or challenge or need is and if you are able to offer an opinion or two about the issue at stake. This is a good way to figure out if their expectations are unrealistic. If that's the case, there's no need to walk away. You can use the meeting to reframe their expectations, politely. This is your opportunity to demonstrate your professionalism and explain realities that your client might not grasp.

Your first discussion should preferably be in person or by videoconference. If several people are decision makers, you should speak to some, if not all of them. The reason is simple: your contract may commit you to working together for many months. You don't want to neglect an important stakeholder who doesn't understand or even want the project to go forward, and who as a result may sabotage it as you go along. This is especially vital with large organizations where the person you start working with could be assigned to another position before your project is completed. It is therefore critical for you to establish relationships with their subordinates or colleagues.

3. The quote

In general, if the discussion is fruitful, the other party will ask you to prepare a quote, which is in fact the formal service offer. The quote includes a detailed description of the work to be done and the price. The estimate can be as short as three pages and as long as ten.

We always precede the quote with a cover letter in which we express our pleasure at having met them and our enthusiasm for the project. This is also a good chance to clarify the meaning of the quote: it is not a contract, but a basis for discussion. Some people react badly to quotes.

It's possible your quote will be accepted unconditionally, but normally there is some discussion and negotiation before everyone agrees on a final version.

The quote should clearly describe:

- **The purpose of the work.** We always take the trouble to summarize what we understood from the discussion we had at our discussion meeting in order to make sure that the purpose of the work is clear. We also include the context in which the work will be carried out and the client's objectives. Very often, there are so many unknowns in the project that it must be broken down into several phases, like doing a feasibility study, including a budget, prior to the project itself. Your description must therefore clarify these steps. Even if it's tempting to be brief here, it's well worth laying things out clearly.
- **Contractual terms.** This obviously includes price, fees, payment terms, deadlines, intellectual property and ownership. Do not neglect to specify whether amounts include taxes or not, because clients don't like surprises.
- **Rights and duties.** This includes setting out issues of confidentiality, opt-out clauses, access to information and people, dispute resolution and the things that you won't do and what they must do. You don't have to mention all the protective clauses that will be in the

contract, but you must be very clear about mutual obligations, particularly with a client who doesn't know much about your business. We prefer to state these points in the quote so that potential clients understand what they are getting into.

4. Negotiations

Your quote will usually lead to further discussion, which may lead you to adjust it or even totally rewrite it—or to walk away. This is normal, because this stage of the discussion often involves some bargaining: the project might cost more than the client was expecting and you might not be promising to deliver the exact results they were expecting. Normally, before you submit your estimate, you should have weighed things carefully.

You should have asked for as much as possible on the best terms, but you should be prepared to negotiate. A client rarely offers you more than you asked for. Correcting an error in the estimate requires tact. We have withdrawn quotes in the past because we realized, after the fact, that we had underestimated the work the project actually required. Of course, in this case we explain the reasons to the client and apologize. In one case, a client accepted a revised price but we had to show them that our mistake was made in good faith.

The final phase of your service offer is the contract, which is essentially the estimate, taking into account your negotiations. For details on contracts, see Chapters 12 and 13.

QUESTIONS FROM READERS

The self-employed student

Can you start your own business while you're still in school?

Jean-Benoît started his career as a self-employed worker when he was still a student, so he can speak from experience on this topic. He was only fifteen, in high school, when he and his childhood friend, Mario, started a tree pruning service in the neighbourhood they grew up, in Sherbrooke, Quebec. The two got the idea when they were trimming hedges for their parents. A neighbour saw them at work and offered them $20 each to prune his hedges. Their parents loaned them the pruning shears and supplied transportation, and the business was up and running in no time. Another neighbour saw them working, then another. Pretty soon they were booked. After doing a little market research, they realized their rates were a little low so they raised them for their next customers. In three weeks, the two pocketed $500 each, a good chunk of cash for a fifteen-year-old in 1979.

The experience made a lasting impression on Jean-Benoît, not yet conscious of how his business was being artificially supported by his parents, who supplied all the equipment at no cost. Jean-Benoît's father also transported the trailer of cut branches to the dump since he and his friend were too young to drive. Jean-Benoît opted to travel the following summer but his friend Mario ran the business for another season.

A few years later, when Jean-Benoît went to university, he decided to start freelancing as a journalist instead of getting a regular summer job. At the end of the summer he had a few assignments, things were just getting going. He knew it didn't make sense to stop the process, only to start it up all over again the next summer. So he decided to keep freelancing year-round while he finished his degree. At the end of his university studies, he had not only mastered the basics of journalism, he had started building a network of clients and other professional contacts and learned the fundamentals of running a small business.

Combining work and school is not a bad idea if you aim to be self-employed. Folks in their early twenties have a lot of energy and few responsibilities, either financial or other. While the university students around him were partying or joining school clubs, Jean-Benoît channelled his extracurricular energy into his future profession. It paid off. Being self-employed while you are studying is a great way to learn to manage your time and juggle deadlines and obligations. The only drawback was that Jean-Benoît didn't shine during his studies, but an academic career had never been his goal. He decided early in his studies that he was going to university to learn, not to perform, and his goal was to become a self-employed writer, not a university professor. On the whole, he got more than what he needed out of his university years.

We've written numerous stories for business magazines about entrepreneurs who started their businesses while they were still in school. Some summer jobs, like student painting, tree planting or waiting tables are ideal because they get you out in the world, or in the fresh air, without interfering with the school year. But if you are thinking of being self-employed after you graduate, starting to work independently in a field related to your studies will also pay off. A Phys Ed student could freelance as a private coach, for example. Julie once wrote a "success" story about a student painting company in Quebec that started out as a business student's summer project and quickly ballooned into a business with thirty employees.

Early in her career Julie worked (on contract) for a student business that had sprouted serious wings. She was an editor at a publishing company, Les Éditions Ma Carrière, which originally produced career guidebooks and morphed into an online job search site called Jobboom. The company was started by two young entrepreneurs from Montreal who launched it out of a grandmother's basement while they were studying in management. The company was later bought out by the Quebec media giant Quebecor.

Students have to be careful, however. You don't have any protection. If you are a student freelancer working as a construction worker, don't forget that accidents are common and injuries, often serious. This is no time to compromise your future. Be careful, take the necessary precautions, and if your activity forces you to take risks on a regular basis, you might consider registering with your provincial Worker's Compensation Board (WCB) or getting private insurance. Rules and conditions vary from province to province. If you have people working for you, depending on your activities, you might have to have insurance for them as well.

A self-employed student should choose a simple activity with flexible working hours that won't eat up too much of their time: it shouldn't get in the way of their studies. Even if a degree is not mandatory for the field you hope to enter (which excludes, for example, people who work in nursing, medicine or architecture), getting a good education is still the best insurance policy money can buy and the best investment you can ever make in your future. Economists have demonstrated this: a university diploma is the best financial investment you can make in your lifetime, period. Quebec economist Pierre Fortin calculated that by the time a university graduate retires, they will have earned on average $1 million more in salary than someone with only a high school diploma. Fortin even calculated the annual return on the investment in university tuition: 19%. It doesn't get much better than that.

Of course, we all hear about the exceptions to this rule—the high school drop-outs, like Magna International founder Frank Stronach, who went on to become a billionaire—but these cases are extremely rare. The statistics don't lie: finish your degree.

11

Everything is negotiable

Starting negotiations on the right foot

Myth #11: "The customer is always right."

There is a reason we devote four chapters of this book to negotiating. Negotiations and contracts are what bring all the parts of your project together and turn them into a business. They are what bring together an idea, its potential in the market, a plan for carrying it out, the necessary conditions for the idea to be realized and your capacity to carry it out.

When it comes to negotiating, you have to throw off the habits you may have learned when you were an employee. Customers are not your boss. You are your boss, and customers are your equals at the bargaining table.

The customer is not always right. Actually, they are often wrong, particularly when it comes to money. It's not as if customers want to exploit you, at least not on purpose. They just want to get the most for their money, which means getting more out of you and your work without paying more. But as a self-employed worker, you want to get the most out of them too, at least as much as their budget affords. You need to be bold and frank in negotiations, but also diplomatic. You should never personally attack the other party, not if you want to develop a lasting relationship with them.

As a supplier, it's important to make sure that you are negotiating with the right person, someone who is authorized to do so. You need to make sure this person has discussed the matter with anyone else concerned. You can figure out how serious a customer is by checking with one of their superiors. If they hedge, you'll know something's wrong.

The four essential conditions

Negotiating is a psychological game in which you are the hero. To succeed in this game, you must understand the principles. Think of them like a set of armour that protects you from being crushed before you've even started.

We've formulated these principles as four rules:

- **The Golden rule.** Everything is negotiable. Always ask, even if you're sure the answer will be no. You have the right to ask, and the client's answer might surprise you. There's no reason to be shy or embarrassed about asking for money or conditions. Talking about money is not dirty. You are not selling your soul or asking anyone to do you a favour. When self-employed workers complain about being exploited, it's usually because they are afraid to negotiate. Either they are too passive about it, or too shy, or have a hang-up about asking for money and think (mistakenly), that "a real pro shouldn't have to beg."

- **The Silver rule.** Always take your time, even—and *especially*—if you or your client is in a rush. We've never forgotten the words of a village elder in a village in Mexico's Sierra Negra we used to visit. He said, "The best way to get things done quickly is to take your time." They were wise words from an old man who'd certainly done more than his share of negotiating over the decades.

- **The Bronze rule.** Don't believe anyone who starts negotiations by flattering you. For creators, this often comes in the form of the catch phrase "You're a natural talent." You may very well be, but this is often an insidious compliment designed to get you to lower your defences and your price. By suggesting your work is somehow "effortless" your client is probably getting you ready for a lower offer (made on the basis that you "must love what you do"). Don't listen to this. You've worked hard to get where you are and there's nothing "natural" about the time and effort you put into what you do. Expect to get what you deserve.

- **The Iron rule.** Heed your instincts and listen to what your inner voice is telling you. If you have the feeling a new customer isn't trustworthy, there's a good chance they aren't. People call it a "sixth sense," a feeling you can't rationally explain. Honour it. If, after your first meeting you find yourself reaching to your pocket to check if your wallet's still there (we're speaking metaphorically, sort of), you might be dealing with a shark. One sign of trouble is when your negotiating partner uses lots of grandiose and unnecessary terminology in a monologue that sounds rehearsed and is designed to intimidate. If you decide to pursue negotiations, be firm and—to return to our original metaphor—keep your hand on your wallet.

It takes two to tango

Negotiating is a game played by two people. It mixes strategy with performance, like playing Monopoly and a piano Sonata at the same time. Both of these skills require practice and you will improve with time. If you want a crash course in the skills, we recommend spending some time in a *souk*, public markets in the Middle East and North Africa that sell everything from jewellery and handbags to spices and veal shanks. *Souks* can be quite intimidating at first. Travellers generally go there with a consumer mindset, to buy souvenirs. They think the objective is to "select" whereas the true purpose of a *souk* is to negotiate. You don't buy anything at a *souk*, ever, without negotiating. It's expected. Travellers feel harassed when vendors call out to them to buy their wares but it's because they fail to understand that the call-out is a vendor's first offer. If you answer them, you are accepting their invitation and you should be ready to talk for a while. They'll give you a price, then your job is to bring it down. Whatever you do, don't disappoint them by capitulating too quickly.

Julie became particularly adept at negotiations in *souks* (public markets) when she spent a summer studying Arabic in Tunisia's capital city, Tunis. In a culture where it was difficult to speak to men without being harassed, she discovered *souks* were a great place to practise her nascent Arabic skills and talk to people. So she dragged the conversations out as much as she could. In the process, she turned into such a formidable buyer that her fellow students started commissioning her to shop for souvenirs for them. Julie would gawk at a bracelet, or a pair of earrings, but shake her head saying they weren't quite right and wait for the price to come down. She would admire a carpet but have to "think over" how it would look in her living room until the price came down.

The discussions can and should go on for long minutes, even hours. The vendors don't mind, because for them it's a natural part of the process of selling. If you accept a vendor's first price, you'll pay too much and insult them with your indifference to the ritual that occupies their days. Bargaining shows that you take them and their product seriously. You communicate the important information that they are not selling to an impulsive fool and they will usually give you the respect you deserve in return.

Why are we talking about *souks*? Not because we recommend you spend inordinate amounts of time negotiating for the fun of it. The key to negotiating in a *souk* is the same as negotiating in any other context: it's a psychological game. The whole art of negotiating boils down to knowing what you want, what your ultimate objective is and then showing interest in an offer while expressing your reservations about it. Like in the *souk*, that gives your negotiating partner some time to think and then come up with a better offer.

As a self-employed worker, you are in the position of the carpet merchant: you want to sell. But if you seem too eager to sell, your buyer will sense your weakness. They'll know you're ready to make concessions. The same goes for the buyer: if you go to the merchant and say you absolutely need to have a particular carpet, the price has just gone up. It's a game with two players. If all you do is make demands, the other person will react harshly and accuse you of exaggerating or threatening them, or, worse, of prematurely ending the negotiation which deprives them of the chance to make a counter offer and tells them that they have been wasting their time negotiating. Of course, if you're up against a good negotiator, they'll keep talking until you're ready to settle. You shouldn't give up easily. If a buyer is asking for terms that don't suit you, it may be worth your while to ignore them for a day or two with the excuse that you're busy, for example.

Basically, negotiating is theatre, though it's much more akin to improv (improvisational theatre) than what you see at the Stratford Festival. If your client is very keen on including one aspect of the contract that you would prefer to take out, accept their position but let them know it bothers you. That signals to them that they will have to grant concessions on other matters that are important to you (e.g. When Julie was buying a carpet in Tunisia she feigned surprise at the cost of delivering it. The seller subsequently knocked a few dinars off the sale price and sold the carpet, probably still at a very good profit).

Former Quebec Premier Lucien Bouchard was a formidable government contract negotiator before he entered politics. He famously said: the sign of a good negotiation is when both parties leave with a little taste of shit in their mouths. Bouchard's choice of language might have been vulgar, but the point stands: in a balanced agreement, both parties have to feel like they lost a little.

For that matter, experience has taught us to beware of overly generous starting offers. Sometimes, for reasons we've never fully understood, buyers go a little crazy and propose a price that really works against them. It happened to us in 2007. Our French literary agent got a French publisher to pay an outlandish sum for the rights to translate one of our books into French: the publisher offered us an advance of 20,000 euros or almost $30,000. It was double what we were aiming for, but who in their right mind would say no to a chunk of cash that size? We should have. We signed the contract and the publisher paid us our first half of the advance. But it turned out that in the rush to acquire our book, the publisher "forgot" that they had to pay for the translation as well, plus travel and lodging costs for us to come to Paris to promote the book when it was published. For some reason it took the publisher a year to put two and two together and realize this would more than double the price of the advance they'd paid us. At that point, the publisher terminated the contract and left us with half an advance and a book with a stain on it (because it had now been rejected from a publisher). The first 10,000 euros they paid was non-refundable, so we kept it, but it took us two years to find another publisher.

Good negotiations generally start when the two parties agree on the matter at stake and some of the general terms. Those provide a framework for going forward. Whether the object of the negotiations is to buy one, two or a hundred carpets, the parties have to stick to the original terms: buying carpets. If you start talking about carpets and end up asking for the keys to the company, you'll have to start talking to someone else (and start the negotiations all over again). More frequently you'll be shown the door.

This was exactly what happened in a famous story of a promising Quebec child singer, René Simard, in the 1970s. Simard had a great voice. His manager at the time was none other than René Angelil, the same agent who would go on to be Céline Dion's manager and husband. Angelil was on the verge of finalizing a contract with a major American record company when he made a fatal misstep: after agreeing to an advance of $100,000, he decided to ask for $1 million instead. The record company abruptly ended the negotiations and Simard had to say *au revoir* to his American career before it even started (luckily, his star status in French assured him a nice local career, anyway).

Sixteen ways to say no

You can't negotiate if you don't know how to say "no." Many self-employed people have difficulty pronouncing this word. They believe they have to take whatever work comes their way, especially when they are starting out. But contrary to what you might think, saying (or hearing) "no" is essential in negotiations. It's very often the magic word that gets things rolling.

If you're afraid of sounding negative, remember that there are many elegant (and even productive) ways of saying "no," and many moments during your negotiations when you can use them. If you are the seller, refusals give your negotiating counterpart a chance, or sometimes an excuse, to make a better offer. If you are a buyer, according to the same logic, saying no can help get the price down. In either case, it might help improve the conditions of the offer.

Here are the sixteen ways to say "no":

- I don't have time
- I can't do it
- I don't understand the order
- The order is not realistic
- It's not in my power to decide
- I'm not interested
- It's too short
- It's too long
- It doesn't pay enough
- It involves too much work
- Such-and-such client pays more
- There were problems with the last order
- My partner won't let me work at that price
- I know of three other buyers/sellers who would be interested
- I can't start working on it until next month
- And, finally, the bomb: I don't like the way you are treating me

There's also another, brasher way to say no, but this requires some explanation. You can say no by striking out offending clauses from a contract and sending it back. We have done this numerous times over our careers when potential clients have presented us with contracts that writers call, "rights grabs." These have clauses along the lines of: "The author yields to the Magazine first publication rights for an article called 'Look out for yourself' for the entire universe, for eternity, on all media including all other rights in the world." We are caricaturizing a little, but not much. We occasionally see contracts like this. They are so greedy they are almost silly. They usually come from inexperienced editors backed up by lawyers who don't know anything about publishing. So, what do we do? We strike out the rights that we are pretty sure the magazine doesn't need and won't make any use of and then we send the contract back to our editor with edits. We write our initials in the margin so they know that we are serious. Sometimes the contract gets sent back to the lawyers. Sometimes that's the end of it.

For that matter, when someone presents a contract right off the bat, without discussing the terms, you should consider that for what it is: just a first offer. That person knows very well (or will learn very quickly) that all aspects of a contract are negotiable. If they don't say anything and act as if the contract is set in stone, it's a negotiating tactic to get you to sign it on the spot. If you let that happen, there's a good chance that you'll come out in a weaker position than if you call them on it and get them to go back to the drawing board. In other words, the person who presents a contract this way is playing a soft game of chicken. It's a negotiation strategy like others, but leaves you with the odious task of having to start the discussion in a contentious atmosphere. Whatever you do, don't be intimidated or embarrassed by this behaviour. The person you are negotiating with knows exactly what they are doing.

Whatever the case, when you say "no" you have to be able to explain why and the more specific you are, the better. For instance, we have established minimum rates below which we simply won't work. The only exceptions are passion projects or favours we're willing to do for a real friend. If you have more than one reason for saying "no," be clear and state each one. Also, the reasons you give for saying "no" must be the right ones: if it's because your last order didn't go well or because the customer isn't offering enough to begin with, there's no point explaining your refusal by the fact that the order is too small or that you don't have time. If your customer decides to meet your demands, you could be stuck working on a big order for an unreliable customer who doesn't pay. It's safer to be forthright.

But when you say "no," it's really got to be a "no." Jean-Benoît once refused a project a friend proposed because he was moderately interested in it and knew he wouldn't have enough time to carry it out properly. The friend did everything in his power to get Jean-Benoît take on the contract: he said he was "stuck," that Jean-Benoît was the only one who could do it, that he didn't have a backup. Jean-Benoît reluctantly agreed to do it, warning the friend that there was a risk it would turn out badly. Unfortunately, this friend got what he was asking for, a bad job, and the work had to be taken back and corrected, which ended up taking even more time. To his credit, the friend admitted that he should never have pushed Jean-Benoît like he did. But for Jean-Benoît, the worst was that he had to delay delivering another writing assignment because of his friend's demands. He should have stuck to his initial reflex, which was the right one, and said a hard "no."

Of course, sometimes the conditions for saying "no" to an offer are just not there. If you are financially tight or don't have much work, you might feel like you are not in a position to be picky. If you are starting out, you may not yet have built the reputation you need in order to do the kind of work you want to do. So be realistic in your negotiations. Just don't shy away from having frank discussions with clients. Engaging in these discussions will give you the opportunity to figure out how much they are willing to buy, or how much they are willing to pay, what their other options are and how quickly they need your project or service.

Don't rush into things too quickly if you can afford to take your time. You should always give yourself some time to think an offer over. Sleep on it at least one night. If you let your judgment be clouded by your initial enthusiasm, you may end up overlooking important points in the work or the contract. Even a few days after you have agreed (in principle) to a contract, there is nothing stopping you from calling a customer back to discuss certain points. If the customer does not want to talk to you, it's a bad sign, and you should call it off if you can. Sometimes this will shock a client back to their senses. But if the customer fails to react, or yells nonsense at you about being unreliable, then you're better off.

Sometimes circumstances will force you to agree to a contract at a discount with less-than-ideal conditions. When this happens, let your customers know that this will be the last time you make these kinds of concessions and explain why delivering under these conditions is problematic for you. Nothing is lost by being honest.

When you start out, you will often have to say "yes" to terms that you know are unacceptable in the long run. That's normal. There's a price to pay for building your reputation. But you shouldn't make these kinds of concessions without at least trying to turn things to your advantage. Go back to our list of sixteen ways to say "no" and find one that fits the circumstances. And as we explain in the next Chapter, on negotiating strategies, there are ways to turn such discussions to your advantage even if the offer does not appear to be negotiable. And remember, there is something better out there and things will be better next time. And with this frame of mind, you're ready to really start negotiating.

12

Nailing down the contract

How to be a winner in any negotiation

Myth #12: "I can only charge the market price."

How much can I get? This is the first question neophytes ask when they get to the negotiating stage of a contract.

Surprisingly few understand what answering that question really involves. Over time, the two of us have come to think of ourselves as "winners" in most, if not all of our negotiations. Since we are self-employed and happy that way, no matter what we do, we almost never come out of negotiations with the short end of the stick. Even if we don't end up with as much money as we wanted, we win. Why? Because negotiations are about more than the price you charge. There can be benefits to getting less work, or more work, or better conditions instead of just more money. We consider ourselves winners if our clients accept our conditions and don't feel like we forced them into anything.

The bottom line is you will always win your negotiations if you understand that negotiation comprises six elements: client expectations, working conditions, rates (or price), ownership, expenses and terms. So there is hope, even for beginners, who don't yet have an established reputation, and for whom price is generally the least negotiable aspect of a contract.

Expectations: Nine questions to answer

No matter what rate you charge, you will always lose time and money if you don't take the time to define your client's expectations—and yours. What's the job, exactly, and what does it entail? These are the questions you need to ask:

- Does the customer know what they want? "I want you to build me a chair" is not specific enough.
- Is the customer asking for something standard, or something out of the ordinary? Do they want you to create a chair that's a fusion of Spanish colonial style and Bauhaus?
- Are they in a rush? Do they need the chair next week, next month or can they wait until next year?
- How much preparation will you have to do? Will you have to spend time tracking down exotic wood to make the chair, or, will the pine you can find at your hardware store do the trick?

You also have to ask yourself the following questions:

- Will you have to put aside other work to finish this contract on time?
- Will the contract require you to make a lot of phone calls or travel?
- Are you taking any risks?
- Is the client open to ideas, looking for ideas or not?
- Is the client asking for high, medium or low quality?

It's important to think carefully about how fulfilling a particular client's wishes will affect your workflow. Sometimes you need to help clients become more realistic about their expectations. At any rate, you should be able to anticipate the challenges and obstacles you may face carrying out a contract. If the job will require greater than normal effort, you need to factor that into your price.

In 1994, a Toronto magazine wanted to send Jean-Benoît to Haiti to interview a minister of the putschist government there. The United States was about to lead a multinational force to restore democracy in Haiti. The minister had a Canadian connection and the magazine thought it would be an original and engaging way to cover the issue. However, the magazine failed to understand how difficult it would actually be to get to Haiti to do the interview. The Organization of American States had slapped an embargo on Haiti, so there were no direct commercial flights there. There was also no way to pay with a credit card. That meant Jean-Benoît would have had to fly to the Dominican Republic and cross the border illegally with a wad of cash to bribe officials to let him into Haiti. It would have been hard to get travel insurance to enter a country illegally and report from a rebel zone, not to mention the high possibility of Jean-Benoît running into the regime's notorious *tontons macoutes* militia who were targeting the dictatorship's political opponents. After Jean-Benoît explained these factors to his editor and told him how much it would cost to go to Haiti as a result, the editor agreed it would be fine to do the interview by phone.

Most people don't know anything about your business. It's the reason so many renovation projects turn into a sour experience for people, even when they have been properly prepared by contractors—because too often people have been improperly briefed by friends who have selective memory about the process. When we start a ghost writing project, we often have to deflate wild expectations about the marketing potential of a book, which really isn't likely to be the next Harry Potter. It's also important to let clients know if their request is contradictory. If you speak to a VP who wants a red sign, but it turns out her partner wants a blue one, the two of them will have to figure out what they really want before they hire you to create it. Never, ever, assume different points of view on a contract will get "worked out" while you are working on it. They don't. And more often, they end up growing into an unmanageable mess that puts the whole contract at risk.

We've said it before but it's worth repeating: always be honest and forthright with clients. Speak up about your concerns, even if you are afraid of offending a client. If you don't get answers to your questions, you will end up with problems that impact the quality of your work and in the long run, tarnish your name. If a client tells you something along the lines of, "Don't worry, we'll work that out later," or "our HR department will take care of it," beware. False assurances like these make contracts more complicated than they are worth unless you factor the uncertainty into your price.

Deadlines are obviously of prime importance to your customer. But they will always be part of your negotiations. We have customers who are surprised when we tell them we can't start working on a project for several weeks or even months. There are times when our schedule is packed and it doesn't make financial sense for us to stop working on one project to start another, especially if we aren't being compensated for putting off other work. People generally understand this when you explain it, so it's best to be clear about your limits up front.

Although part of your job as a self-employed worker is helping clients assess their needs, there are limits to how much of this you should do. You have to be careful not to get sucked into helping a client figure out what they want. That's not your job unless you are being paid for it. When people approach Julie for help writing a book, she generally gets them to agree to pay her to write a book proposal first. They will need a formal proposal into order to get a publishing contract, and the process of writing one allows them to understand what the work of writing a book will actually involve. Unless you have such a formula, it's your client's responsibility to define and communicate their objective and their expectations and yours to judge if they make sense. The customer shouldn't end up feeling like part of your job to help them make their plans (unless you start with a consulting fee).

If the customer really doesn't know what they want, then you should break up the contract into separate stages or phases or deliverables, and negotiate a price for an initial consultation to help them define what they want. There's nothing unusual about this. Engineering firms always negotiate a fee to do preliminary studies before building a bridge. The preliminary studies can include financial or feasibility studies. In general, if it's going to take us more than an hour to figure out what a client wants we think we should be paid to do pre-research to clarify the order. Clients are often happy with this since it gives the some time to make up their mind before they commit money to a long-term project.

If you end up with a client who really can't decide what they want, make it clear to them (in writing) that they are giving you an open mandate and that they will accept and pay for whatever you do. Making clients face this often shakes them into making up their mind. There's no need to adopt a defiant tone. Stay calm, but be clear: you don't want to waste their time or your own. If the client refuses to define what they want but won't agree to pay for an undefined order, this is another red flag. Working for them will be risky so it has to be worth it.

If you are talking to a potential client and they don't want to sit down to discuss details of the project or product, they are asking you to do for them, consider that a red flag. The only exception to this if it you happen to be talking to the wrong person, i.e. a person who isn't authorized to negotiate with you in the first place. You will save a lot of headaches by making sure you are talking to the right person.

Thinking preventively

Mediation specialists, who spend most of their time settling contractual disputes, have a very simple word for all the other elements of negotiations. The word is prevention.

Jean-Benoît's brother, who is a lawyer, once told us, "When you go to court, you have already lost, even if you end up winning. That's because it costs time, money and energy." Prevention is never a waste of time, energy, or money. Going to court, or doing arbitration or even mediation, is like going to war: no matter how good the reasons are for fighting, wars cost more than peace.

We have been self-employed for the better part of three decades, and neither of us has ever had to go to court or use mediation or arbitration to solve a conflict with a client. One reason we've been able to avoid this is that we pick our customers carefully: as much as possible we write for well-established publications and clients. The other reason we have been able to avoid escalating disagreements into outright conflict is that we are good at spotting potential sources of discord early in our talks with clients, before we have signed anything. We make a point of identifying sources of conflict in our working relationships upstream and steering around them. We don't wait until it's too late to find mutually agreeable solutions to differences with our clients. We do this by applying the logic of the six-point negotiation system described below. For more on mediation, see Chapters 13 and 14.

Working conditions

A friend of ours, Paul Bernier, is a prize-winning architect who designs beautiful houses. One of the reasons for his success is that over the years he has learned how to avoid conflicts with clients. In a typical case, a couple hires him to make a plan for their home, but when he meets with them to discuss the plans, they start arguing over what they actually want to do. And there are even trickier cases, like when Monsieur and Madame don't argue, but constantly contradict one another. When Monsieur says white, Madame says black. Paul has learned from experience to avoid being drawn into his clients' conflicts. When it happens, he politely informs them that he can't work for them unless they agree ahead of time on what they want. An architect is neither a marriage counsellor nor a mediator (and Paul knows better than most architects since his wife Joëlle is a lawyer who specializes in mediation).

In addition to the clients' expectations, there is the issue of the clients themselves. You will spend time with them, sometimes a lot of time. Are they reliable? Can you talk to them in a productive way? Are they flexible? Do they return emails promptly? These are important questions. If the answer is to any of these questions is "no," and it looks like communication will be a constant struggle, this should be reflected in your price.

One of Julie's first ghostwriting clients was a great communicator (it was her job), but had an unpredictable schedule that made it hard to actually find time to speak to her. This was important, since the project was based largely on interviews with her. Unfortunately, Julie was a relative beginner and didn't anticipate how much time she would need to spend just booking interview times. Julie learned, through experience, to get a sense of how available clients are going to be before she signs anything and then to factor it into her price. It's also helpful for clients to understand up front what kind of a time commitment their project will require.

There are customers who are absolutely inflexible about certain things, like quality, but turn out to be very flexible about others, like deadlines. Sometimes it's a question of personality and sometimes it's because of their own time constraints. You need to learn to quickly recognize the conditions that will hurt your ability to perform a job and possibly, your health.

If there's one thing a reasonable customer should understand, it's that you can't be in two places at once. Telephones and Internet may allow you to negotiate a shipment of cloves from Dar es Salaam while you write a report from a hotel room in Yellowknife. Airplanes mean you can fly to London in less time than it took to load the trunks onto the Titanic. Thanks to the Internet, you can work from virtually anywhere and this has become even more acceptable since the pandemic. But none of these technologies have made it possible for you to be in two places at once. Exchanges may be fast and efficient, but you can only solve one problem, in one place, at a time. You might want to explain this to certain clients before you sign a contract with them.

If you are working for a company where several employees need to approve your work, you should negotiate the number of approvals (or in our case, revisions) you will have to deal with ahead of time and *ask the company to appoint a single contact person to communicate with you.* A freelance speechwriter working for the Ministry-of-Changing-Ideas will quickly find themselves in hell if they have to deal with nineteen different political attachés who disagree about the message or tone of the speech they are trying to write. The speechwriter should stipulate, during contracts negotiations, that the nineteen attachés have to agree on corrections before they communicate them to him, *through a single representative.* Then they have to understand that this will require longer deadlines, because it will be time-consuming on their end. You should always insist on dealing with as few respondents as possible. Otherwise, you will waste many (uncompensated) hours untangling contradictory feedback, or worse, end up embroiled in office politics. Office politics are not part of your job. You aren't an employee.

C.C. madness

We thought it would pass, but here we are, three decades after the invention of email, people still send other people indirect messages using the "c.c." function, short for "carbon copy." Some people put it to good practical use and use it tactfully. Others abuse it and become repeat offenders.

When misused, the c.c. function can quickly turn it into a communicable disease that infects relations between colleagues. People use the c.c., for example, to passively offload responsibilities by drawing people into an issue that's not really their problem. Or they use the c.c. function to demonstrate how hard they are working and how much more they are doing than everybody else. Some employees c.c. their colleagues to say indirectly what they don't dare to say in person.

The risk with the c.c. is that it makes "too many cooks" in a project. We have had clients who c.c.'d ten colleagues with a draft of a text we wrote. When they do that, it's sending the message that their colleagues should give individual feedback on our work. In those situations, we end up with ten sets of contradictory, unreconcilable edits from people whose feedback was unnecessary because they weren't involved in the project from the outset and don't understand what the objective is. Then we have to figure out how to tactfully tell them we are not interested in their thoughts.

We are talking about email, here, but, of course, this syndrome is also true for Google docs, Slack or any other platform that allows for sharing documents.

That's why it's important to stipulate in your contract negotiations exactly with whom you will be communicating for the duration of your contract and who will be authorized to fiddle in the Google Doc. Feedback on progress should come from this respondent, not from the entire staff. Why? First, it's not your job to manage the staff. Second, you're the one who suffers from the sloppy use of c.c. or "over-sharing" of documents. If you don't set these rules down early, you will quickly find yourself bogged down in, or actually get caught in the crossfire of somebody else's, internal politics. Dealing with your client's HR problems should not be part of your mandate unless that it what you are being hired to do. And even then, you should set ground rules over whom and how many people you will be communicating with over the course of your mandate.

Just as our architect friend Paul refuses to be a marriage counsellor for his clients, you can't afford to get caught up in the infighting and power struggles that preceded your work with a client. We avoid this problem upstream by stipulating in our preliminary discussions that a company will appoint a single person to collect and synthesize feedback on our work and report to us with one set of comments and corrections.

When the project is underway, your contact person needs to understand that they cannot c.c. everyone involved in the project in every email they send you. If they insist on doing this for internal reasons, you should insist that they c.c. their colleagues in b.c.c., the hidden version of c.c. You need to send a clear message that you won't get involved in their internal communications unless you have been hired to do that.

Although the possibility of a lucrative contract might make you feel like you are suddenly more "available" than you thought, remember: time itself is still not compressible. You might be able to stay up for forty-eight hours in a row to finish a juicy $12,000 contract, but you can't go on for weeks working like that no matter how much you are being paid. So deadlines should enter into your negotiations. If you are tempted to turn down a contract because the fee isn't worth the time it will take you, or worth putting aside other work to finish it, consider coming back with a price that will make it "worth it" for you. How will more money help? You might be able to hire an assistant or buy specialized machinery. However, the cost and trouble of working this new way should also be reflected in your fee. Sometimes customers are remarkably flexible when they are faced with refusals based on logistical factors or deadlines that are too tight. If they really want to work with you, sometimes they'll go a long way to make it happen.

Sometimes clients get involved in matters that are none of their business and make demands that are not related to the work you are doing for them. This usually happens because they have made the mistake of thinking they are your boss, not your customer. For example, they may complain that you don't get to the office every morning at 9:00 a.m. But unless it's in your contract, there's no reason (beyond any practical ones, of course) for you to respect a time schedule. For instance, if you have been hired to produce a study for a client, you must deliver the study regardless of the conditions under which it is produced. But since the client is not your boss, they cannot dictate to you how to do the work. They can't demand that you write the report in their offices, for example. You organize your time the way you want to. On the other hand, if a client asks you to come to six, one-hour meetings that require you to make six round trips between Edmonton and Calgary, should factor in the six-day trips required. A client who expects you to always be on call and available whenever they need you will either have to pay a premium for that service, or be firmly put back in their spot. It's a lot easier to do this when you make the conditions of your work clear from the start.

Setting your rates

In Chapter 5, we explained how to calculate your unit cost or rate, but bear in mind that there's no such thing as a "real" price. The real price is whatever a customer is willing to pay. A serious customer will not be offended by you asking a high price, especially if your reputation justifies it. However, if you are asking for more than the going rate, or what a client is expecting, you should be prepared to offer solid arguments to justify your price, like testimonials of past work and fees you were paid for similar work in the past.

Prices should always be discussed in relation to the industry standard, so you should start by knowing what this is. In advertising or commercial writing, for example, the basic rate is $100/hour. Beginners are always tempted to ask for less, but this is a mistake. If the client has confidence in your writing, you should not offer your services at a discount. If you have a price in mind, add 25% and wait to see what happens. If you have the choice, an hourly or daily rate is usually the best deal, especially when it's difficult to predict how complicated the job will be. For instance, if you work in crisis management, and the City of Belleville calls you to settle a blockade of the Canadian National Railway like the one that took place in 2020, it probably wouldn't be a good idea to charge a fixed fee of $2,000.

On the other hand, package prices are interesting when you can predict how long a job will take. In general, this is easier and more profitable for experienced workers. To determine the price, you need to know how to estimate (and count) your time, and to do that, you need experience. You should determine a reasonable maximum time frame for the package: i.e. determine how many hours you can work until you start losing money. A $300 order that you think will take half a day to complete won't be profitable if you are still working on it the next day. When you are negotiating a fixed price, be sure to clearly delineate the tasks involved and the schedule so your customers can't "expand" the job as you go along. A client who asks you to write a brochure cannot add, "production of the annual report" to your tasks midway through the contract.

The fixed rate you charge should be based on the value of the work you are doing, not on what it costs you to produce it. If the going rate in your business is $150/hour, it would be a mistake to only charge $100/hour because your work independently from home and you have no overhead. Your client does not need to know what it costs you (or doesn't cost you) to supply or service them. Clients also judge you partly based on what you charge. If you lower your fees, they might feel they are getting less, or lower quality. Charging a fair price becomes a question of maintaining a professional image.

Some clients know the market rates for what you are selling and refuse to pay anything above these rates. Fair enough. You should use the same logic and set a standard rate for your work, like "When I work at my normal price, it's only for jobs over $1,000." When our pipes froze one January morning a few years ago, our plumber told us he'd charge us $70 an hour, but only for a minimum of two hours of work. In other words, we couldn't expect to pay less than $140 for him to "pop over" and fix our little problem, even if it only ended up taking him thirty minutes to actually solve it. It just wasn't worth his time for less than $140. We thought this was fair. An NGO who asks us to fly to Ottawa and stay overnight to make a half hour presentation the next morning should expect to pay us for a day and a half of work, not the half hour it takes to make the speech.

If you have two clients competing for your services, you can also use this factor to raise your price. Just don't disclose the name of the competitor in case the two customers know each other and figure out a way to lower your price by joining forces, maybe by sharing your services.

Sometimes you have to be inventive. A customer who refuses to pay more than the standard hourly rate for a service will sometimes agree to pay a surcharge or to barter for another service. For example, you can negotiate a discount on the design of a software program to manage gas stations in exchange for a free one-year gas voucher. That would be worthless if you use your bike for transport, but lucrative if you drive an SUV. Another trick is to throw in a bonus gadget or additional service. For example, the public relations consultant could take a look at the client's marketing and advertising materials while she's at it; it's not her field, but she certainly knows more about it than her client does.

And remember that if circumstances force you to work at a discount, you should *never* offer it. Let clients ask first.

Ownership

The question of ownerships of rights doesn't come up in all negotiations. For example, if you sell a shipment of carpets to someone, it's understood that they own the carpets. But if you make a video for a company, you may retain ownership of the images, or the right to use them. And these could become a source of revenue elsewhere. We talked about intellectual property in Chapter 4, but now we'll discuss how to put a price tag on it.

Negotiating intellectual property is not like negotiating the price of a job or service. There is no set price for intellectual property. Some creators' associations provide price lists for articles, photocopies and scripts. But those are just benchmarks. The right price, again, is whatever the buyer is willing to pay.

Most of the time, clients don't actually want ownership, they want exclusivity. They can have it, but they have to pay for it. Exclusivity can mean a number of things. Do they want you to refuse work with their competitors? Does their contract prohibit you from taking on other work in the same field? Or limit you to certain competitors? Or give the signatory a right over what you do in the future. Your first job is to figure out what exactly they mean by "exclusivity." Whatever it is, exclusivity comes at a premium, because such contracts limit your business and bind you, personally. This kind of contract actually may turn out to be quite lucrative, but if you decide to go in this direction, make sure your client understands that they are still hiring a supplier, not a contract employee. In other words, even if you agree to some form of exclusivity, your client is not your "boss."

One variation might be to negotiate exclusivity for one aspect of your work, but not for the rest. For example, if you are a photographer, a customer might want all your fashion photos but nothing else. That contract won't stop you from taking and earning money selling pictures of cars. But your compensation should always be proportionate to the level of exclusivity requested, and you should be ready to put a dollar figure on this.

Logically, if a customer wants full and complete ownership of your intellectual property (in what is called an assignment or transfer of rights), they should pay more than a customer who just wants to use your product in a limited way (a license). For example, a client might want a single copy of a picture or article you created, or the right to publish it one time (or for an exclusive period, after which you can continue do whatever you want with it). Between assigning full and partial rights, there are an endless number of possibilities for selling intellectual property. The more intellectual property rights a customer asks for, the more they compromise your ability to exploit your idea and earn income from it in the future. So they should pay a higher price for them. Part of these royalties should be claimed in advance of the income your customer expects to generate from your intellectual property. This can be paid in the form of a down payment, or what we call in the book industry, an "advance" (on royalties). It is worth selling a lot of your intellectual property to a customer who has the potential to create a lot of revenue with it. That will benefit you in the form of royalties. But it might be a better idea to hang onto some of your intellectual property because you will be in a better position to make use of it down the line.

When we are negotiating book contracts, for instance, we generally retain the rights to French translations because we know that we will be better than our English-language publisher at turning those rights into a lucrative revenue stream. We know the French-language publishing world and French-language media much better than any English-language publisher does. That gives us a better shot at finding a good publisher and getting media exposure for our work. Generally English-language publishers have allowed us to retain the French rights to our work because those rights are not worth that much to them anyway and want to spare themselves the trouble of finding a French publisher.

Conversely, someone may have a better ability to make money from your intellectual property that you do. Take the case of the person offering a course in mental arithmetic. They may just want to sell a book that explains their lessons. But maybe one of their clients, a bank, asks for the audiovisual rights. Why would the bank want these rights? Maybe it wants to film the course for employees who can't make it to the "live" course. The audiovisual rights were worth nothing to the owner of the manual, but now they are worth something because the bank has a good idea and the ability to put those rights to use. In that case, it makes sense to sell the audiovisual rights to the bank (obviously with restrictions). At the very least, the owner can authorize the company to use the audiovisual rights, to show the recording or DVD to their employees (and to no one else), for an additional fee.

This example highlights another important aspect of intellectual property negotiations: before you sell your rights, always consider who can generate the most money using them. For example, in the case of a course on mental arithmetic example, the bank would be in a much better position than you are to create and distribute a videoconference to its employees. But the bank would not be in a better position to turn the course into a documentary movie, a television series or an audiobook. So the author should never sell any audiovisual rights to the bank other than the ones it requires to film the course for its own employees.

Let's take another case: say you invent a new type of robot crutch that "walks all by itself." You then secure a patent for the robot crutch in every country in the world. Does that make you the best person to produce, sell and distribute the crutch in all those countries? Probably not. Your invention will be worthless in a country unless you have a local representative who knows the market. It is better to own 1%, 5% or 10% of a bakery than it is to own 100% of a bun. According to that logic, you are better off assigning the intellectual property rights for your robot crutch to someone who can make them profitable in a specific location. Your robot crutch business will only make money "on its own" if you can find people who know how to turn the patent into revenue.

Normally, when you have a choice, you should always try to sell the minimum of your rights, not the maximum. Why would you include the audiovisual rights to your mental arithmetic course in a contract with someone who doesn't even know how to make a documentary film and has no contacts in the field? At the very least, before signing, you should ask them what they plan to do with the rights, and whom they know who can help them do it. There are situations where you have no choice but to let the rights go (some publishers usually demand all rights in exchange for publishing your book). There are other situations where it is not worth retaining the film rights because there is no potential for making a film anyway. But if you can foresee a potential use, you should at least let your negotiating partner know that you have no intention of giving away these rights for free (or that they have already been assigned). If they want the audiovisual rights, try granting them a temporary (one-year) non-exclusive license (which gives you the right to do what you want). Don't forget to include a percentage of royalties on that, and, why not an advance on royalties?

We occasionally find ourselves negotiating with greedy clients who insist on acquiring full rights over whatever we are writing for them. Our philosophy is that these clients can have all the rights if they are willing to pay us enough for them. If they insist on acquiring them without extra compensation to us, then we try to get some exceptions in return, like a license to use the work on our own website, or in future books. In effect, it's like selling them our house, but still being able to live in a clone of our house and redecorate it or rent it out to someone else if we feel like it. In other words, we get paid well and, on top of that, we keep the benefits from the property we just sold.

One last word of caution about dealing with patents: sometimes people who hold competing patents will approach you to acquire the right to yours. If this is the case, be sure to find out what they plan to do with it. The person may have no intention of actually commercializing your invention; they might just want to take a potential competitor off the market.

Charging expenses

Customers rarely reimburse overhead costs such as paper, pens, ink, telephone service. However, special expenses for the job certainly are refundable (e.g. flights, hotel stays, driving long distances, couriers, long-distance or international calls, renting or purchasing special equipment). In that case, your client may want to put a limit on your expense budget, and that's fair.

Remember, however, that you should always negotiate refundable expenses ahead of agreeing a contract. If you wait to talk to your clients until you have incurred expenses, they will be in their right to refuse to cover them.

Car travel should be reimbursed at a rate that you and the client agree on ahead of time. The Canadian government pays its officials $0.58/km for the first 5,000 km and $0.52/km after that. This fee covers all expenses, including gas and depreciation. If you drive 12,000 km for clients, you'll earn more than enough to lease your BMW.

Your client should reimburse you for any charges you incur owing to whims of their own, or you should add a fee for these whims up front in your package rate. Maybe the company Blank Drawings Inc. commissions you to design and deliver 1,200 laminated flash cards, but stipulates in your contract that the cards must be printed by a brother-in-law of the company's founder in Picton, Ontario. In this case, you'll have to add travelling back and forth to Picton an undetermined number of times to your work. Make sure the client agrees to reimburse your time and travel expenses for these trips. You are not the Ministry of Development of brother-in-laws' businesses.

The only justification a client might have for refusing to reimburse you for special charges is paying for the charges out of pocket, on their own. You can do this by, for example, acquiring your client's courier number and making sure your bills go directly to them. Workers who build furniture or houses usually get the customer to order the material directly so the bill goes straight to the customer and doesn't pass through the builder's own accounts.

If a customer refuses to reimburse expenses, period, you should think twice about working for them. At the very least, you should point out to them how unfair that is. They probably wouldn't want to lend you their own car for the business trips you are making on their behalf, so why should you use yours for free?

Some customers have strict policies in place about reimbursing expenses. One might reimburse car trips from Edmonton to Red Deer (155 km), but not from Red Deer to Calgary because it's less than 150 km. Others will ask you to return property you bought at their expense. Fine, but make sure you take these policies into account when you are negotiating your fee.

It's always good practice to be economical when you are incurring expenses for a client, but there's no reason to go crazy being frugal. A customer who expects you to make a return trip from Winnipeg to Minneapolis should pay your mileage and compensate you for the time it takes to make the trip (fourteen hours for the return trip, not counting time at customs). Taking the bus or train or flying instead of driving might be more expensive options, but they give you the luxury of being able to do something else while you are travelling. Don't be afraid to ask clients to pay for a solution that suits you better. It may be more economical for them anyway. Taking the bus to Minneapolis may mean, you can get your work done for them more quickly.

Don't be afraid to remind a reluctant client that you do cover costs that are never reimbursed. Clients used to send documents by mail at their own expense. Now they send PDFs that you have to print in colour on your own printer. We all know how expensive printer cartridges are. Long-distance phone calls used to be expensive, but fees were detailed on bills so you could pass them on to clients. Now they are included in a plan for monthly services so you pay it yourself. Internet and wireless technology have made everyone's lives easier, but self-employed workers have ended up absorbing a lot more business costs than they used to, so charge whatever you can (legitimately) charge to your clients.

Always beware of a client who tells you that all your expenses should be included in the fee. If you are providing a service, agreeing to this could be suicide. If the client insists you include expenses in your fee, then you should jack your fee up accordingly.

Terms and conditions

The terms and conditions of your contract are as important as the fee itself.

Let's say Esso wants to commission you to write their annual report, their annual information form and prospectus. The job would pay US $100,000, and you have six months to deliver. To meet the deadline, you'd probably need to hire a researcher and a proofreader and spend fifteen days doing interviews with executives. Esso agrees to pay your expenses and even offers you free gas for a year as part of the contract. The problem for you is, unless Esso pays you up front, you'll run out of money long before the deadline. And that's not taking into account the amount of time huge companies like Esso take to process and deliver payments. By the time Esso pays you, your banker might not be in the mood to extend your credit line. In addition to paying a few thousand dollars in unexpected interest, you will run the risk of having to file for bankruptcy for a project that you delivered on time.

Okay, this might sound like the freelance worker's version of a disaster movie, but unfortunately, things like this do happen. There are two ways you can reduce the financial shock of contracts that last for months: you can negotiate advances or scheduled payments and get your client to reimburse your expenses as they come in, ideally before you even have to pay the bill.

For big projects that take months to complete, you should insist on being paid for your work in instalments. We use this system for any assignment or contract over $2,000. It's the only thing that makes it possible for small independent business like ours to stay afloat while working on large projects. You can even negotiate a percentage—10% or 20%—at signature. Sometimes customers agree to pay 50% of the fee as an advance (on signing the contract). Sometimes, because of their own budget constraints, or because they want to file an expense in their current financial year, this suits clients just fine. Other clients are reluctant to put any money forward before they see results. Your contract should then specify that you be paid in stages, according to results. A client who refuses this request is not being fair. All self-employed workers can greatly benefit from laying down these types of conditions, which are common.

When it comes to intellectual property, it's important to insist on advance payment for strategic reasons. You want whoever buys your intellectual property to exploit it and make money from it. The bigger the advance they pay, the more incentive they will have to make sure their investment (and yours) pays off. This is the logic of the book or film industry. Agents ask publishers for big advances for their authors partly to ensure that publishers will make an effort to promote the resulting books (to recoup their costs). In other words, if a client doesn't use your intellectual property, they will have wasted their money buying it. There's no immediate risk for you. If the results don't live up to anyone's expectations, you won't have to reimburse the fee.

One other tip: always verify the time frame for payments of your invoices ahead of time. A customer who pays in five days is better than one who pays six months after invoicing. If you are dealing with customers you don't know, you should include in your contract that invoices are payable within thirty days. Self-employed workers love clients who pay quickly because it reduces their need to rely on credit. If necessary, make sure your client understands that if you are not paid promptly, you are essentially subsidizing their business (e.g. by using your own credit line to survive while waiting for them to pay). You should be able to send your invoice to the accounting department as soon as a job (or an instalment) is approved. Your cheque or direct payment should then be issued without delay. Logically, anyone who pays later should pay more. It's our policy not to start a second contract with a new client until the cheque for the first job has arrived.

Be very wary of clients who say, "We'll pay you when we use your work." A client might ask you for an illustration for an advertisement, but only want to pay for it when the ad has been published. Nothing justifies this approach. If the client ends up cancelling the advertising campaign, you will not be paid. There's no reason you should pay the consequences for a client's decision to change plans. Some of our magazine clients have tried a "pay on publication" policy over the years. When they do that we just stop writing for them. We can't afford it. It's a sign they are not very professional. And sometimes they never publish our work.

One variation of the package is a unit price (e.g. per page, per photo). This can be interesting if you and your customer agree ahead of time that these fees apply to units "delivered" and not units, "accepted." For instance, it is not uncommon for photographers to be commissioned to produce three photos for a client who really only wants one and who decides, after the photos have been supplied, that they will only pay for the one photo they want. Clients are known to resort to shady practices like this when they are in financial trouble.

"Are you solvent?" We have occasionally asked clients this question. It shocks them, but it is a very effective way to send the message that we're serious about not taking risks when it comes to being paid.

It's not uncommon for start-up companies that are not on very solid financial footing, or companies that are simply in financial trouble, to try to lure beginners in a field to work for them for little or no money, or make it conditional on their project taking off. They use arguments like "working for us will help you get established," and promise to repay you with eternal gratitude or maybe future paid contracts. Sometimes there are good reasons to work for these companies. It actually could pay off in the long run, for your reputation or the legitimacy it brings you. But if you are tempted to participate in such a project, you should at least touch base with one of their suppliers to see if they pay quickly—or at all. If you don't trust them, you might ask them to put sufficient funds to pay you into a trust account.

You can also negotiate a clause for compensation in case of early termination of the contract. If your services are no longer required because the client's situation or strategy has changed, they should at least pay for the work up to termination of the contract and a compensation fee for lost work. All large contracts should include an early termination fee, and you should not hesitate to ask for one in your contract.

Self-employed workers who are just starting out will likely have a hard time getting an early termination clause included in their contract. If customers have any reason to doubt your ability to deliver, they will be sceptical about this and you can't blame them. You'd be sceptical in their shoes. If they agree to the clause, it will probably be on the condition that you provide them with proof of your progress at regular intervals. This is usually done in the form of regular progress reports. This is fair, but get it in writing.

13

Contract basics

What you need to know before you sign a contract

Myth #13: "Verbal contracts have no value."

Even when your client sends you a final contract, one you've carefully negotiated, it's not time to let your guard down. The reason contracts are important is that they frame your relationship with your clients. If it's not in the contract, then it's outside legislation that applies.

Newfoundlanders learned this the hard way in 1969 when Quebec's hydro utility Hydro-Québec presented them with a contract to buy 5,000 megawatts of power from a dam it was building at Churchill Falls, in Labrador. The contract would be binding until 2041. Since Hydro-Quebec was spending a billion 1969 dollars to build the dam, when Newfoundland signed the contract, they believed they had given Hydro-Québec the short end of the stick.

Newfoundlanders had barely pulled the corks out of the champagne bottles when they realized the contract had no indexation clause. That meant Hydro-Québec would be buying electricity from Newfoundland and Labrador Hydro at 1969 price prices, for the next seventy years. In other words, the more time went by, the less Hydro-Québec would pay for the electricity being produced in Churchill Falls. It was a golden deal for Hydro-Québec that promised a supply of 5,000 megawatts—one seventh of the total power of Québec's power grid—for seventy years at bargain basement prices. Newfoundland challenged the contract before the Supreme Court of Canada, three times. And three times the judges concluded that the contract was more solid than the dam.

There are good contracts and there are bad contracts, just like there are good customers and bad customers. Do you need to have a contract with each and every client you deal with? Some very large real estate deals, after all, are sealed with nothing more than a handshake. Millions of Canadian couples live together without a written contract to divide assets like their house or their pension fund in case of death or divorce (especially in Quebec, which has the lowest marriage rate in the country). So it's fair to wonder if it's worth the trouble of having a contract for a three-hour translation job.

Verbal versus written contracts

Actually, the question of whether to have a contract or not is the wrong question. Even if it's not written down, you do have a contract with your clients. In the thirty years we've been professional writers, we have written around 2,500 articles, reports and columns, published fifteen books and written two documentaries for film and radio. Most of this work, at least 98%, has been researched and written under verbal contracts only — although some have an adjunct written contract pertaining to the copyrights aspects. The same could be said of speaking engagements. But for all our books and documentaries, we sign lengthy, complex contracts that are negotiated with the help of an agent.

In any business, you should have a written contract with clients in the following cases:

1. If the job or order is complicated or difficult and if it will take a long time to execute the work, or if it involves complex rights (like copyright or any kind of property).

2. If you are dealing with a customer who doesn't know much about your business or appears to be confused about the nature of the job.
3. If the job is for a large sum of money, or involves a lot of people or responsibilities.

(If the job is pressing and you need a written contract, it is possible to start to working before you have written and signed a contract, with the promise that a written contract will follow quickly. But you should only do this with customers you know and trust.)

If the order is simple, of limited scope and duration, if it doesn't involve intellectual property, if your counterpart has a good reputation and if the sum of money at stake is not enormous, a verbal contract is much less trouble and probably sufficient.

But even a written, signed contract won't save you from scammers. The contract might be written on titanium foil in gold ink, but it won't fully protect you from a dishonest customer who has no intention of respecting it, either in spirit or letter. These dishonest customers will find endless ways to throw the validity of a contract into question when they want to get out of it. They'll claim it was "too detailed" or "not detailed enough" or that "working conditions have changed." Our philosophy is that there is no point in signing a contract with someone who can't keep their word, anyway. We'd rather dive into a job confidently than wade into it watching our backs. With trusted clients, disputes tend to get settled as they pop up. Verbal contracts are sometimes preferable in this case because they are easier to adapt, if necessary, to changing circumstances.

Also, when customers hear "contract," they think, "lawyer." Let's just say that's not usually music to their ears. Smaller companies are especially averse to suppliers who insist on legally defining every single clause of their contract. Customers are allergic to excessive paperwork, and who can blame them? They might think you are the type of person who spends more time tweaking contracts than actually producing results. Neither clients nor the self-employed workers they hire for work are huge fans of paperwork.

That's why you need to remember that contracts don't have to be written down to be valid.

The verbal contract

We've alluded to it often, but let's say it clearly: contrary to popular wisdom, a verbal contract has legal value. Yes, A VERBAL CONTRACT HAS LEGAL VALUE.

Too often, self-employed workers are fooled into imagining the opposite. The verbal contract is based on the mutual good faith of the parties who negotiate it and the mutual reliability of their memories. Unfortunately, no one's memory is as foolproof as a written document. Yet this drawback can be compensated for with witnesses and supporting documents that prove a verbal agreement took place.

The important thing to understand is this: a verbal contract exists if you can demonstrate a "contractual relationship" between you and your client: that is, that you have agreed on price, a schedule, terms and even changes to these while the work was underway. An agreement is all it takes to establish a legal relationship, and ongoing correspondence on the subject is irrefutable proof that you reached an agreement. Maybe it wasn't final, but you had one.

Imagine a worker who shows up unannounced and starts to repair your fence without you asking them: you're going to send them away unless your fence needs to be repaired and you decide to go ahead with it. In that case, if you agree to let the worker continue, if you bring them water, or lend them your tools, a contractual agreement exists, even if nothing is actually written down.

Remember: in front of a judge, it's your word against your client's—or the validity of your respective writings and witnesses (more on this in Chapter 17). The only things required to make a verbal agreement binding are an offer, acceptance and in Common Law jurisdictions (outside of Quebec), "consideration" of the offer. This won't be hard to prove in most cases. Any correspondence, reports or plans you made while working for a client will help prove your claim that there was a verbal (interchangeably called "oral") contract. The Internet, which has largely replaced oral communication, works to the advantage of self-employed workers since most communication is written. That makes it easier to establish the existence of this contractual relationship. An advance payment that was negotiated and received, even if it's small, is also proof that a verbal agreement was reached: customers don't send spontaneous gifts out of the blue.

Even when the verbal order is specific, with a trustworthy partner, it's a good idea to summarize your understanding of it in writing and send it to your client for approval. Sometimes you misunderstand details and this is a way of clarifying conditions. Sometimes either party's ideas evolve following a discussion and this gives you a chance to document changes. At the very least, a written summary provides evidence of the verbal contract.

It may be that the original order requires you to begin working immediately without waiting for an advance payment, or discussing the substance of what you will be doing. In this case, write to the client at the earliest opportunity. When the customer calls you for information, answer by email. A tacit confirmation of your contract can result from an email exchange as innocuous as "Hi Zac, I'm going away for the weekend, but don't worry, your project is moving forward nicely. Ciao. Nick." All Zac has to answer is, "OK. Nick," and you have evidence there was a contractual agreement in place.

To further bind the other party, nothing prevents you from writing a letter that summarizes the agreement. The written record summarizes the parties' obligations on paper (see the example on the next page). You will note in the example that there are several sentences that force the client to show their consent. The penultimate paragraph asks the client to consent, but even if they don't, they will have difficulty arguing, down the road, that they didn't owe you anything. If they go ahead with the work, they have implied consent.

You don't need to have your client's permission to write a report like this and the client shouldn't take offence if you do. Your letter just establishes that you and the client are on the same page. It's in everyone's interest.

An example of a written report

Dear Customer,

I am writing to confirm the details of our talk this morning.

You have ordered a brochure and information package about your dandelion harvesting service and you have provided me with some very useful contacts. I thank you for that.

As discussed, the length of the brochure and information package should be 1,700 words altogether. I will suggest ideas for illustrations, which will be done later by a third party.

We have agreed to a fixed rate of $1,000 for the work, plus travel and long-distance phone charges. You agree to pay me an advance of $300 next week and I agree to supply the final revised text by February 28, 2023. As this actual date is a weekend, do you want the text for the 27th or March 2nd?

In our discussion, you suggested a number of sources you wanted me to talk to, but since we spoke, I discovered that some of them have passed away. Do you have other ideas or should I find new sources myself?

[Optional paragraph: If you are still satisfied with the terms and conditions above, could you sign this letter and return it to me? I'll start working right away. If I have not heard from you by the time I receive your advance, I will assume these terms and conditions are satisfactory to you.]

Hoping for a quick reply, I send you my best wishes,

Flora Root
8 Weed Street, Grassville, NS
P0T 2G0 Canada

The written contract

The written contract formalizes the contractual agreement. Each party signs it. Each page, each addition and each deletion in it should be initialled by both parties. The (numbered) clauses detail the task, payment and settlement in case of dispute. All the points covered during negotiations must be included in the contract because the written contract takes precedence over any prior verbal agreement. The form of the contract can vary widely. Almost all professional associations provide at least one example of a standard contract.

An important point to determine at the outset is, who will draw up the contract, the buyer or the seller? There are no rules about who should do it. Generally speaking, if you know more about your business than your client does (often the case for us when non-writers hire us to write something for them) the responsibility will fall on you. However, the client may have a standard contract that they use and adapt for different projects. Either solution is acceptable. Before drafting the contract both parties need to have a discussion or exchange in which they agree on general terms of price, the amount of the advance payments, ownership and duration of the contract as well as any exclusions or terms that are specified in the contract.

A contract does not have to be drawn up by a lawyer to be legally binding. However, you may want to have a complex contract checked by a lawyer, especially the first time around. An experienced colleague or your professional association might also advise you on the main points you should include, or to which you should pay particular attention and the justification for clauses that may seem superfluous or unnecessary. When it comes to contracts, the devil really is in the details.

Because it is necessary to include so many details, writing a solid contract can be a slog and test your patience. But stick it out. It will be worth it. A good contract is one that will survive the passage of time, including changes of directors. So it has to take into account as many scenarios as possible over a long period of time. The contract will cover non-delivery, delays and poor work, non-payment, bankruptcy, any unforeseen defects and lawsuits that might arise. This does not make for a pleasant read, but like a good marriage contract, your work contract should set out the terms necessary for a harmonious divorce. You are making a serious mistake if you interpret a thorough contract as a sign that your client is trying to take advantage of you. Generally, the purpose of a contract is to protect everyone who signs it. It provides the rules of the game in case things go wrong, for both parties. In practice, this means that even if the signee is fired from their job two days after you sign your contract, their successor will be bound by the contract anyway, whether they agree with it or not.

The contract also gives you the opportunity to establish rules that will work for you. For example, in publishing, contracts always stipulate that if our publisher goes bankrupt, the rights to our books will unconditionally return to us, the authors. This clause protects us from our books being passed from one publisher to another without our consent—or worse, being passed from one bankruptcy trustee to another.

Although you may have agreed verbally on certain terms before signing it, you'll only see how different conditions fit together when things are on paper. In their rush to finalize a contract, a client may have slapped terms you agreed onto a preformatted standard contract without reading them over. It's up to you to spot contradictions.

Remember, a contract is a bargaining position. If a customer you are used to dealing with verbally suddenly offers you a written contract, out of the blue, ask them what prompted the change. Always ask why. It may be that they realized you are so helpful to their business that they are suddenly afraid of losing you. If they want to secure you with a contract, you should negotiate a fee increase. But they may also be slyly trying to get more from you than they had before. This has happened to us numerous times. Legally, when a newspaper or magazine publishes one of our articles, they are only buying a licence for first publication rights. Legally, they can't store or resell the article with those rights. They can only publish it. When Internet began making it interesting for publishing companies to store articles in databases and resell them in the late 1990s, publishers started asking journalists to sign copyright contracts that gave them more than what they used to purchase. They called these "electronic" rights and pretended they were worth nothing at the time but might be in the future—at which point they vaguely promised they would remunerate us for them. Many journalists rightly balked at these contracts. Others, ourselves included, used the new contracts as leverage to increase our fees.

The nature of the contract you sign may be dictated by the business you work in. It will therefore be written to take into account the specific legal or cultural constraints of your industry. For example, hairdressers and plumbers rarely have written contracts for the work they do with individual customers in their salon. But hairdressers who work for a TV chain doing actors' hair on set will definitely have one. No one works in the TV industry without a written contract.

Your contract may also have to comply with a pre-negotiated collective agreement. In principle, when you hire a plumber, they will charge you the hourly rate prescribed by their trade union. Singers and actors who are members of the Alliance of Canadian Cinema, Television and Radio Artists (ACTRA) must work according to minimum standards the union has negotiated with producers. Producers adhere to these standards by paying their dues and hiring only artists who are ACTRA members in good standing. An artist member, who works for a non-recognized producer or in conditions that don't meet the minimum negotiated by the association, will quickly hear from ACTRA.

Reading between the lines

The first thing you need to do when you receive a contract is, read it. Most people who end up with a bad, exploitative contract didn't actually read it before they signed on the dotted line.

Never sign a contract under pressure. Always read it twice. If it's a big contract, sleep on it between readings and once again before you sign it. In the thrill of the moment, when you land a sale and are offered a contract, the excitement might cause you to overlook details. Never ignore nagging doubts about things. They could turn out to be quite important. How many creators and inventors have been exploited or even put out of commission because they gave away the rights to all their future work? If you miss something important, you will be entirely dependent on your client's good will to adjust the original contract. No self-employed worker ever wants to be in that situation.

Always check the following points in a contract:

1. **Time and territory.** Always set a limit on these. If you don't, you may be penalized for the rest of your life.
2. **Ownership.** Make sure you define the rights you are assigning. Although it is implicit, we like to add a sentence in our contracts stating that any rights not stipulated in the contract are excluded. It's a good way to firmly stake out your territory.
3. **Penalties.** If possible, include a penalty for breach of contract. Read the clauses carefully. You could be bound to some of them even after the contract is broken, for example, if you promise not to solicit the client's competitors for the next three or five years. In other words, make sure that there are limits to the limits the contract imposes on you.
4. **Employment relationship.** If you only have one customer, make sure your contract does not imply that you are employed by this customer. This could have a significant impact on your work status (see Chapter 6) and as a result, on your tax status.
5. **Conflicts.** Anticipate them. Don't stick your head in the sand. No one is immune to having problems with clients. Your client may start out in perfectly good faith, but a lot can happen if the person you are dealing with is fired, promoted or just moves on. They might be replaced by someone who doesn't like you or your service, or thinks you are too expensive or doesn't understand the nature of the deal you had struck. Your contract should include a mediation clause and perhaps an arbitration clause, because going to court is expensive.

The contract should be consistent with your goals. For example, if a bank asks you to set up a training course in mental arithmetic but wants to own the rights to the materials you produce for the course, as well as the rights for the course itself, you won't be able to take your course anywhere else and make money from it. Unless, that is, you specify in your contract that the rights the bank is buying are *non-exclusive*. That is, the bank could acquire such a license to your course and materials, but allow you to continue to run the course for other clients anyway, or that they pay a royalty.

It is also a good idea to check for harmless-looking clauses that may actually penalize you. It may be legitimate for a client to ask for a "right of first refusal" for future works and you might not think this is a big deal. It may also seem reasonable for the contract to stipulate that the contract be "renewable by tacit agreement." But if you put these two clauses together, the result is that you are tied to your client for life without the possibility of renegotiating the contract!

Mediation or arbitration?

In the event of a serious dispute with a client, a mediation or arbitration clause forces both parties to try to reach a compromise before going to court. Mediation and arbitration have developed as alternatives to the courts. They are faster, (sometimes) cheaper and confidential. However, before you agree to this, you should understand the difference between the two. Arbitration is not a more "serious" form a mediation. They are both considered forms of alternative dispute resolution, but arbitration is something completely different. We discussed this with a friend, Joëlle Thibault, who is a lawyer by training and a professional ombudsperson.

- Mediation occurs between two consenting parties who disagree but still want to maintain their relationship. This is the business equivalent of marriage counselling. Mediation is a renegotiation carried out by a third party called the mediator. It results in a new agreement being reached between the parties. If mediation fails or if the new agreement is not respected, you can either try it again, proceed to arbitration (see Chapter 14) or go to court (see Chapter 17). Simple mediation can cost between $1,500 and $2,000. A complicated case could cost up to $5,000. Rates for this service range from $200 to $300/hour.
- Arbitration is similar to a private justice system. The arbitrator is to your business relationship what the judge is to your marriage: after

you use an arbitrator to solve a conflict problem with a client, you will no longer have a business relationship with that client. The arbitrator follows very precise rules. Their decision is not an "agreement," but an "award" that binds you and may even be enforceable in court. Good arbitration done by the book costs a minimum $ 15,000, at a rate of $350 to $450/hour.

Many contracts include an arbitration clause that commits the parties to both mediation AND arbitration. However, in almost all cases, arbitration is not in the best interest of self-employed workers so you should limit the remedial clause to the mediation clause if you can.

There are four reasons you should choose mediation over arbitration:

1. If you have done a good job negotiating your contract and taken as many potential friction points into account as possible when you did this and if you manage to keep good communications with your client, you probably won't need a judge or arbitrator to solve the conflict.
2. The court that is most likely to hear your case is the Small Claims Court, which costs next to nothing (see Chapter 17). Arbitration, on the other hand, could cost you the price of a new car. As a bonus, some Small Claims Courts even offer you a one-hour mediation session for free.
3. Arbitration is most interesting to large companies who are concerned about their public image because it offers a confidential form of justice for the same price as going to court. It won't necessarily be advantageous for you.
4. Arbitration can have the effect of blocking any recourse to the courts, a disadvantage if you ever want to appeal the decision.

For the average self-employed worker, situations where arbitration is more advantageous than going to court are rare. One exception may be if you have a very, very large contract involving huge sums of money to be paid over a long period of time. In that case, arbitration could cost less than taking your case to the court—but even that is a "maybe."

Sign on the dotted line

For a contract to be binding in Common Law, it must generally include an offer, acceptance, consideration and mutual intent. Rules in Civil Court are formulated differently, but the principles are basically the same.

A contract in which all the clauses are imposed by one party without any possibility for negotiation will only be valid if you accept it. Technically, this is called a contract of adhesion. It's also known as a "boilerplate" or "standard form" contract. When making their decision, courts take in consideration the possibility there was unequal bargaining power, unfairness and unconscionability at play when a contract was negotiated.

In principle, when a client presents you with a contract, you should not consider it a final version, written in stone. Offering a contract is almost always a negotiating position. You should never sign a contract blindly. You can strike out clauses that don't suit you and initial your deletions. If they are reasonable and justifiable, these changes will usually be accepted. You just have to make sure that the other party also initials the changes or deletions.

If a client tries to make you sign a contract on a "take it or leave it" basis, they are probably not a good client. They might even be dangerous to your business. If they won't negotiate a contract up front, imagine how they might act when a difference arises about the work itself, which it inevitably will. When you are starting out, you may not have a choice but to sign the contract as it's presented. But even if your bargaining power is limited, you should at least try to limit the scope of the contract, or it's time frame, or improve some of the conditions in it as much as you can. Otherwise, you could end up being bound to your client with very bad working conditions, for a very long time.

The polite and constructive way to refuse a contract is to say that you are ready to negotiate but that the terms being proposed are not yet acceptable. Be clear about what you want. If circumstances (cash flow problems, slump in business) force you to sign it anyway, your customer will not be able to feign surprise when you drop them for someone else who is willing to negotiate the terms of a collaboration. When they realize they might lose you because they weren't flexible in negotiating your contract, they might become more flexible.

If a customer wants to continue working for you and opens the door to renegotiating your contract, then, of course, you should use the opportunity to get more money and/or better conditions. But take your time and proceed with caution if your primary goal is to preserve the bond with your customer (if it's a good customer, this bond is always valuable). If the customer is too eager, ask them what the rush is. Everything is fine as long as you are still talking. You might even get your customer to talk more than they want and inadvertently supply you with a strategic advantage for your negotiations. If you keep your wits about you, you may very well reach a much better deal.

Operations 3

14

Keep on talking

Because negotiations don't end when the contract is signed

Myth #14: "I'm bound to the contract."

Magazine writers like us face a peculiar conundrum when they are starting out. You submit a paper you've been working on for weeks, or maybe months. When your editor sends it back a few weeks later, it's covered with red highlights of corrections and comments. Horror-struck, you go ahead and enter the corrections and answer the questions and then send it back, convinced you have failed your first real test as a writer.

Then the surprise: the editor calls back and asks you to write another story. And you wonder, did I do a good job or a bad job? Is this, "congratulations" or, "I'm giving you your final chance"?

Jean-Benoît asked one of his early editors outright. He was stunned by the answer. "First," the editor said, "it's my job to correct you. Second, you have done three things that 90% of freelancers don't do. Your first draft was well written, it was well documented and you delivered it on time." Whew.

If you can meet these basic requirements, you'll be one of those self-employed workers whose phone never stops ringing. Clients will share your name with their competitors. You won't even have to sell yourself: you'll be offered your pick of jobs so you can quickly become selective about which ones you want to do and which ones aren't worth the trouble.

You'll recall from the Introduction chapter that businesses have five functions: Sales, Operations, Research, Finance and Management. After setting yourself up, doing research, selling and negotiations, it's time to produce.

Although it is likely that the goods you deliver will evolve into something different from what was originally planned, doing good work and delivering on time is essential. The ability to do so, in any field, is a strong selling point. If you can't do this, clients may opt to work with someone who delivers with less flare—but delivers on time. We know editors who deliberately work with less skilled writers than their more talented peers because the less skilled ones are much more reliable.

Customers are looking for suppliers who can:

- Deliver the goods
- Not make much of a fuss in doing so
- Deliver on time

Learn the skills of good communication

No matter what your field is, there is one thing that you'll probably never learn in your training: how to communicate well with your customers. Good communication is not just important; it's very often the key to producing high-quality work. Good communication is what makes it possible to manage the difficulties and small or large crises that come with any work contract. Good communication is also essential to the never-ending negotiations that are the essence of a self-employed workers' career. Even when you have signed a contract and are doing the work, the negotiations with your customer carry on. Why? Because unforeseen issues pop up while the work is being carried out, things change and sometimes you learn about something that you didn't know when you signed your contract.

Being able to do quality work and respect deadlines are advantages, in themselves. But sometimes circumstances force you to adapt a project in mid-process. Houses turn out to be missing a part of their foundation (a friend of ours actually discovered this in the middle of renovating his two-story house). The facts of a story aren't quite what we thought they were when we started our research (this happens to us all the time). Whatever the discovery, it changes the nature of the job and calls for renegotiations, sometimes of your fee, sometimes of the deadline, sometimes both. To successfully renegotiate, you need to be comfortable communicating information to your client.

For instance, in our field, we have often had to renegotiate deadlines or even the length of a text that was assigned, sometimes midway through writing it. It actually happens pretty regularly: we are assigned a five-page story on a topic, we do our research, find out there's more to the story than our editor knew at the outset and end up submitting ten pages. We sometimes manage to convince our editor to double the length of an assignment (which means double the fee). But we can't just spring a story on them that's twice as long as what they assigned as a *fait accompli*. We have to communicate what's going on as soon as we know the terms of an assignment could change. By the time we submit the ten-page story, our editor has already agreed to the new terms. It can be in everyone's interest to change the terms of a contract while it's in the process of being executed, but you have to communicate well to make it happen.

In almost every case where we have had problems with people we hired, the issues popped up because of poor communication. We discovered a general contractor we had hired to renovate our upstairs apartment was working on many other contracts simultaneously. But we didn't realize this until he was falling behind in his work for us. Had he told us about what he had on the go when he started, we very well may have hired him anyway and just given him more time (and asked our future tenant if she could move in a little later). Maybe we could have worked around his constraints. (Instead, the whole thing escalated into a horrible fiasco when we had to call the police because unpaid workers from his other sites started showing up at our door asking for money he owed them.)

Don't try to hide it when a new development is going to affect your work. People are people. Your clients will understand if you have a sick child or ailing parent or if you have to take the afternoon off to find a plumber because your toilet is blocked. Stuff like that happens to them too. Everyone knows there are things in life that can't wait. But if you hide your problems, you'll end up submitting your work late. You may even end up not doing a great job because you're in a rush, and *that* means you might lose a client.

Good communication is not just talking. It actually starts with good listening.

Listening is so natural that we take it for granted. People who teach the famous Toyota management model often insist on the art of asking good questions. But what's the point if you don't listen back? The reason listening is so hard for so many people might just be neurological. Brains think way more quickly than mouths speak. So your brain is constantly distracted by seeking more information—while often missing the information that is at hand.

Most students in business schools receive absolutely no training in listening (the idea behind becoming a leader is that you talk!). The few professionals who are trained to listen properly, such as social workers, know that listening well is not a passive exercise. You have to listen not just with your ears, but also with your eyes, your body and even your heart. This is because most communication is actually non-verbal. When someone tells you they are "fine," they can mean the absolute opposite. The actual meaning has to be gleaned from their tone or gestures, or even the context. You have to pick up the non-verbal elements in order to give meaning to what others say.

Any experienced self-employed person will tell you that half the cases of jobs or contracts that went poorly, started with poor listening. They didn't pick up the early signs of trouble. In fact, when the look back at what went wrong, they often realized too later that they missed signals that were pretty obvious.

And naturally, they often realize that if even when they did pick up the signals, they failed to heed them, or act on them. That's where the "talking" part of communication becomes essential.

We have hired self-employed workers ourselves over the years to do all sorts of things for us: clean our house, help us build a social media presence, build a new deck in our backyard, fill out our income tax returns, design a website and negotiate books and film contracts for us. We have learned over the years that even when the workers we hire are very good, we can't just hire them and leave them on their own. We have to keep an active eye on whatever they are doing for us, whether it's to correct mistakes, or clear up misunderstandings or just make sure they understand what they are supposed to be doing for us. But the ones we liked and called back were those who made an effort to communicate while they were working for us. Constant communication is the only way to make sure that the product delivered meets our expectations. Our guidance is necessary, but theirs is too.

The art of adapting

There are two reasons it's important to establish good communication with your customers. One: it makes your life easier. Two: it allows you to negotiate and adjust your client's expectations to real working conditions, on the ground. Even during the production stage of your work, you need to stay in communication with your customers like a pilot does with air traffic control. The only pilots who don't talk to air traffic control are bush pilots, whose job it is to land wherever they can manage. There's no need to pretend you are a bush pilot. If you aim to land on the runway with your cargo in one piece at an agreed time and not disrupt traffic, or bring in the emergency fire services, you need to keep the communication lines open with air control.

Most beginners are afraid to communicate with their clients after they start working a project. Beginners tend to work with their cards very close to their chests—usually too close. They either think they are "bothering" clients when they initiate communications mid-process. Or they are afraid of looking like they aren't on top of things. They don't want to show signs of "weakness." Of course, what's really going on is that beginners lack confidence and are afraid of disappointing their first customers. Whatever the underlying motive is, this attitude will end up hurting you. You have to give your customer regular signs of life while you are working for them and keep them informed about your progress. If you were working in the same office with your client—that is, if you were an employee—regular updates would happen more or less spontaneously in daily conversations with your superiors. But as a self-employed worker, physically removed from your client, you have to make sure this communication happens on your own. You have to make the effort. Customers don't fear anything as much as a supplier who never gives them a sign of life. If the order went out on March 1 and your client expects delivery by 5:00 p.m. on May 1, and they haven't heard a word from you for over two months, they'll be nervous as the deadline approaches. No one wants to be in that situation. What would be more terrifying to air traffic controllers at a major airport than a pilot who doesn't report their flight status? Imagine the stress for everyone involved.

There are two reasons customers get afraid when they aren't getting regular news from a supplier. First, they know that there are a thousand and one things that could delay the job. It's Murphy's Law: anything that can go wrong will go wrong. There's only one thing worse: something actually does go wrong and your client doesn't hear about it until it's too late to solve the problem. Then they are stuck having to arrange an "emergency landing" (which will be more expensive and troublesome because they will most likely have to find another supplier). Of course, your customer will be happy if you just deliver on time. But you will still be considered less reliable than the self-employed worker who checks in with occasional progress reports. It's reassuring to hear how things are going. Even if you are working in proximity to a client, always make an effort to keep them informed about how your work is going. Remember, a self-employed worker is nobody's subordinate, so no one is supervising you.

But there's another reason to communicate regularly with your client. We call it the "drifting client." Good clients are passionate and committed to what they do, and always attuned to developments in their specific field. Because of that, the ideas they have about a service or project they commissioned are bound to evolve over time. Sometimes these ideas actually take a whole new direction between the time you sign with them and you deliver. This can become a serious problem if you are unaware. Keeping up regular communications gives you the time and opportunity you need to manage their expectations. Consider this: during World War II, more naval fighter planes were lost as a result of navigational errors than because the enemy shot their planes down. What was going on? Pilots would arrive at planned takeoff sites to discover that there wasn't an aircraft carrier there. The culprit was bad communication: no one thought to tell them the aircraft carrier had moved to another location.

For the freelancer, the "drifting client" issue poses the biggest problem at the beginning of your career, when you don't have as much experience managing expectations—helping clients understand and define their needs—and you don't have the experience you need to pick up the signals that your clients' ideas are shifting. Rest assured, problems with drifting clients can easily be prevented with a simple solution: stay in touch with your client. You don't need to have years of experience to be able to do this: all you need is honesty and a phone or their email address.

But what do I say to clients?

Normally, once you and your client have agreed on the expectations, the price, the terms and the deadline of a job, you can consider that the order has been "placed." Yet remember, the contract you sign is actually nothing more than a flight plan: it does not replace actual inflight communications. You and your client will have to continue discussing things as your work progresses.

What do you need to talk about? We describe the main things below, but the purpose boils down to four goals.

- First, you need to reassure the customer that you are a competent professional.
- Second, you have to ensure them you have remained in control of the project.
- Third, you need to put yourself in a position to be able to renegotiate aspects of your contract as the situation evolves.
- Fourth: you need to protect yourself in the event of disagreement or non-payment (see Chapter 17).

Through frequent communication, by sending reports and showing your plans, you will gain a lot of control over your work orders. Clients will trust you more. You demonstrate over and over to them, as you are going along, that you are competent. Even in cases where clients back out of orders—it's not fun, but it happens—thorough and thoughtful communication shows you are a real pro who has no time to waste. And they'll remember that.

The preliminaries

Let's return to the flight control metaphor—it's working well. You should start communicating with your client as soon as you exit the hangar. Don't be ashamed to check in (by email is fine) when the flight is about to take off. Maybe you already know you'll need more time than you originally thought. Better to say so now than to wait. The customer, who is often more flexible than you think, might grant you an extension without you even asking for it. Reasonable delays are normal: your customers are constantly experiencing and asking for delays themselves. At any rate, deadlines are often more benchmarks than absolutes. Julie once worked as an editor on a six-month contract with a small publishing company. The deadline she gave to her writers was two weeks earlier than what she actually needed to comfortably meet her own deadliness with the printer. She gave her writers "fake" deadlines so that if, for whatever reason, they were running late, she knew she had some leeway and could negotiate comfortably and civilly with them. That lowered the stress level for everyone.

Don't second-guess your client. Normally, your first discussions with your client should just allow you to establish the client's flexibility (about deadlines or any other production issue). It's a good policy to be honest if there are any circumstances you can foresee that might affect your ability to deliver. You might have to delay starting work because you are put off by the scale of the order, or because you are hesitant about some detail or another. If that's the case, it's better to say so right off the bat than try to hide it! It will catch up with you. Your customer may have thought things over, in the meantime, and had the same concerns. In any case, reporting problems is a sign of professionalism. If an engineer discovers at the outset of their project that their client is trying to build on sand, they should say something, so the client can either adapt the plan or cancel the project altogether. If a pilot realizes they don't have enough fuel for a flight, they should certainly say something before hitting the runway.

After starting, it's a good idea to phone, email or write again to your client to either confirm that everything is progressing as planned or let them know that the plan needs to be changed. If your client is not available, insist on getting the message through via their assistant or secretary. Don't worry about "unnecessarily disturbing" your client: it is their job to deal with you and they'll appreciate getting the information they need to do so. They may be very busy: so leave a message or write to them.

Sometimes you discover early in your work that some of the assumptions you and your client had about a project were totally off track. Clearly, you both misunderstood something about the job. Sometimes it even turns out that your client doesn't need your services, after all. When you hit these kinds of road blocks, don't procrastinate and don't just forge ahead blindly. Communicate your concerns to your client right away. They may be disappointed, and you might lose work, but they'll appreciate your honestly and forthrightness. They may even turn around and offer you work on another project or compensate you for the preparation work you have done (especially if the project was their idea in the first place or if you turned down another client to work on it). Again, don't think sharing your concerns about difficulties you encounter in the project will make you look like an amateur. It's the opposite. Speaking up shows that you are confident and experienced and have good judgment, all of which boost your credibility in the long run. Challenges and obstacles are normal, even inevitable, and everyone knows that. Only incompetent workers avoid or neglect reporting problems. We all know how this can lead to disasters.

If you are dealing with inexperienced clients, you will almost certainly have to repeat explanations you have already supplied. They need to understand what steps you will need to go through to arrive at finished product. We call it "educating" customers. We do it with just about any client who isn't a writer, editor or translator.

Get it in writing

Written communications can really make your life and your job easier. They can also protect you by allowing you to control how things proceed with a customer: you can make sure they follow through on their commitments. Documents also allow you to travel back in time and understand and explain how a decision was made.

By doing this, you gently take control of the situation. Getting things in writing also helps build your client's confidence in you. It's also your best protection.

If your customer refuses to pay you, or changes their mind about a project without consulting you, you will be glad to have things in writing. All the written documents you have produced (including emails) serve as proof that you were acting in good faith and had agreed to a plan. So the customer cannot turn around and claim that you misled them, or that you changed your mind halfway through the project without notifying them, or that they hadn't actually agreed to the project or its terms in the first place (although they can always claim that the quality of your work does not meet their expectations, which is possible).

In short, creating a paper trail can save you a lot trouble (and money) if a dispute arises with a client (see Chapter 17). This is very important. You don't need to advertise that not all your written communications are carried out strictly for your client's benefit. Just keep the paper trail in your archives and hang onto it for a while even after you have received your cheque.

The progress report

Any self-employed worker who produces or delivers a service over a lengthy period of time should take the time to write a progress report to their client midway through a project even if this is not required contractually. When work on a big project is at about the halfway point, we produce a report that is essentially a roundup of the situation. In journalism, this means explaining what information we have found, whom we have talked to, how our ideas have changed, if they have, and what remains to be done.

For larger projects, this report can sometimes be several pages long. It's possible to make your report verbally as well, but the written form is preferable for the reasons we discussed above. In addition, a written report gives your client time to study it at their own leisure or pass it around to colleagues or other interested parties for input if they need it. The written report is also an opportunity to dazzle your client with your ability to summarize and explain your work. That generally has the effect of making them trust you more. Yes, progress reports are a hassle. Projects are usually picking up steam by the time you write a progress report (otherwise there would be nothing to report on) and it can be a little painful to slow down and document what you've done. However, rest assured, such reports will very likely save you time later.

We can't count the number of times have we been saved by good communication. One memorable case was when Jean-Benoît wrote a progress report for a magazine editor just before he was leaving for holidays. When he returned two weeks later, Jean-Benoît sensed that something was wrong. It turned out the editor had been expecting a much more thorough investigation than Jean-Benoît had realized but had not been clear about this when he assigned the story. The editor had the honesty to admit his mistake. He cancelled everything and compensated Jean-Benoît for the preparation work he had done. If Jean-Benoît hadn't made a report of his work along the way, he only would have realized the problem when it was too late to find a mutually satisfactory solution.

This kind of situation often arises when people go on holidays: the person who places the order takes off and puts someone in charge to evaluate the final results, even though that person was sometimes not part of the original order and almost invariably sees things differently. The only way to prevent the problem is to take control quickly: find out who will be replacing your contact and discuss the details of the order you were given with them before directly, ahead of time. That allows you to get the "substitute" on board with how you see things before the work is submitted.

The same logic applies when the person who places the order with you retires or is fired. Find out who their replacement will be as quickly as you can and start the communications with them. Be proactive. Don't wait.

So far, you have "bothered" your client at least three times and they are delighted. They know what you've done, and what, if any, problems you might have in delivering your work. They have heard how things are going and what new stuff turned up during your work for them. They no longer have lingering doubts about your talent or ability to deliver: they can see you are close to the finishing line. Basically, they trust you. Their only worry now is whether you can deliver a result that will be polished enough that they won't have to pull up their sleeves and work on it themselves after you hand it in.

The plan

The next step is crucial. In order to complete and deliver work in its final form to your client, you must start by making a plan, outline or prototype for approval.

There is no such thing as "spontaneous creation." In journalism, boiling down a thick file of documents to eight written pages can be downright traumatizing (you always have to cut, and it's often things that are really interesting!). When we were studying at university, and at the beginning of our writing careers, we both had the mistaken belief that a plan was a few notes scribbled on a sheet of paper. It's not. Real plans are elaborate and lengthy—between a third and half the length of the final written work. Once in a blue moon an article will come together more easily and with less planning than we anticipated, but that's usually when we spent a lot of time thinking it over and organizing our ideas in the first place. Most of the time we plan articles carefully, even elaborately. Only amateurs dive into things blindly, whether in writing or any other activity. For that matter, in most of the cases where we ended up in a conflict with a client (editor), it was because we started writing before we were sure what we were doing, what we wanted to say or how we wanted to say it.

Don't be afraid to show your plan to your client, especially if you are a beginner. In most cases, they will appreciate a solid plan, a good prototype or in some cases an outline of what you are doing. It will reassure them, not the opposite (as beginners often fear). It will give them a sneak preview of what they are getting and a chance to make input if they want. They can also pass the plan on to their colleagues to make sure everyone knows what's coming and is on board with it. It's preferable to hear objections at this early stage rather than later, or even on delivery of the final product.

However, there is something you need to be careful about, especially when you are dealing with inexperienced clients. Before you submit a plan or especially an outline, make sure your client clearly understands that this is not the final product. Illustrators and graphic designers frequently run into this problem. They send in a few sketches and then a client calls them back within the hour threatening to cancel the contract because the work is "sloppy." Remember, there are people out there who don't understand that creation is a process that happens in stages. These folks imagine that finished logos just pop out of graphic designers' heads. Many people assume good writing happens spontaneously as well (it really, truly, doesn't).

There's nothing lazy or sloppy about an outline. It's a necessary stage on the way to a finished project. But beware: if a client doesn't understand this, seeing (or thinking they are seeing) a "half-done" job can really shake them up.

Curiously, when the clients do understand the purpose of a plan or outline, these documents often become powerful sales tools that convince them to order more of what you are selling.

The beta version

So now you are "clear to land," as the air traffic controllers' time-honoured formula goes. However, pilots don't relax until the plane is on the runway and neither should you. You still have to keep communicating with air control.

Why? For any number of (legitimate) reasons, the final product might turn out to be quite different from the original plan. Perhaps you only found out about a key piece of information after you started (as writers, this is a frequent hazard); new facts come to light; you may have found a way to tighten up your ideas; or maybe you came up with an entirely new idea. If that's the case, don't hesitate to send in a "first draft," also called a "preliminary," "beta" or rough version. Whatever you call it, use the word "version" and not "draft," even if that's what it is. We have many clients who are willing to read a beta version, but not a draft. Submitting a "beta" version allows you to test something, you're not sure about without coming across as sloppy or incompetent. Be careful, however: some customers are a bit quick to judge and won't react well to unfinished work. You have to be careful of clients zooming in and fixating on details (things that can still be corrected or changed) instead of seeing the big picture, which is usually what you want feedback about. For instance, in the case of writing, certain clients can't help but correct spelling or grammar mistakes, or worry about slight inconsistencies in Canadian and UK or US spelling ("honor" or "honour"?) They are unaware that these really are "details" and will be cleared up in a later stage of the creative process, namely, the copyediting stage. Writers know those are matters for copy editors and that it's not worth fretting about mistakes until it's the right time to correct them. But some clients can't stand anything that's not "final." It's up to you to figure out their tolerance level. With time, you learn to recognize which clients deal well with draft versions and which don't.

Handling misunderstandings: Think before you write

With Internet and the web, we write more than we ever have. But writing is not always the best way to solve problems with other people. For the same reason that we recommend supporting your sales effort with written documents, we strongly urge you to keep your criticisms OUT of writing, at least initially. Ideas may end up drifting into oblivion, but written words never disappear. Misunderstandings that could have been cleared up with a simple phone call, or a brief in-person meeting, end up taking on epic proportions when they get hashed out in harsh written words in emails. The syndrome is even worse when third parties get involved in the emails through the famous carbon copies (c.c.).

A slightly negative comment that would have gone unnoticed in a conversation will turn into a long-lasting bone of contention once it is written down. And if the person you are addressing decides to answer you in writing, watch your relationship go down in flames.

The problem is worse if your client is not self-employed, like you, but an employee of a company. Your client is bound to share the comments with their colleagues, and then the whole situation just gets worse. If you feel the need to criticize a customer or members of their staff about a particular point, never do it in writing. Handle the issue by phone or in person. The reason is simple: you are alone and your client is probably several people. Written criticism is easy to pass around. Nothing is better for hurt feelings or pride than getting other people to see how you've been mistreated. Your written criticism of one employee may alienate everyone on the team at the receiver's end. Remember, when there is a conflict, the blame will usually go to the person who isn't there—the outsider, or you. Being an outsider, you should never run the risk of looking like you are trying to erode your client's team spirit in any way. When one member of their team is attacked, the others will tend to stick together, even those who agree with you. Remember: their loyalty will go to the person who pays them (and their colleagues).

So how should you handle a problem with a client? First, figure out whether the problem is about your relationship with the client or about the contract with your client. If the actions of your client or their employees have violated the contract, you should definitely take the time to write them down, referring specifically to the contract. If the problem is that someone's behaviour is making it difficult for you to do your work, you should discuss this rather than writing about it.

On the other hand, circumstances may force you to write to everyone you are involved with in a project. This will be the case if you need to give instructions: for example, "Everyone sends their comments on to X," or, "don't include me in your c.c." In this case, try to avoid pointing fingers at anyone.

If an employee is harassing you, you should first notify the person or their supervisor, communicating verbally. However, you should avoid embarrassing them in front of their colleagues: team spirit is a strong force. People on a team might agree with you in private, but in public, shift their loyalties to their colleagues out of solidarity. The exception would be cases of serious abuse—and even then, you never know.

Whatever you do, when you start having problems with a project, do not use writing to take any specific person to task publicly (and by "publicly," here, we mean even a very small group). The person you are singling out could end up suing you for defamation and damage to their reputation. This rarely happens, but if you don't control what you say to, or about, this person you'll be asking for trouble.

If you have a legitimate beef and feel that you need to confront your client in writing, take the time to write down your thoughts without recrimination. Stick to the facts. And then, don't send it right after you write it. Sleep on it: print it out, put it on the corner of your desk and re-read it with a clear mind the next day. Once you see your frustrations on paper, you will probably realize how futile it is to communicate them to your client in this form. At the very least, you will see how to better frame the issues in order to protect yourself from recrimination.

Remember that the goal of communicating a problem is to solve it, not to win your case. There's no point in setting the house on fire when all you want to do is fix it. It is possible for a relationship problem to get out of hand and compromise your ability to fulfil a contract. But again, because the problem is affecting the contract, you must notify the client as soon as possible and you must stick to the facts.

Managing conflict: Consider mediation

A professional mediator would tell you that, in the last three chapters, we've actually been talking about what's called "interest-based negotiation" (also called "win-win"). Interest-based negotiation means reaching a mutually acceptable outcome that is mutually beneficial to both parties. You need to keep those principles in mind when you sign a contract, but also while you are carrying out work for a client.

The principles of interest-based negotiation can be summarized as follows:

1. If you have a problem, do not be afraid to talk about it.
2. You have enough imagination to come up with solutions to everything.
3. Keep your objectives in mind rather than sticking to your position.

4. Make a distinction between the problem and the person with whom you are discussing it.

5. Always keep the lines of communication open.

To respect these five principles and keep the gears running smoothly during your contract, you have to be careful not to let your self-interest get out of control. Interest-based negotiation only works well when you are really, truly acting in good faith. In other words, if you constantly communicate with the aim of getting an edge over your customer, they'll see this sooner than later and understand that you are not really negotiating in good faith. Your primary goal should be to deliver and do what it takes to prevent disputes. That doesn't mean you always need to put aside your own interests. Just weigh them against other factors and keep the overall picture in mind.

All business relationships go through rough patches. Nothing runs perfectly smoothly all the time. There will always be friction. Sometimes it will be minor, sometimes it will grow like a virus and threaten your relationship with a long-standing client, but trust us, friction will always be there.

When you find yourself involved in a serious dispute that puts your relationship with a client in jeopardy, it might be because in your negotiations, you failed to consider what potential sources of friction might arise. You or your client might end up refusing to bend on a point that was forgotten, omitted or just not clear in your contract. Or perhaps the terms and conditions of the job changed radically over the course of the work. The dispute might even arise from a combination of any or all of these factors.

Ideally, everyone would like to be able to settle their dispute without terminating the business relationship. That's the goal of mediation. Arbitration, as we explained in the previous chapter, is like a private legal court: if you are using arbitration, it means the relationship is already over. Mediation is basically just a means for renegotiating a contract by enlisting a third party. It is as simple as that.

You and your negotiating partner must choose the mediator together on the basis of their knowledge or impartiality, and both of you must trust him or her. The mediator will follow an established procedure that starts with both parties signing a mediation agreement. Mediation typically involves two types of sessions: joint sessions (where the parties are present and explain themselves) and caucuses (where the mediator confers with one or other of the parties individually). Some negotiations are conducted exclusively in caucus meetings. Others only happen in joint sessions. Some mediation cases can be wrapped up in an hour, though most cases take a few days, and some even weeks. You won't be in mediation for years.

A good mediator also uses something a judge or arbitrator never does: creativity. An arbitrator or judge can only make a decision within the boundaries of the contract; they can never venture beyond them. The only question they are trying to answer is, was the contract respected? But the mediator, on the other hand, assumes that the contract is itself under threat and that the relationship must be saved. They are therefore ready to quickly explore avenues beyond the contract, according to the real goals each of the parties is pursuing. Though it amounts to renegotiating the contract, mediation is an interesting option if you are having trouble with a customer who you don't want to lose.

Mediators don't decide anything and don't award anything to either party. Instead, they get the parties to come to an agreement. The resulting signed agreement constitutes a contract according to the law. If the other party does not respect the agreement, then they can take it to arbitration or to court. We hope you will never have to resort to mediation, but as they say, it happens in the best of families.

15

Open "till the wee hours"

It's the small things that count

Myth #15: "You can never say no to clients."

All baseball fans know the name Yogi Berra. Between 1946 and 1989, he was catcher, manager and coach of the New York Yankees and then coach and manager of the Mets and the Houston Astros. But even if you don't pay attention to baseball, you've certainly heard one of the many aphorisms he sprouted over his career, including the most famous: "It ain't over 'til it's over."

If Yogi Berra had been a self-employed worker, his maxim probably would have been: "It ain't over *even after it's over.*"

Why not? Just ask any experienced self-employed person and they'll tell you, projects don't really end. And that's a good thing. Because if there's one thing successful self-employed workers all do well, it's to provide top-notch after-sales service.

What keeps customers coming back to self-employed sales and service providers is quality work, of course. But customers also expect you to perform a host of small gestures specific to their line of business. We're not talking about little courtesies like sending customers Christmas cards—although those are nice touches and can be very effective tools in some fields. No, most customer satisfaction comes from a potentially long list of after-sales services they receive. Frequently giving clients a sign of life over the course of your work for them is one, even if all you do is check in to make sure the poster you designed actually looks right when it's taped to the wall. In journalism, editors appreciate freelancers who read their publication. Illustrators who show that they are sincerely interested in how their client uses the images they produce will be always preferred over designers who don't give a damn what clients do with their work after it's delivered. It's the same thing in any other field: you should be proud of your work and proud to work for your client, and you should communicate this to your client.

There is no such thing as perfection in this world. Doing good work also means revising, adjusting and reworking projects without grumbling about extra work—up to a certain point, of course. Some customers are too shy to actually express their dissatisfaction about a job, so it's in the interest of every self-employed worker to get ahead of the curve and ask for customer feedback, or even anticipate having to do some tweaking after finishing a job. The reputation of a self-employed worker depends on little things like this. A client may not have the nerve to tell you they had a problem with an aspect of your work, but rest assured, they'll want to get their frustration off their chest somehow or another. They might very well do that by telling one of their competitors (who is a potential customer for you) about how dissatisfied they were. Since your reputation is by far the best visiting card you have, you should do everything you can (again, within reason) to protect it. That means reaching out to make sure customers are happy.

In short, if a client asks you to make a small adjustment to a piece of work, even if you regarded your work as finished, don't balk at the idea. Your first reaction will probably be: "It's my masterpiece, don't touch it!" But step back for a second and think about it. You can probably learn something valuable from listening to your client's feedback. The change they are asking for might even improve your project or service, maybe in a way you never thought of. We always ask our editors to make corrections directly on our work. Sometimes this ritual really tests our patience. But more often than not we end up with a better understanding of how that client thinks and what their expectations were, or are. At the very least, our clients know we are open to changes, new ideas and being challenged and that we are committed to doing good work and even improving it. We show them that it's "not just about the money."

Whether or not you have the last word on what you deliver depends on the contract and the customs of your business. But you should always insist on seeing how your work is being used and how it has been modified. Maybe a client will go on to make 14,000 copies of your mental arithmetic notebook and resell them ("because we loved it so much!"). That will clearly violate your contract. Perhaps the marketing plan you produced for client was sabotaged when they replaced the photo of Heidi Klum with an ostrich. You need to control the use of anything that has your signature on it and anything that you intend to use and sell to other customers. Doing this kind of follow-up can bring about uncomfortable conversations, especially if your client was not as satisfied as you thought they were, but you are always better off finding out about problems and fixing them yourself than trying to undo some terrible mess someone else has made of things. If you bury your head in the sand and refuse to face a problem, you will very likely end up in a bush fire that you can't put out.

You also may spot a defect, after delivery—maybe even if your customer is happy. This is normal: you worked hard on the project and lacked the distance to objectively evaluate it at the time of delivery. One, two or three weeks after we deliver articles (which in the magazine business means, before they are published), we welcome the opportunity to read them over and check our facts and numbers or rethink our title. This is a lot easier than worrying about whether things are alright or not. Sometimes we find problems before our customers do. They generally appreciate this mark of professionalism more than they worry about the actual mistake or problem.

Avoiding after-sales abuse

We're not saying you should be a prisoner to your client's every whim. On the contrary, you need to be able to stand up for yourself when it's called for. When's that? If your client blames you for doing something they explicitly asked you to do against your warning (and didn't end up liking), that's their fault, not yours. If they gave your poor instructions, you should tell them so. The only thing they might be right about, is blaming you for not pointing out their mistake earlier—if you saw it. But you're not to blame if the client never really knew what they wanted, or changed their mind mid-process. In creative fields, that can happen as customers become educated about the creative process (by watching and talking to you about your work).

It's possible a customer might also cross the line and misuse the product you supplied. This is a problem for you, especially if your name is on the product. How you react will depend on whatever field of business you are in. If you were doing a marketing campaign and the photos that you chose to accompany a text were altered, there is nothing you can do about it unless otherwise specified in your contract. On the other hand, if a customer signs a license to use something and then goes on to actually modify it, you are justified in refusing that modification. You may have to take off the kid gloves and put on the boxing gloves.

This kind of problem is, fortunately, quite rare, but we've occasionally had to demand the removal of a paragraph the editor added to our text. We insist here on the verb "demand": under copyright law, we are the owners of the text. A taxi driver who owns and is responsible for their vehicle has the right to refuse customers who don't respect their property, or even the rules of taxi riding. Sometimes you will need to make your customer bend. But try to avoid provoking unnecessary confrontation, except in extreme cases, and only when you have solid reasons for doing so. Confrontation may mean you'll lose the client.

In a nutshell, be polite, but firm.

The best time to land another sale

Many self-employed workers love what they do so much that they forget they also have to sell.

A job well done is your best selling point, but it is also your best selling *moment*. It's okay to be proud of signing your first contract and delivering the merchandise. But don't forget, you'll need many more contracts like that a year to earn a living. So, you need to find a way to work AND sell.

Though it's exciting to get a new contract, beware of taking on too much work at the same time. Beginners often fall into this trap, mostly due to insecurity. When Jean-Benoît was in his "apprenticeship" period in journalism—which was unusually long because he was doing a university degree at the same time—he often ended up with a workload that put his time management skills to the test. He ended up neglecting his studies as a result. He also let himself become too dependent a few clients, which meant he didn't develop effective sales skills. They were beginners' mistakes, but he learned from them.

We discovered early in our writing careers that the best time to sell a new project to an editor is right after we submitted the final version of whatever we were writing for them. If the editor is satisfied with what we did, this is the best moment to signal our availability. Editors are usually receptive to new pitches. However, this means that by the time we complete a book or article, we have to be already thinking about what we are going to pitch next.

Being self-employed is like cooking: whatever you have on the front burner has to get most of your attention, but while you are cooking you can't forget what you have on the back burner, or in the oven, or sitting on the counter, or in the fridge. In other words, you have to occasionally step away from the stove to tend to the rest of the food in your kitchen. You also have to be able to answer the door when it rings.

When self-employed workers start out, they often make the mistake of letting their sales efforts lag while they work on their first big contract. Some workers are actually afraid of approaching other customers, thinking they might lose the customer they are presently working for, or make that customer feel like they are less of a priority. This is another example of behaving and thinking, "like an employee." If you want to survive as a self-employed worker, you have to be looking for work, or at least keeping an eye out for opportunities, all the time. It has to be a way of life. Your customers won't be offended. As a matter of fact, they will respect you more, knowing that you are busy and sought after—and that they could lose you to another customer if they're not careful. That's why it's actually a good idea to advertise the fact that you are working for someone else, too, or that you are talking to other clients, whether current or prospective.

Your customers need to understand that you work for other people and accept the fact that you will sometimes have to put your work for them on the back burner to tend to someone else, unless, of course, there is a clause about this in your contract (in which case you should be compensated for making this sacrifice). To return to our kitchen metaphor, if a customer gets upset because you are working for someone else at the same time, they are behaving like uninvited guests in your kitchen. And you should politely instruct them to leave.

Every week, you should do at least one thing to reach out to new clients: make a phone call, or send an email. Social media posts don't really count here but it's a good habit to post regularly. To have stable income, you need to do this as part of your regular professional activity. You have to have a hand in sales all the time. Prospective clients will appreciate being approached by a self-employed worker who is obviously busy: it's a sign that your business is running well and that there is demand for what you produce or offer. But it also shows that you are organized and can juggle many tasks. As the saying goes: if you want something done, ask a busy person to do it. The busy person may have less time, but they know how to use what they have in order to get things done. Of course, you also have to demonstrate that you can live up to the expectations you create. You need to be able to follow up quickly when someone requests a quote or information about your product or service. If you approach customers, then leave them hanging instead of following up swiftly, you will have to start the process all over again later—from scratch and possibly with them doubting your abilities.

The intensity of your sales efforts will depend a lot on the nature of your market and how regular your income is. Do your clients want occasional, one-time jobs or are they looking for someone to do ongoing work? The construction sector works according to major contracts over long periods of time, but requires little or no follow-up (ideally, anyway). When the job is finished, the self-employed construction worker packs their bags and head to a new site, perhaps with the hope that the customers will call them back for future projects. Construction is a business that usually has waiting periods between contracts, especially since homeowners generally do their renovations in warm weather, not in the middle of winter. Singers, actors, musicians and all performing artists have the same problem: their businesses have seasons that depend on the schedules of the venues in which they perform. The communications sector (radio, television, newspapers), on the other hand, has no season. It requires a continuing, steady stream of written texts, advertisements, photos, images, illustrations, comic strips, video and more. In this field, you might not need to spend as much time on sales because most customers will need your services all year round. However, you should be on the lookout for new clients, since publications go out of business, and editors get fired or change jobs.

Even when you get off to a good start in your business, the fear of running out of work is bound to hit you at some point. It happens to ALL self-employed workers, throughout their careers. It's just part of life. Your contract ends one week and you have nothing on the agenda for the next week, or month. The best thing to do is not fret, but take advantage of your new-found free time to do some sales. Having some time between jobs gives you time to call back old clients and offer your services. Those clients may have a burning, immediate need and be delighted to hear you have free time. They may place an order with you right off the bat, or they may refer you to a friend, colleague or competitor who they know also needs your services. Don't be shy. Potential customers are always looking for someone good who can do something for them.

To make sure you have a constant flow of work, you should always have several orders placed, or contracts underway, simultaneously. Of course, this means learning to spread your work out at a pace you can manage. This is a learning process. Don't take on six different contracts that have to be delivered on the same date. You may be able to pull off the impossible once or twice in a year, but you can't keep it up over the long run. It's not a question of experience, but of simple logistics. Work on a contract gets more intense the closer you get to your deadline. When you are planning your workload, you should keep this in mind. In an ideal world, you should be able to structure your schedule to spread work out evenly ahead of deadlines. Unfortunately, real life sometimes throws a wrench in plans and messes up the most meticulously thought-out schedules. Your client might not be able to stagger their work the way you can. Still, you should aim to create an even working pace. The further your deadline, the less a job will monopolize your time and prevent you from working on other contracts simultaneously. No one really likes a tight schedule, not you and not your customers. Remember that on the day or days prior to handing something in, the finishing up process has a way of monopolizing your time and attention. Customers may call you six times to find out where things stand. It's human nature. Make sure you can take the time you need to do things right.

Five Scout Virtues for doing post-mortems

Even when business is going gangbusters, specific projects might fizzle or die. It's important to learn to look squarely at failures when they happen. Self-employed workers who blame other people for all their difficulties rarely succeed.

We have met self-employed workers who chronically complain about the "boss." That just tells us they are inexperienced. They don't know their "boss" is actually their customer. If, as a self-employed worker, you find yourself at the mercy of a customer who treats you like an employee, it's your own fault. Understanding the nature of your relationship with clients is fundamental. There's no place for prima donna-style indignation with your customer. The worst thing you can do is to dismiss your customer's criticism on the basis that you "have other satisfied customers." That attitude will lose you customers over the long run, unless you're truly a genius—and even then, there are other geniuses out there who have a better attitude about client relationships and will get your business.

Prudence dictates that self-employed workers should act as if they are *not* geniuses, even if they are. Real geniuses don't need to pretend they are.

For that matter, self-employed workers should always be in a learning frame-of-mind. They should instinctively put themselves in learning situations whenever they can, to pick up information, however they can.

In our case, practically every time an order has gone wrong, we realized (later, sometimes much later) that it was at least partly our fault (that's where humility comes in). We might have failed to face up to a situation when we saw things deteriorating, or failed to assess the risk in working on a particular project—in other words, we should have known better! But at the end of the day, the problem can be traced back to the fact that we failed to live up to one or more of the qualities we list below. From what we've seen among our many self-employed friends and colleagues, this is usually true for them, too.

These are the Five Scout Virtues for the self-employed:

1. **Humility.** This might be the most important virtue of the self-employed worker. People tend to misunderstand what humility really means. It doesn't mean being submissive or servile. Mother Teresa was a humble woman if there ever was one, but she also raised millions of dollars for her cause. She proved there's no contradiction between being humble and selling yourself. But like her, you still need humility in order to carry out your work well. Learning always takes longer than you think. By the time you are finally earning a decent income from your work, you will be just starting to master the basics of your field (the learning curve get flatter, but you're always on it). You may have a great idea, but it might just be "decent." You need humility to see the difference—which doesn't prevent you from getting out there and selling your idea.

2. **Tenacity.** It takes a lot of tenacity to hang in there as a self-employed worker. You will face adversity. There will always be some setbacks. So you need to keep pushing forward. Without tenacity, you will have a hard time finding the energy you need to go out and knock on doors, maybe hundreds of times, to sell your wares. Tenacity doesn't mean being stubborn and obstinate. Nor do you have to be a perfectionist.

You have to be able to live with the imperfections of your idea and your work; in some cases, you even have to be able to admit that your idea won't work (see "Humility," above . . .). Sometimes this is the only way to find a better idea. Admitting mistakes doesn't mean you are giving up. It means you are willing to change your idea in order to make it work.

3. **Honesty.** Honesty is essential in the relationships you build. If you think that you need to be a shark to be in business, think again. It's not true. Don't assume that your customers and competitors are trying to take advantage of you. They're not. Your customers expect you to give them the straight story about your plans, but they also want you to be honest about potential problems that pop up. Maybe you didn't fully understand their order. Maybe you're afraid you won't be able to meet the deadline they have set. Whatever the problem or issue, be honest with your customers about it. Start by admitting the problem. You won't last long in your business if you play with your cards too close to your chest or go about things with a siege mentality ("They're out to get me"). It doesn't mean you always have to tell the whole truth, but your client should have the information they need in order to be able to make decisions.

4. **Boldness.** Don't assume that just because you are small, your services will only interest small companies. Large companies could need them too. The most important thing is to understand the true potential of your idea. Sometimes it's worth being bold and approaching a client who might seem a little out of your league. You might fail, but you will probably learn more about your market in the process. Yet be careful, because being bold does not mean being reckless. You should make sure you have a reasonable chance of succeeding before approaching potential clients.

5. **Curiosity.** Curious people are always up to date on new developments in their field. They are always able to carry on an intelligent, open-ended conversation with their client and not just about the business at hand. Curious people get excited when they make a breakthrough and suddenly understand a problem or come up with a new idea. Curiosity projects optimism. Sound too spiritual for the business

world? Maybe you should take your cue from the Japanese. After they return from business trips, Japanese employees are expected to produce what is called a "wonder report" for their company, in annex to their main report. The wonder report is about things they learned that don't have any obvious connection to the trip's stated purpose. No one should be surprised that the Japanese are so skilled at reinventing products that other cultures thought were old news.

16

How to be brazen

Sending out invoices with a light heart!

Myth #16: "The client is the boss."

Jean-Benoît had a memorable conversation a few years ago with a freelance colleague who was trying to create a union for freelance writers. Over the course of the conversation, the fellow repeatedly referred to the "damn bosses" who didn't pay freelancers fairly.

Jean-Benoît spotted the flaw in the union activist's reasoning immediately and explained: "First, the person you work for is not your boss. That person is your client. And second, the client doesn't pay for you. They pay for the service or product you are providing and they pay for it when they are billed. It's an entirely different power dynamic than when you are an employee."

The colleague stared back at Jean-Benoît, speechless. (He never did succeed in unionizing self-employed writers, for that matter.)

In the many, many discussions we have had with self-employed workers over the years over different topics, we have often noticed that beginners hesitate to send bills to their clients. Some actually wait around to get paid and never end up sending a bill. When we ask them why, they often explain that they find it pretentious, even aggressive. Of course, it's nothing of the sort. Billing is not just normal. It's expected. Rest assured: your clients send bills to their customers.

The bottom line: a self-employed worker should always bill clients promptly and should never ask anyone's permission to do so. You are in business. Does Bell or Hydro One, or any service or utility company, ever ask *you* if they can send a bill? They'll occasionally ask you if you are satisfied with their services and they may ask you how you would like to receive your bill—by mail or email. They may ask you how you would like to pay it—by cheque or direct deposit. But they sure won't ask you if they can send it. Some companies even add a surcharge now if you want to get your bill by mail. You should follow their example. Normally, the client should receive your invoice when you deliver the final version of your product or service or when they approved it, unless you've negotiated to be paid in staggered instalments over the course of a longer project.

In short, if you want to get paid, you have to send an invoice. If you don't, how will your customer know what they owe you or when it's due? If you don't send them a bill, you will rely entirely on their presence of mind, good faith and memory to pay you, and we all know how reliable these are (not). Your client could completely forget about paying you, in absolutely good faith. At the very least, the invoice is a professional reminder that the time has come to pay. And the client requires an invoice for their own accounting records anyway. So, by sending a bill, you are helping them too.

When he was starting out, Jean-Benoît actually wrote articles for three whole years before he sent his first invoice. Like many young writers, he had the mistaken belief that there was something pretentious, something too "businesslike" about creative people like him sending out bills. He thought he would come across as self-important, or money hungry and he was afraid of offending his editors. And naturally, they paid whenever it suited them. But after three years, he realized his hesitations really came from being insecure. And just like that, the reasons he had for not sending bills suddenly seemed downright silly.

But even then, Jean-Benoît remained a little timid about sending invoices to clients. He still thought about his editors as "bosses," not the clients they actually were. He thought he had to be sure editors were happy with his work before sending a bill—not a good idea, of course, because it gives clients an excuse to put off, or even avoid paying you altogether. In his defence, Jean-Benoît's approach was typical of beginners who still doubt their abilities. Eventually he started mailing invoices the day he delivered his articles. Today we send our invoices as Word documents (or sometimes PDFs if it's required) in attachments to emails. We send the invoices in a separate email from the finished text. It's important to send the invoice separately from the product being delivered, mainly so it has a clear heading in their email box ("Invoice for," followed by the name of the project). The documents will in most cases go to different departments so if you send them together, customers who opened one text might forget to click on the other icon, and the invoice may get lost in the process—this has happened to us a couple of times. Our clients aren't any sloppier than people in any other business. They're just editors who are in a rush to see and publish our wonderful prose (that's what we tell ourselves, anyway), so sometimes they're forgetful.

The only exception to this invoicing policy is when we submit a first version of a story of a text to be "reviewed." In this case, we really aren't (yet) sure the text meets the client's expectations and we want to get their opinion on it. But if a client tells us that they are satisfied, then off goes the bill.

Invoicing customers quickly also helps you keep on top of your own finances. Cash flow is one of the biggest financial challenges for self-employed workers and for many companies, period. Waiting for a $5,000 payment is great, but it's better if the cheque arrives in ten days rather than in three months. The faster you get paid, the less interest you'll pay on the money you have to borrow on your credit card or credit line to cover your costs. For example, we often run up travel or research expenses for an assignment. We try to bill these as soon as the money is spent. We don't necessarily wait until the entire assignment is done. If you get in the habit of doing this, you'll find some customers will reimburse expenses quickly enough, often before the payment is due. This, of course, improves your financial situation in general. It's a good habit to get into. We once refused an assignment because of the amount of money we would have had to put forward to cover expenses. We just didn't have the financial wiggle room to foot that kind of bill, even temporarily. Unfortunately, after refusing the assignment, we went through our bills and discovered that the reason we were short on cash was that we forgot to send invoices for previous expenses incurred for the same client! Damn! We got more systematic and organized about sending bills after that. Now we put them in specially marked folder and go through them regularly to see what's been paid and what we have coming in.

Even though you don't need to get anyone's permission to send a bill, you should be careful not to overdo it. You have to respect certain limits. For instance, you can only charge the exact amount you and your customer agreed on at the beginning of the project and not a penny more unless your client agrees to increase the fee. We knew a researcher who once sent a client a bill for $13,000, which was four times the amount they had originally agreed on. The job required more time than either party originally thought but the research failed to communicate this while he was carrying out the work. Instead, he just sprung it on his client after the fact. This is not a good way to treat your clients and not a sustainable way to do business.

Sometimes the invoice may be the only interaction you have with a customer that's "purely business," especially if you work on the basis of verbal agreements instead of a written contract. All the more reason to take care when writing this important document. Always remember that your client's accountant was not in on the discussions you had with your client, so the accountant might require information that goes beyond "the obvious." Make sure you break down what you are charging and explain each part. The invoice has to be clear and contain all the information a bookkeeper will need to get it authorized and then process it.

When we were starting out, we used to send generic "Bluenote" invoices to our clients (the ones with carbon paper in them). They looked official (at the time) and we figured they were better than just writing an amount on a sheet of paper and mailing it. Before the turn of the millennium, we started sending a standard Word doc with our and our clients' full contact information on it. Later, we hired a graphic designer to create a formal billing template for us with our company logo at the top. Today we have templates with the billing address and names of each of our clients on it so all we have to do is fill in the amount we're charging, change the date, add an invoice number and basic information about the project and *click,* it's gone.

The standard invoice

Invoice 18981029
October 29, 1898, Montreal

To: Sherlock Holmes
c/o *Murder and Mystery* Magazine
1234, Enigma Boulevard
London Ontario N0L 1G0

File: Investigation into the death of Conan Doyle

Done by: The Polygraph S.E.N.C.
27 My Pleasure Crescent, Laval-by-the-Sea H7Z 0P6

Fee	$5,000.00
Minus January payment (excluding taxes)	($1,000.00)
Minus February payment (excluding taxes)	($1,000.00)
Minus March payment (excluding taxes)	($1,000.00)
Balance	$2,000.00
GST: 5%, # R123456789 =	$100.00
QST: 9.975% #9876543210 =	$199.50
Total	$2,299.50

[Optional *Copyright: As stated in the contract.*]
Payable upon receipt.

Please make the cheque payable to:

The Polygraph Company,
27 Pleasure Crescent, Laval-by-the-Sea
H7Z 0P6

Thank you.

Nine elements of the invoice

We had a client who insisted that we send him invoices in PDF format, with a company logo. These details may be nice professional touches, but there are neither necessary nor mandatory for invoices. Sometimes, clients have silly internal policies. To have legal value, an invoice must contain the following nine elements.

1. The word "invoice" must be stated clearly at the top, in capital letters so your customer won't mistake your bill for a grocery list. Some companies require a six- or eight-digit invoice number or even a purchase order number. If you don't have a system of your own, use the date (for example, 2022-01-25 for January 25, 2022). This will also make it easier to keep track of invoices and find out whether they were paid or are outstanding. Big corporate customers like this system, too (and your company logo). Some clients may require you to have a purchase order (PO) number. In that case, that number must appear prominently on your invoice, because it will be required for processing it. (We generally put it in large bold letters at the top right corner of the invoice.)

2. The date must appear. This will be used in case of litigation, so you can demonstrate that you were acting in good faith and your creditor wasn't. It also helps you keep track of payments, particularly overdue ones.

3. The name and address of the purchaser, and name and title of your contact person. It is always a good idea to find out precisely to whom you should send an invoice: sometimes it's the president of the company, but sometimes it's the purchasing manager or the controller. If your client is a large company (or a university), this must be done correctly. Otherwise, your invoice can end up getting lost and your payment delayed (this has happened to us many times). However, when you are invoicing a third party (someone other than your contact), be sure to write the name of your contact on the invoice in case there's some kind of mix up.

4. The name and address of the seller (you), and name and address of the person in whose name the cheque is to be issued in case this is a different name. For instance, we ask for cheques to be made out to

our General Partnership, so we indicate this information clearly—the name of the GP followed by the address—on the invoice, even though the address is the same as our own.

5. Basic information about the order. Describe the object and the basis for pricing—a fixed price, a single unit or an hourly rate—and then the sequence—if it's the first or second instalment for the payment—as well as the calculations that led to the balance owing. After the total, indicate whether any other invoices will follow, for example, for expenses incurred during the work. If your invoice is for an agreement made subsequent to the contract, write, "As agreed on this date."

6. Ownership. In addition to including details about the service for which you are invoicing the client, it is useful to stipulate what rights you are granting the client. This is particularly important when you are selling a product or service that has an intellectual property dimension to it: unless you negotiate otherwise, you are deemed by law to have sold only the minimum, i.e. a license for first publication. However, it is still a good idea to state that this is the case. Since respect for intellectual property is essentially based on asserting your own rights to it (there's no copyright police out there catching intellectually property thieves), your clients should not be able to claim they didn't know they were only buying limited right. Simply refer to the contract using a formula such as "Intellectual property rights as specified in the contract XYZ." NEVER ATTEMPT TO SUMMARIZE INTELLECTUAL PROPERTY RIGHTS ON AN INVOICE. If you try, you many end up contradicting the contract you previously negotiated and signed, and the invoice may well override the contract since it is a later agreement. Make it clear.

7. Your GST and PST numbers (or HST if that's the case). These are required by law if you charge these taxes. (Chapter 19 is all about taxes.)

8. The amount of taxes (GST, PST, HST), discounts granted and total amount owing. Don't make your customer scratch their head trying to figure out what they actually owe you. Again, make it clear. If you have given them a discount, enter it clearly as such: the client should be reminded that you have done them a favour and understand that this may not always be the case in the future.

9. Conditions of sale. This usually means writing, "Payable upon receipt," or "Payment on acceptance" at the bottom of your invoice. That means that the customer must issue the cheque as soon as they receive your invoice, not whenever they feel like paying you, or only after they use your product or service. If you don't include these instructions on your invoice, it may take longer to get paid. All invoices, whether for an advance, or research, for compensation or service fees, should be paid upon receipt or acceptance unless you have negotiated something else with your client.

You are not under any obligation to include your social insurance number on an invoice, though some clients may ask you for it when they are issuing your first cheque. Some clients mistakenly ask for social insurance numbers under the (false) belief that you are an employee. All you need to do to in order to correct the misunderstanding is to send an invoice. If you are collecting HST (or GST and PST/QST), they don't need your SIN.

As we said earlier, invoices must not contradict the contract you signed with a client. So, if you went to the trouble of negotiating payment on acceptance in your contract, make sure you don't write "payment due upon use" on the invoice. This is also true for intellectual property. But again, if the rights in the contract are complex, DO NOT TRY TO SUMMARIZE THEM on the invoice. Just refer to the contract with the old "as specified on" clause.

Invoicing expenses

The invoice you send for expenses will differ slightly from your invoice for fees. Again, large companies may have a particular format for these, often a form. It is payable upon receipt and always accompanied by copies of the receipts (not the originals) for the amounts you are being reimbursed (see example on next below). The invoice must supply details of each expense item on separate rows, grouped by category (e.g. "travel," "taxi," "documentation," "meals," "hotel"). Make the total for the amount of each row of expenses in the last column. The more clearly you write it and the more detail you provide, the better: this reduces or dispels any doubts your customers may have about what you are billing them for. Since some of your receipts may only have the total amount on them, including taxes, you may want to include amounts before tax or with only GST where that is the case. The other option is to include a spreadsheet showing how you calculated each expense with applicable taxes and showing the gross amounts and applicable variables. A good bookkeeper can do that job for you, but you can also find all the equations you'll need in order to do this yourself in Chapter 19.

We invoice expenses to clients—sometimes before the work is finished—at the end of the month when we do our bookkeeping and have gathered all our receipts in a folder. Getting reimbursed for expenses can make the difference between a tricky end-of-the-month situation and decent cash flow. That's why, when we return from a work-related trip, we send the invoice for expenses to our client right away.

The policies about what expenses can be reimbursed vary greatly from one client to another. Whatever they are, their eligibility should be agreed on contractually. You absolutely need to enquire about them before you start a project with a new client. There's nothing to stop you from billing things that aren't covered, but you should always be prepared to have to justify the expenses if you are asked to.

Sample expense report

Dr Watson—July 25, 1898

PROJECT: Police Secrets
Amounts (taxes included):

- Telegraphs (Jan. Feb.) $132.28 Travel (Guelph, Quebec City, Beamsville, Regina)
- Carriage rental $131.90
- Inn $54.00
- Hay $39.00
- Valet $4.39

Personal carriage ($0.33/km)

- Hull (June 19) 420 km = $138.60
- Saint-Bruno, Saint-Hyacinthe (July 3) 163 km = $53.79
- Saint-Hubert (July 18) 24 km = $7.92

Meals $14.20

Total $567.08
GST #123456789 included
QST #9876543210 included

Occasionally, a client will ask us to supply original receipts. In this case, we just say no. Only employees have to supply their bills to the boss for reimbursement. The boss can justify needing them for their own tax purposes. But you are not an employee and you need your original bills for *your* tax purposes—you never know when you may get audited. Your invoice is the only original they need. The client is in their right asking for clear copies of your receipts, or seeing the originals, but they cannot hold on to them. If your client is ever questioned about this, they can always refer the inspector to their supplier (that would be you). But you'll find yourself in an unfortunate situation if you don't have the original receipts: the authorities will count your refunds as (taxable) income but will also make you pay tax on the deductions you are claiming, for which you no longer have proof!

We recently had an editor client who demanded original receipts. After much discussion, we realized that the order to collect original receipts had come from the accounting department. So, we discussed it directly with the accountants, who totally understood the situation once we explained it. And they were satisfied with our invoice and copies of our receipts, end of story.

17

Customers to avoid

How to handle customers who don't pay

Myth # 17: "You should never offend a client."

Magazine Editor: "You shouldn't have wasted money sending a registered letter. I never got your bill in the first place . . ."
Freelance Writer: "Well, that's funny, because I remember talking to you about the bill two months ago when I handed in my article."
Magazine Editor: "Oh, right. I guess I forgot."
Sure.

Luckily, we have rarely had to listen to these lame excuses for not paying our invoices. But we have heard it enough to recognize the backpedalling of a client who knows they have run out of acceptable excuses for not paying an overdue invoice.

There are two types of clients who don't pay: the ones who are in good faith and the ones who aren't. It's pretty simple. The first type are folks who get distracted easily. They're basically absent-minded, or disorganized, maybe a bit stingy, but basically honest. The second type are easily distracted, absent-minded, disorganized and stingy—but they are also liars. The second type tend to be victims of nefarious forces that blow invoices off their desks straight into trash cans. Or some version of that.

Sometimes a phone call is all it takes to set an honest client back on the right path and get them to make the payment. When you are faced with the second type of non-payer, there's no easy solution. That's when the golden rule of negotiations comes into full force (see Chapter 11): the customer is not always right. Really, truly. When you are doing business with this kind of creep, you have to remember this rule. And act in consequence.

The good news is this: if you act preventively and follow our advice from Chapters 1 to 15, this should never happen, or only very rarely. In thirty-five years of doing business, this kind of problem has happened to us about three times. The bad news is that when it does happen, you have to act on it.

Whether they are honest or dishonest, the client who doesn't pay has the same effect: by holding on to the money they owe you, they force you to finance *their* business. That's why you have to be uncompromising, even fierce in dealing with them. You should never apologize for taking the steps necessary to get paid. Clients who don't pay don't deserve anyone's sympathy.

Nothing is harder on the morale of a self-employed worker than realizing your customer has negotiated in bad faith. When you negotiate and complete your contract in good faith, you expect the same back. If things go awry and you realize your client is acting in bad faith, be ready to declare war. The arm-wrestling match that follows will be one of the worst things you'll ever go through as a self-employed worker—especially since these situations often bring additional costs and, of course, you lose a client in the process. Fortunately, it should be rare.

Check the facts

Before declaring war, you should call your client to see if there has been a mistake or a misunderstanding. It is almost certainly the case. Accounting departments change and change rules, and people go on holidays. Keep calm, be polite and breathe through your nose until you know what happened.

In most cases, the bill really was misplaced or the person responsible for paying it went on holidays. This is not the most professional behaviour on the part of your client, and it's definitely not acceptable, but these things do happen. However, if you are feeling pushback from the client when you enquire about your bill, be firm. You might want to point out that if they owed money to Bell or their hydro company or some other utility, they couldn't use an excuse like, "I was on holidays" for not paying their bill, or avoid paying it late. True, you're not a utility, but they should have had the courtesy of warning you.

Another common reason invoices don't get paid is that your client has an employee whose singular mission is to find irregularities or mistakes in bills. If this person finds a $4.37 error on your expenses bill, they will put your invoice in a pile with others to be "rechecked." Payment of the bill will hence be delayed. If this happens, there's no need to fly off the hook: for one, the bill-checking employee might be right about the mistake. The best approach in this case is to congratulate them for their keen eye and make a note to yourself to double-check your next invoice before you send it. Sometimes a customer may reject a particular expense if you didn't negotiate it ahead of time. If that's the case, it's your fault and you should correct it.

Sometimes the error is theirs. The policy of the accounting department is that invoices should be submitted in PDF form, but the person you billed didn't tell you and you sent an invoice in Word so the bill was automatically discarded. This is called bad internal communications.

Of course, there's also the possibility that your customer is simply not satisfied with your work. If that's the case, try to find out what the issue is. Maybe their grievances are well founded, maybe not. If they are, try to reach an amicable agreement. You should write everything down in either case, the same way you would for an investigation of any type. But stay calm. You may really want to hold on to them as a client, but you may also end up doing work for them at a different company (people switch jobs). It's a surprisingly small world out there.

One of our best clients started not paying a while back. Since we do a lot of work for them we did not realize they owed us a total of $7,000 for four or five jobs we'd done for them. After some unfruitful back and forth with the client, Jean-Benoît wrote that he was concerned and informed them he would need to file a formal summons. In the exchange we learned that their finances were bad because of another parent publication that they had to close. This was consistent with problems they had already expressed. They admitted that they were losing freelance contributors because of the problem, but urged us to be patient because things were turning around. A week later they paid us the first $3,000 of what they owed us and then, three weeks later, we received the remainder. They are still a very good client. So, it pays to be firm, but also understanding up to a point—if the story they are telling you makes sense.

How to spot a red herring

You do have to learn to spot dishonest customers and their delay tactics. You could be dealing with a crook who knows all the tricks. They will ask you in a fake innocent voice why you didn't send a bill. Or they'll request an itemized bill without specifying what you need to itemize and then not pay it once again. When you ask them why it wasn't paid, they'll complain that you didn't supply the right details. The variations are really infinite but they all boil down to the same thing: diversion tactics.

Beware of the customers who only pay you part of the amount you have invoiced. If you receive a cheque from them for part of the amount, check to make sure it doesn't say "final payment" before you cash it. If you do deposit it, you will be deemed (in the eyes of contract law) to have accepted a "new condition" as part of your contract, even if this contradicts the original contract. It's a better idea to photocopy the cheque (for your records), return the original to the client with the invoice and ask them to kindly pay the full amount as agreed. If you absolutely need to cash the cheque—say, because you're having a cash flow problem—make sure you cross out the words "final payment," photocopy the cheque before cashing it and notify the client in writing that you have done so. But it still might be a good idea to consult a lawyer before you do this, especially if it's a big cheque.

Not all bad payers are crooks, but all of them deserve to be told that their excuses and vague answers to your questions are unacceptable. If the client is clearly playing games with you, you need to call them on it. If you have doubts, send them a new bill with a mistake, like $500 more and/or with interest added. If you see the "lost" bill reappear miraculously, you'll have a better idea of whom you are dealing with.

Here are some examples of how to handle other situations:

Client: "I thought the first payment was for a whole bill."
How to react: "No, it wasn't. Check the invoice. It says, 'first instalment'."

■ ■ ■

Client: "Can we negotiate?"
How to react: "No. We negotiated before I started working for you. The only thing I'll negotiate now is the interest rate on the money you owe me."

■ ■ ■

Client: "I'm having financial problems."
How to react: "I am too, because you owe me money. I want to be paid, and quickly."

■ ■ ■

Client: "My boss didn't authorize the order."
How to react: "That's not my problem. It's your problem. You'll have to work that out with your boss, who is responsible for your actions."

Alternative reaction: If this is the case, I don't get involved in your internal dispute. A promise is a promise, especially when it's on a signed contract.

■ ■ ■

Client: "It's too expensive."
How to react: "You agreed to my price."

■   ■   ■

Client: "You didn't give us what we asked for."
How to react: "You had ample time to clarify your expectations while I was working on the project."

■   ■   ■

Client: "The company closed."
How to react: it's usually the former owner who's in charge of closing a business. They keep what's left of the assets. If the business has closed due to bankruptcy, consult the trustee to find out what the rules are regarding being paid.

■   ■   ■

Client: "The business has been sold."
How to react: there may have been a change in ownership while you were working for them, but that doesn't change the fact that the business is responsible for paying its accounts. You should send a formal notice to the former owner. If they told the new owner there weren't any outstanding accounts at the time of sale, they'll be in a fix and likely want to settle things quickly with you. After that, notify the new owner about the situation.

Don't turn the other cheek

If your client turns out to be dishonest or, at the very least, fails to meet their most basic obligations towards you, you will have to act immediately. Every self-employed worker has to deal with bad payers at some point in their career. The first time it happens, almost everyone makes the beginners' mistake of turning the other cheek.

The very first thing to do is to suspend work you are doing for them and tell them why. This can be hard for beginners in any field. Instead of sticking the customer's nose in the mess they have made, beginners tend to ignore the problem for as long as possible, hoping it will solve itself. Beginners generally want to be accommodating. Experience teaches you to set limits. Sometimes beginners will even take a new order in the hopes the problem with the old project will work out if they maintain the relationship—we've made this mistake and regretted it. It's called "turning the other cheek," or "giving them another chance." It may work in love (though probably not), but it definitely doesn't work in business.

When you are self-employed, there's no time or place where it makes sense to turn the other cheek. You won't be getting anything in return and you'll be opening the door for clients to take advantage of you over and over. Remember, you are not in a subordinate relationship with respect to your client. Your only bond with them is a contract to deliver a good or service and, ultimately, get paid for your work in the form of a cheque. Do you really think it's a good idea to take a second assignment when a client hasn't paid for the first one? Why should you put up with overdue accounts? You won't be "hanging on to a job." You'll be signing up to do more work for someone for free.

For that matter, it is always a good policy not to start a second contract with a new client until you have been paid for the first one. If you have ongoing work with that client, be ready to stop working for them and to explain why. We talked a lot about communication in Chapter 14. It's important to master and use these skills when things go wrong too. If you can't do this, you will end up painting yourself into a corner, quickly.

Jean-Benoît vividly recalls the first time he went into debt because a client didn't pay him. It was 1990. The editor owed him $1,100 for two stories she had published six months earlier. This editor informed Jean-Benoît that she was late paying because the magazine was having financial problems. Jean-Benoît then made a classic beginner's mistake: he took on another assignment from her while he was still waiting for the cheque for his first story. Her next excuse was that she had lost the bill. This time

Jean-Benoît returned his invoice with a late payment fee tacked to it and stopped working on the third assignment. Miraculously, the editor suddenly relocated the original bill (the one without the extra charge)! The next thing Jean-Benoît heard from her was that she sent the cheque "that morning." When it didn't arrive, Jean-Benoît understood then that he was truly dealing with a dishonest client who wasn't going to pay. Seriously, how many letters are really "lost" in the mail? Not many. Jean-Benoît did get paid, a full year and a half later. The only thing he did right was in cancelling the third assignment from the editor.

The three steps for collecting overdue payments

There are collection agencies who will do this dirty work for you, but they aren't cheap. And in any case, they will expect you to complete the first steps of the collection process before they take on your case so, it's a good idea to understand the basics of the process.

There are a number of steps you should follow before you take a client to court for non-payment of an invoice—this is the heavy artillery that should only be used in extreme cases. If you follow these steps, you may not need to go to court at all.

Make a first phone call or send an email signalling that the invoice is due and you need to be paid immediately. If this doesn't get results, make sure all your subsequent communications are done through registered mail. Doing this sends a very strong signal to your client that you are no longer giving them the benefit of the doubt. This has worked for the couple of times we have had to do it, and it's the only way advised by lawyers and collection specialists.

Keep in mind that as you progress in these steps the level of antagonism will gradually increase. Step 1 and step 2 send the message that you still hope to maintain your business relationship with your client. If you are already fed up and ready to throw in the towel on the relationship, you can skip 1 and 2 and go straight to step 3. But if you do this, you will be sending the client the message that they have already passed the point of no return.

The steps that follow also apply to cases when you find that someone used your work without payment or authorization.

1. **Send a bill.** Don't underestimate the power of a good old-fashioned invoice, especially in cases where you discovered a company has been using your work without your permission. You are the owner, and no one can excuse breaking the law by claiming ignorance. That said, ignorance happens, so a user may not have thought about the commercial intricacies of copyright before helping themselves to your intellectual property. A bill will be a good way to educate them.

2. **Send a statement of accounts**. This is also known as a "payment reminder," and is a document that shows the details of what's being charged on an invoice. You should add a note to this explaining that you will suspend work on ongoing projects for the client until the first invoice is paid. Attach a copy of the original invoice and contract if applicable.

   If there is an intellectual property issue involved in your work, state that the license will be valid only when the fee for its use has been paid. It may be useful to quote the article of law or send them a link with information on intellectual property. If the client goes ahead and uses your work anyway, they will be knowingly committing a violation. Be careful, however, as this can be a double-edged sword. The customer might agree to your request, then simply stop using your work. In that case, you will have to argue that they are obligated to pay you for its use. That can get messy.

   You are also entitled to start charging interest. However, while this approach may get your customer to realize the extent of their mistake, it may also make them dig in their heels, which means you will have to go to court to get what you are owed. But you might have had to go anyway.

3. **The formal notice.** This is the heavy artillery. This legal document instructs a client to pay you what you are owed (see example below). This step marks the point at which legal interest (what the government allows you to charge the clients as interest on the overdue payment) will be charged. In the event of bankruptcy, this document may place

Sample formal notice

<u>**WITHOUT PREJUDICE**</u>

Mr Paul Lisson
Unspeakable Enterprises Inc.
33 Rocky Avenue
Troubletown (Manitoba) R3T 2N1

<u>**Subject: Formal notice. Contract # 96-8-24**</u>
<u>**Invoices for December 3, 2016, and December 23, 2017**</u>

Sir/Madam,

After delivering the service you ordered, I'm still waiting for payment of the amount stipulated in the contract and billed one month ago (SEE APPENDIX).

You are hereby formally required to pay this invoice within ten business days of receipt of this letter, failing which legal action will be taken against you without further notice or delay. We are willing to hear a proposal for settlement.

PLEASE ACT ACCORDINGLY.

Yours sincerely,

Marilyn Duenow
7 Still Waiting Boulevard,
Rapid Falls (Sask.) T1R 1N6

Attached: Invoices of December 3, 2016, and December 23, 2017

c. c. Your shareholder
Mr Arnold Boss, President and Chief Executive Officer,
Reliable Enterprises Inc.
Ms Jean Honour, lawyer
First-Class Law Firm

you among a company's official creditors—the rules regarding this vary between jurisdictions. However, your claim could always be contested. For about $40 (though it can be much more depending on the jurisdiction, the complexity of the case and the amount involved), a lawyer will help you file a formal notice and attach their signature. It's impressive but not compulsory, legally speaking. You can prepare a formal notice yourself that's perfectly legal, as long as it meets the standards of the genre.

A formal notice is always brutally specific. The first paragraph summarizes the problem. The second states your requirements and supplies a reasonable deadline for settlement. If it's complicated, you can subdivide the second part into separate parts. All the addresses of the persons concerned must appear. The mention WITHOUT PREJUDICE in capital letters means that you do not have to limit your lawsuit to the amount required and that the letter will not harm your ability to pursue other remedies. Do not forget to sign your formal notice. The formal notice does not have to be limited to one page. The time limit does not have to take into account "working days" but it is acceptable to specify this.

We're including a lawyer's trick: formal notice letters should always be terse. Just set out the facts: you delivered the product or service, you haven't been paid, your customer has to pay you, and here's the deadline. Although the temptation may be strong, avoid long explanations, recriminations or any language that sounds like a complaint. It's risky. If you end up in court, a skilful lawyer (on the other side) will use this against you and weaken your case.

Another trick is to state your willingness to hear a counterproposal. This doesn't bind you in any way, but it is a demonstration of your willingness and good faith in trying to solve the issue outside the courts.

And a word of caution: while your letter of notice may obliquely threaten the costumer with legal action, avoid making threats of any kind. The letter should NEVER state that failure to pay could, or will result in criminal or penal proceedings, or anything that sounds like that. Why not? Because that amounts to extortion. As a private citizen, you can't appropriate powers that belong to the police, prosecutors and the legal system: they are the ones, not you, who decide what criminal behaviour is and what isn't, and what action is required. No matter how bad a situation gets, you can't take justice into your own hands. If you make threats, your creditor's lawyers will definitely use it against you. That said, there's absolutely nothing preventing you from actually filing a complaint about your customer to the police.

A formal notice should always be sent by registered mail. And do pay the extra charge at the post office to obtain a copy with the recipient's signature. You can use this to demonstrate to a judge that your client received the notice (claiming "not to have received" notices and invoices is a classic delay tactic). It will also help your client understand that you are very serious about getting paid and that you won't be easily intimidated.

An even more powerful, but more expensive way to deliver your letter is by a bailiff, i.e. hand delivered in person. You can send a bailiff to deliver a notice while your client is having dinner with their banker or, even better, when they are in the middle of delivering their weekly press conference. The message will get through, especially if you pay the extra charge to have the bailiff read your formal notice to the client in front of everyone there and then have your client sign a receipt. Sure, this will cost a little more, but it will be deeply satisfying (especially if you manage to discreetly slip into the audience and watch the spectacle unfold). It may actually be necessary to resort to using a bailiff if your debtor refuses to receive any registered mail—a common manoeuvre used by high-flying crooks.

Going to court and the alternatives

After sending a formal notice, you'll have to make a decision: either take the next steps yourself, have a lawyer take care of the process or get a collection agency to handle the file for you.

In exchange for a commission of 10% to 40% of the amount you are collecting—all depending on the difficulty of the work (it costs more if you are dealing with a runner)—this kind of agency will harass your client for a month or two. Most collectors charge a percentage of the amount they collect. These professionals are familiar with all the legal means they can use to be convincing, like pointing out to a debtor that a bad debt could damage their reputation with the credit agencies. If you mandate the agency to do so, they will negotiate a settlement on your behalf, or refer you to a lawyer if the client continues to resist their approaches.

You can also use a cheaper, pre-court alternative: mediation (refer to Chapters 13 and 14). This will be your first move, of course, if there is a mediation clause in your contract. But here's the catch: the other party may refuse mediation. That will leave you no option but to go to court.

Courts provides three types of remedy: an injunction, a criminal prosecution or a civil suit.

We will quickly brush over the first two options and then focus on the civil suit.

- An injunction is a permanent or temporary court order to stop an offence and force the other party to comply. The injunction does not provide any monetary compensation, but it is particularly useful if the crook you are dealing with needs your product or copyright to keep carrying out their activities. And it is especially justifiable if the activity in question is one that harms you. A crook who defies an injunction risks going to jail or a paying a large fine.
- Criminal prosecution is like the atomic bomb you use in cases of clear theft. You won't get compensation, but you may get sweet revenge. However, as we said before, and we'll repeat it: while carrying out efforts to recover what is owed to you, never threaten the other party with criminal prosecution as this is tantamount to extortion. It's frustrating because you know you are in the right. However, you will regret making threats if they end up giving the crooked client a way to turn the case against you.
- A civil lawsuit allows you to recover what you are owed, plus damages, plus interest, plus court costs, provided, of course, that you win, but it takes time and costs money.

In carrying out legal actions, you have the choice between several institutions/tribunals, but the most likely is "Small Claims" court.

CUSTOMERS TO AVOID **287**

Small Claims Court

The court you are most likely to use is the Small Claims division of your provincial court where you can settle smaller claims at little cost and with minimal red tape. To initiate a lawsuit in this court, all you need to do is fill out a form. The information should be easy to find at the website of your provincial justice system. The amounts you can settle for in Small Claims Court vary in Canada—e.g. the upper threshold is $7,000 in Quebec but up to $35,000 in BC. If your client owes you $8,000, the Quebec Court will allow you to reduce your claim to $7,000 so you can make the claim in Small Claims. However, you cannot divide a $14,000 claim into two $7,000 claims to be able to have access to Small Claims. Depending on your jurisdiction, other conditions may apply. For example, in Quebec the pursuant cannot be a corporation or partnership that employed more than five people in the twelve months before the claim is made. It can take anywhere from three months to a year to process the claim. We know of a claim that lasted more than two years because of delays, a change of jurisdiction, a retraction of judgment and a summons mistakenly sent to the wrong people. You do not need to have a written contract. In fact, small claims judge a large proportion of issues over verbal contracts, but they may require that you bring in supporting documents, rather than only witnesses.

Small Claims Court also allows you to present your arguments yourself without lawyer, and they often forbid corporations from using one, too, in order to level the playing field. Judges may even act as a counsellor.

When one considers the many constraints of arbitration or high tribunals, or even mediation, recourse to Small Claims Court, which is almost free of charge, is the best option for most cases of non-payment. In some provinces, this court even offers a mediation service—one hour, free of charge—to help opposing parties find common ground before going to court. This could be advantageous because while an arbitration decision is final, mediation produces a negotiated agreement, not an award. Mediation is therefore not prejudicial to a possible Small Claims remedy if your client does not end up respecting the mediation agreement.

Most Small Claims Courts allow people to reduce the value of their claim in order to use the small claims channel. But you can always go to a higher court, like a provincial court or superior court.

When you go to "big court," it's necessarily going to be more expensive. There is no "in between" option: you cannot have your brother-in-law-who-really-understands-the-law represent you. This stands to reason: like doctors, who have a monopoly on diagnosing patients, lawyers also have a monopoly on representing people in higher courts. If you are suing as a company or a partnership, you will have to use a lawyer. In either case, an outside perspective will help you see all the angles of your case and to make sure you follow the procedures correctly, for one, because it is not always possible to appeal a decision. Even lawyers have to use lawyers!

There are a few ways to reduce the bill at this stage. You may be able to convince an association or organization representing you to support you in your lawsuit and pay the lawyer's fees on your behalf. Some non-profit associations may also offer representation at a fraction of the cost of a private lawyer. If your case is particularly scandalous and/or promises high visibility, a law firm may agree to represent you pro bono or for a percentage of the settlement.

Any judgment in your favour gives you the power to collect your debt within prescribed limits. But this is no more a magical solution than sending another invoice: even after a judgment, crooked clients still might use the same tricks they employed the first time in order to get out of paying you. They might send you a cheque for a portion of the total and marking it "final payment," for example. Legally, cashing that cheque could be interpreted as a form of out-of-court settlement.

Remember: once a crook, always a crook.

Managing 4

18

Making wise deductions

The truth about what you can deduct from your taxes

Myth # 18: "I should deduct as much as I can."

"So, what can I deduct?"

If you ever overhear people talking about this at a party, you can bet you're in the company of new self-employed workers. The possibility of being able to write things off inevitably makes new, or aspiring self-employed workers salivate. That's one reason why we decided to address the question right off the bat, in the first chapter of this section on management practices for the self-employed. Figuring out what's deductible will influence many other decisions you make about how to manage your business. The self-employed spend as much time—or maybe more—talking about their taxes as they do mulling over whether to incorporate or not. But before you decided anything, you need to know what Canadian tax authorities have already decided for you.

So here we go. Self-employed workers are entitled to tax deductions that are specific to businesses. When it comes to deducting business expenses, many employed workers envy freelancers' "privileges." However, as we will see, there are many limits to what you can deduct. First of all, what exactly do we mean by a "deductible expense" (for those of you who don't know already)? These are expenses that you have already incurred in the process of carrying out your work, which you then subtract from your gross business income in order to establish the amount of your personal income and therefore, your taxable income for a given year. The more expenses you deduct for your business, the lower your net income will be and the less personal tax you will pay. In Canada, we apply the principle of progressive taxation wherein personal tax rates increase proportionately to the size of incomes. That means you should take all the deductions you are entitled to, since each expense you have (that contributes to the income of your business) will lower your taxable income as well as your tax rate.

Okay, so exactly which expenses are deductible? Unfortunately, there is no pre-established, all-purpose, definitive list of what is deductible. That would be nice. Instead, tax authorities expect you to use your own judgment to figure out what's deductible, working from a general principle (and as we'll see, a number of rules).

That principle is: you are entitled to deduct, either in part or in full, all professional expenses that contribute to your "expectation of profit."

Okay, so what exactly is an "expectation of profit"? It sounds a little vague. What it means is this: the expenses you deduct must be for good or services that enabled you to generate income or reduce other expenses. When you are trying to decide what expenses "enabled you to generate income or reduce expenses," it can be hard to draw the line between personal and business expenses. In a way, buying groceries gives you an expectation of profit: how can you make a profit if you don't eat? For most people, groceries are what you have to buy to stay alive. To determine what is deductible and what's not, apply the following rule: if it's good for Esso, then it's good for you. Esso pays for the meals an employee eats when they are on the road, but not for the caviar (or chips) that an employee eats at home with friends on Saturday night. However, if the friends invited on Saturday are actually legitimate customers, then you could deduct the caviar or the chips.

Contrary to what Sherlock Holmes might say, there is nothing "elementary" about the art of making business deductions. You have to use your common sense and apply deductive reasoning (no pun intended) when deciding what's deductible. You might also want to consult a tax professional if you are looking for tricks that you wouldn't have thought of on your own (probably money well spent, since there are some tricks). Is that expensive designer suit you purchased to accompany a prestigious client to the annual Golden Scarf awards banquet for the Dawson City Chamber of Commerce deductible? Maybe. But then, you also wore the suit to your daughter's wedding. There's no clear-cut answer. Some clothes might qualify as partly or fully deductible, but certainly not your entire wardrobe, even if you wear special clothes to meet clients every day. The reason groceries and clothing are not deductible is simple: these things are necessities of life, things you have to pay for anyway. However, uniforms are deductible. And if you are running a cooking school, then some of your groceries may be deductible, but certainly not all of them.

Along the same line of reasoning, while a land surveyor would probably have to work very hard to justify claiming the purchase of a wide-screen TV (or any TV, for that matter) as a deduction, an actor or screenwriter could make a good case for it. The actor could even justify deducting a cable subscription, a home theatre sound system or streaming fees. In other words, when it comes to taxes, everything is relative. A land surveyor who also has a radio show could deduct both their stakes and their new radio.

When it comes to deductions, there's a lot of margin for manoeuvre. You don't need permission from the tax authorities to *try* to deduct any particular expense. When you file your income tax return, you are not required to provide any supporting evidence: not receipts, nor a solemn declaration, nor a floor plan of your house to determine if the amount you are claiming as "your office" is accurate. You are fully within your rights trying to claim daughter's crayons as a business expense—if this is justifiable, for example, because you run a daycare centre or a school for mental arithmetic. In other words, you can "give it a shot." As a general rule, it is a good idea to try to claim all the legitimate deductions you are entitled to. If you don't subtract all legitimate expenses from your income, you may pay extra tax for nothing (see the box below). And remember: all expenses must be deducted in the income tax declaration of the year they were incurred. Income tax allows you to spread a loss over years (more on this in Chapter 20), but you can't do this with expenses—with the exception of depreciation in value (more on this below).

However—and here's the catch—you will have to justify these deductions if a tax inspector questions them. That's called an audit. A good friend of ours ended up getting audited and had to pay back $50,000 in taxes (including interest and late penalties) because she failed to keep her receipts for deductible expenses (we discuss the filing period in Chapter 20). The receipts you supply must be actual receipts: tax inspectors will not accept credit card statements, they require actual paper receipts, preferably with full info. A good receipt must have the purpose of the transaction, the seller's contact information and the seller's sales tax numbers if they charge them. Since the CRA is known to audit entire industries according to their assessment of "risk factors," there is an argument for not pushing it. They might inspect your industry the year you deduct your daughter's crayons. You won't see it coming. Note that because so many people got in the habit of deducting huge restaurant expenses, the government has considerably reduced the deductible portion of restaurant meals from 80% to 50% and then, in Quebec at least, it's limited to 1% of your overall sales figure. So be reasonable, otherwise the Finance Minister will tighten the screws even more—and for everyone.

So, what actual expenses are deductible, then? The detailed tax guide provides certain categories, but there's nothing preventing you from adding more categories depending on your line of business. For example, a graphic designer might spend a fortune on paper, while a surveyor could spend a lot on stakes. If you're an electronics technician, you may have categories of expenses related to carrying an inventory. As journalists and authors, we have considerable travel and documentation expenses. Our accountant did a double take in 2004 when we deducted almost $20,000 in travel expenses (but they were absolutely legitimate: we spent most of the year on the road researching a book) and almost $5,000 in documentation expenses (we had to buy a lot of books for our research). They were legitimate expenses and we had the receipts to prove it. That's simply what it had cost us to research a book on the French-speaking world. To back up our "expectation of profit," we had our publishing contracts and proof of substantial advances from our publishers.

Take note that the amount you can deduct varies according to whether or not you are registered for the GST/PST-HST. In some cases, the amount is with taxes and in others it's without (we explain why in Chapter 19).

Keep in mind, however, that among deductible expenses, some can be deducted in full and others only in part. There are also some that you should never deduct, even if you are entitled to do so.

The case for using deductions

There are people who don't take all the deductions they are entitled to on principle. Their altruistic reason goes like this: "Since I paid for my own pencils when I was employed, how can I justify deducting them now?" The problem with this reasoning is that as a self-employed worker you'll have to pay for much more than just pencils. You'll see! Expenses add up. In other words, if your expenses are legitimate, there's no reason not to deduct them. When you were employed, your company certainly did.

Need more convincing? Watch how the numbers work with Mr Proud and Ms Profit. They are claiming the same gross income ($50,000) and have the same expenses ($15,000). If Mr Proud doesn't use any deductions, he will have to pay $15,400 in taxes on $50,000. If Ms Profit uses all the deductions she can, she will only pay $9,300 in taxes on a net of $35,000. With the extra $6,100, she can go on a trip to Iceland, or reinvest the money in her business.

	Mr Proud	**Ms Profit**
Gross income	50,000	50,000
Expenses	15,000	15,000
Expenses deducted	0	15,000
Net income	50,000	35,000
Total paid (taxes)	15,400	9,300
Net income after taxes and expenses	19,600	25,700

* These amounts are increased by mandatory contributions, but do not take into account other deductions, credits, refunds and contingency obligations.

In a way, Mr Proud "pays twice," since he already paid sales taxes on the items that constitute legitimate business expenses. Look at the last line: at the end of the year Mr Proud only has $19,600 left in his pocket, which is $6,100 less than Ms Profit has in hers. The difference isn't just that he's paying taxes on legitimate expenses he incurred but the fact that he did not want to deduct them from his income. Mr Proud's position only has an advantage—though it probably costs him more than it's worth. That is: by inflating his net income in this way, Mr Proud improves his bottom line (i.e. his taxable income), at least on paper.

Raising his bottom lines does have advantages. It increases

- how much Mr Proud can borrow from the bank,
- his RRSP and CPP contribution limits,
- his parental leave coverage limit and
- his wage loss replacement coverage limit.

All these amounts are calculated on net business income, after deductions. Reducing your income as much as possible does have a few disadvantages.

However, there are also risks involved in keeping your declared income high for these reasons: a higher taxable income won't necessarily translate into more money at the end of the line. Mr Proud is still paying $6,100 more in taxes per year. Also, when it comes to borrowing capacity, by inflating your income on paper, you could appear to be doctoring your accounts, which may, in turn, be considered committing fraud.

The fourteen items that are 100% deductible

The following list of deductible expenses is not exhaustive: nothing prevents you from adding categories according to your needs.

1. **Office supplies.** Notepads, agendas, scissors, paper, printer cartridges, external cameras, keyboards, USB keys, headset, earbuds, computer mouses and so on. Computer software also qualifies, but not the computer itself (see the section on depreciation in this chapter).
2. **Telephone/smart phone.** Long-distance calls, service charges, telephone and line rental, service plans, Internet access. If the phone you use for business is also your residential line, you should exclude personal calls. However, you can still deduct a realistic proportion of the basic service fees for business use.
3. **Transport.** Taxis, buses, trains, subways, but also stamps, courier services or car rentals—in short, everything you need to get someone or something from point A to point B, *for business.*
4. **Advertising.** Include everything that gives your business exposure here: advertisements, business cards, letterhead, condolence flowers you send to a client who lost a family member, Christmas gifts for clients, supplies for office parties. Website expenses also count here.
5. **Debts.** When a client fails to pay their bill, you can deduct the sum from your income, provided, of course, that you counted it as income in the first place.

6. **Business taxes, fees, permits, membership dues.** This category of deductions includes expenses for anything the government or your professional association requires you to have in order to carry out your practice. Some professional or union dues, however, are only deductible as personal expenses. Just be careful not to deduct anything twice, as both a personal expense and a business expense.

7. **Training.** The government has strongly encouraged professional training in recent years. A seminar, workshop, night school class, a book that helps you run your business better (like the one you are reading) all qualify as deductible expenses as long as they are relevant to your practice or field of business.

8. **Travel.** Hotel expenses, airfare and car rentals are eligible in full, even if your client has reimbursed them. The problem with combining work and pleasure, like extending a work holiday or taking a spouse along, it that you have to prove that you were actually travelling for work. This excludes expenses incurred for your spouse or children. If you come back with a contract (or a refusal letter for a contract you were trying to get), you can prove that the travel expenses were made in "expectation of profit." Some fraudsters make up bogus refusal letters. This could attract authorities' attention. If you combine a work trip with a holiday, you should deduct only the proportion of the trip that was actually devoted to work—like, three out of seven days, say. In that case, transportation to and from the destination is still deductible, because you *had to get there for work reasons.*

9. **Conferences.** You are entitled to deduct expenses for exactly two conferences a year—no more. Eligible expenses include transportation, registration, accommodation, meals (at 50%) and mandatory dues.

10. **Honoraria.** Sometimes you have to hire other self-employed people, say, to set up a website or fix a computer system. If you entrust the work to your spouse and pretend you paid them—a common tax evasion technique—the spouse will have to declare the income from the contract. You may have to explain what work was actually done. It's not a great idea, even if your spouse really does fix computers for a living.

11. **Consultation fees.** Any consultations with professionals (lawyers, accountants, engineers) made in the course of your work are fully deductible, as are consultations with a computer programmer or a collection agency. However, if the consultation is personal in nature (e.g. couples therapy), it is not deductible. Fees for preparing your personal income tax return are not eligible unless the accountant charges you for a consultation (i.e. not actual work on the report), or unless your personal tax is complicated by your business to the point that you need to consult a professional.

12. **Maintenance and repair expenses.** This deduction excludes your car and your house, but applies to any repairs you have done to your tools, computer, telephone, copy machine, etc. After all, these devices are as indispensable to your work as the bathyscaphe is to the oceanologist's work.

13. **Insurance.** Office and liability insurance are 100% eligible as a deduction, as is insurance for specific items related to work (office, liability, extreme risk).

14. **Financial expenses.** Bank accounts and credit cards are expensive. You can subtract 100% of the fees for an account that is used exclusively for business purposes, as well as for the interest on a loan related to your work, such as a line of credit or loan for operating funds from the total cost of your account.

Expenses that are partially deductible

Certain expenses related to your home, your car and renovation costs are partially deductible. However, there are specific limits to these.

1. Rent

This varies. A commercial office is 100% deductible, as are its utility costs (gas, electricity, coffee maker, maintenance, toilet paper). A home office in rented accommodations is deductible in proportion to the surface you use for commercial activities, plus the proportional amount of heating and housekeeping expenses. If you own your home, you can deduct fees and costs associated with your mortgage, but not with repayment of the capital. The deductible portion is, again, calculated according to the proportion of the surface area of the house that you are using for your office. Tax authorities set a few limits for deductions related to home offices: the surface area allocated to the workspace cannot exceed 50% of the rented space.

Take care when you are calculating these amounts: deductions for home offices are highly scrutinized by tax authorities. In the case of a residential office, if you try to add access to the toilet, stairs and kitchen outside the office to the calculation of space you may have to fight it with tax inspectors to get it accepted.

Office rent expenses need to be presented in the following categories: rent (or interest on mortgage payments), heating, electricity, taxes, services, insurance. Be specific about every expense. Breaking expenses down carefully will be good protection if, and when, you end up being audited.

2. Cars

The deductible portion of a car should correspond to the proportion of your overall mileage that you did for business. There is no ceiling on the rate, but be careful. You will definitely catch the eye of tax authorities if you claim something like 75% of your car expenses as business deductions. The percentage is determined by the percentage used for work and you must have kept a log of kilometres driven for professional reasons.

Deductible expenses can include gas, license fees, insurance and repairs, but not the purchase price (see the section on depreciation), the trailer hitch or the trailer—unless you specifically need a trailer for your work. Contrary to what many people think, the same rules apply to rental cars (they are not entirely deductible).

In the case of both car rentals and office rentals, tax authorities ask you to break down the amounts according to fixed categories. For the car, these are leasing costs or interest on loans, gas, maintenance and insurance, parking and tolls.

3. Meals and entertainment expenses

The maximum deductible amount for meals is 50% of the costs incurred for work meetings in restaurants. For entertainment, you can deduct 50% for certain clothes (rarely) and theatre outings (if you go with a client or buy tickets for them). If you overdo it, for example by deducting 5% of your sales figure, you should make room in your schedule right away to meet with an auditor: they will come after you (and whatever you do, don't invite them to a restaurant to talk about it). If you are a food critic or chef, you may justifiably declare a higher level of meal expenditure as "research expenses." Always write on the back of your restaurant receipt with whom you ate and what the purpose was. It can be hard to draw the line between food and entertainment and expenses for advertising, travel and conventions, so the best practice is to carefully document the purpose of each expense you claim.

What you shouldn't deduct

There are also certain expenses that you are entitled to deduct as business expenses, like personal insurance (for your salary, disability, travel and health). But don't do it.

Why not? In the case of salary and disability insurance, the compensation provided is calculated according to a tax-free value. For example, if the insurer pays you a disability pension of $2,500 per month, you pay no tax on this amount. But if you have claimed the premium as a deductible expense, the compensation paid will become taxable, which will significantly reduce the net amount. In other words, if you deduct your salary and disability insurance expenses, the tax authorizes will take it back just when you need it most.

Life insurance is normally nondeductible unless a lender or client requires it. And even in that case, it's not 100% deductible.

As to personal health insurance, it simply does not qualify as a deductible business expense, but don't worry, it can be deducted as a personal expense.

Figuring out the depreciation puzzle

The way tax authorities see it, some of your biggest expenses, like buying a computer, office furniture or tools, are not actually "expenses" at all, but "investments," or "assets," i.e. goods that have a resale value.

You can never deduct the full amount of these expenses, but only the part that corresponds to the value they lose every year. This is called depreciation. There are no clear rules about what constitutes an asset, but accountants assume that a piece of equipment or furniture worth more than $200 should be considered an "asset." The GST-PST/HST paid on assets are 100% deductible in the first year.

As for calculated depreciation, the tax authorities use various methods (see below).

The same logic applies to car purchases, except that the portion of the depreciation you can deduct corresponds to the proportion of the mileage allocated to your business. Several documents from the tax authorities list the percentage you are allowed to deduct. Revenue Canada has established fourteen categories of depreciable assets, while Revenue Québec divides them into eighteen categories. For the self-employed worker, there are two main categories.

1. A car and computer equipment are deemed to depreciate by 30% each year.
2. Furniture, tools that cost more than $500, equipment and machinery are deemed to depreciate by 20% each year. It is possible that some percentages may vary according to government policy. Your accountant will know when this is the case.

There are automatic calculators available on the web that you can use to quickly calculate depreciation. You can also do it "by hand" (see Chapter 20, "The Income Statement," for an example of how). In either case, it's complicated. A calculator has to take into account a lot of information: gross amounts, net amounts, taxes, the date of acquisition (for your first year of fiscal period, your depreciation should be proportional to the number of months you've been in business), the applicable depreciation percentage and the formula of amortization.

On top of that, there are three types of calculation: linear, declining balance or proportional. As a consequence, we let our accountant handle this.

- **The linear formula.** You deduct a fixed percentage over a certain number of years. Linear, also called straight-line depreciation always starts from the initial value and reduces the value of the asset to zero after a predetermined number of years. When you reach zero, your asset is deemed to be worthless and the depreciation allowance is terminated.
- **The declining balance formula.** Here, the percentage is not calculated on the initial value, but on the residual value. Take a computer (30% depreciation) for which you paid $1,000. At the end of the first year, it is worth $700. At the end of the second year, it is worth $510—not $400—because the 30% is calculated not on the original value ($1,000) but on the remaining value ($700). So, in theory, the property will never reach the value of zero.
- **The proportional formula.** This is a mixture of the previous two, but also takes into account the number of hours an item is used on an annual basis.

You must keep your list of depreciated assets up to date. And if you sell your equipment for more than its residual value, you must add the profit to your income! On the other hand, if the price is lower, it represents a loss and therefore an additional amount you can claim as a deduction. The same logic applies if the property is destroyed in an accident or a disaster, or if it has been stolen or lost: its residual value constitutes a loss that can then be added to your expenses.

A few good reasons to go easy on deductions

The more expenses you deduct, the more you reduce your net business income, which in turn will reduce your earned income (which you report for tax purposes as personal income). This reduces the amount of taxes you pay.

This is why all self-employed workers face the (strong) temptation to push the limits and get "creative" with deductible expenses. There are costs to this. Aside from the obvious risk of getting caught by the tax authorities, being creative in claiming deductions poses a very real financial problem, particular with regard to banks, insurance and contribution limits for pensions.

Banks use your net income to determine your borrowing capacity. Insurance companies use your net income to calculate your salary insurance. The government uses your net income to determine your RRSP limits and contributions to the government pensions plans as well as benefits like parental leave or unemployment insurance or universal daycare programmes.

If you go to extraordinary lengths to reduce your income, artificially, by claiming every remotely legitimate expense you incur, you could very well end up losing out financially in the medium or long term by lowering the benefits to which you're entitled. A disproportionately low net income will not correspond to your real financial situation so you won't be able to borrow as much, get insured for your real value, make RRSP contributions proportionate to your real income or get as much money for parental leave as you need to take time off with your newly adopted twin daughters (that was us and we thankfully did get a good number of months of parental leave each). Unless, of course, you've managed to save up and not spend all that money you tried to save with tax deductions. But seriously, what are the chances that you've done that?

In recent years, some banks and insurance companies have agreed to increase the net income of workers who work at home by about 10% to take into account the cost of their rent and vehicle deductions. But if you are overdoing it with deductions and ask your insurance company to take into account personal deductions that were illegal or at least abusive, a fussy employee there could very well decide to call you on it and report you to the authorities.

In other words, deductions are a double-edged sword, and it's up to everyone to decide: if you want to maximize your deductions, you will pay less tax, but your earnings and financial capacity will be deemed to be lower and there will be disadvantages to that. If you minimize your deductions, you may end up paying taxes on your tools (which are theoretically deductible), but this increases your borrowing capacity, insurance coverage and your RRSP contribution limit.

And there's one more issue that may make overly creative tax deductions problematic: it could increase the taxes you'll pay if you sell your home. In principle, the capital gain on the sale of your main residence is tax-free. This is obviously not the case for commercial real estate. So if you have a home office and have deducted a considerable share of it as rent, that share becomes taxable as a capital gain when you sell the house. The larger the share of your office on your property, the more tax you'll pay. Other considerations come into play in this calculation, but it's another reason to be careful about claiming deductions. If you get carried away, you might end up losing out.

When taxes are your best friend

How charging sales tax can make your day

Myth #19: "I shouldn't bother with GST."

Anyone who was an employee in another life is likely to share the same feelings about GST (goods and services tax) and its provincial cousin, PST (provincial sales tax), Quebec's QST or HST (harmonized sales tax in the provinces that have combined them). The new tax scheme got such bad press when it was introduced in 1990 that most Canadians still aren't over it more than three decades later.

But for self-employed workers—who, remember, run businesses— these taxes are a heaven-sent opportunity. They totally work for us. The first thing you should do when you start your business is call the Canada Revenue Agency (and Revenu Québec in Quebec) and register for your own GST/PST or HST numbers.

Technically, the GST and PST/HST are both VATs, or value-added taxes. This means that the tax actually paid to the government is not the tax collected from the customer, but the difference between the tax collected and the tax paid on deductible expenses. The taxes collected and the tax deducted are calculated through separate accounting processes, which is fairly simple to manage with a spreadsheet program that we will discuss a little later.

Do you have to register to collect GST-PST/HST? Businesses with annual sales of more than $30,000 have to. Businesses making less than that should, in our opinion. Here's why.

Four good reasons to charge GST/HST

From a business perspective, the GST/HST/PST/QST is a pretty great tax for self-employed workers. Any self-employed person—being a business of their own—should be able to benefit from charging it. Here's why:

1. You'll pay less tax overall

Because you are registered to collect sales tax, it's your customers who refund the tax paid when you purchase your goods or supplies. Regular people cannot do this, but businesses—including yours—certainly can. If your customers are, in turn, registered for GST and PST/HST, then they can get their taxes reimbursed by their customers—but that's their business! If you are not registered to collect GST, the tax you pay on the material you purchase—so, basically on all your business expenses—will come straight out of the fees that you charge for your product or service, except that nothing will come back to you from your customers to make up for it. Applying the same logic, if you don't make a profit in one quarter or year, the government will actually reimburse you for part of the taxes paid on your expenses (see the next box).

The advantages of GST-PST/HST

Compare the cases of Anita (who is not registered for HST) and Roberta (who is registered for HST at 13%)

Anita's gross income:		$30,000
Deductible expenses (HST included):		$10,000
Net income:		$20,000

Anita therefore pays income tax on $20,000.

	Gross income	Net of tax	Taxes
Roberta's gross income	$33,900.00	$30,000.00	$3,900.00
Deductible expenses (Including HST)	$10,000.00	$8,849.56	$1,150.44
Net income	n/a	$21,150.44	$2,749.56

Roberta ends up with $1,150.44 more net income. What miracle made that happen? It's simple: her deductible expenses and income are no longer counted in the same column as her taxes.

Explanation: GST and PST/HST are value-added taxes, in other words, taxes on profit. The calculation is separate from that of revenues and expenses. In practice, this means that a person like Anita, who does not collect taxes, pays GST/HST on her expenses like everyone else. But because Roberta claims HST on her fees, she has the right to use the HST she has collected to reimburse herself for the HST she will pay on all her business expenses. In other words, it's Roberta's clients who end up paying her taxes on the expenses she incurs for her business! Look at Roberta's tax column: she only remits to the government $2,749.56 of the $3,900 collected. That's why Roberta ends up earning more money than Anita does!

Who said the HST was a bad tax?

2. It looks professional

Many self-employed workers take advantage of the clause that allows businesses with sales under $30,000 to avoid collecting GST and PST/HST. This is a serious miscalculation. In not doing so, you immediately project the image of being an amateur who earns less than $30,000, and many potential clients will instantly judge you as either not successful, not well established or not very committed to what you are doing. You also imply that you are working under the table. Needless to say, solid, well-established clients generally want to do business with other solid, well-established freelancers, or at least bone fide professionals. Beginners can help their cause and make themselves look less amateur by demonstrating an understanding of standard business practices and charging GST and PST/HST. As the saying goes, success attracts success. Better still, governments offer some advantages to smaller businesses that charge GST and PST/HST, as we'll see below.

3. Prevention is the best medicine

If you decide not to collect the taxes, you might end up in a real pickle if your business suddenly starts doing better than expected. For example, say you are anticipating $25,000 in sales, but a contract at the end of the year pushes the figure up to $35,000. Suddenly, you have to charge GST. The government will give you one month to get your registration numbers in order to do so. As soon as you are eligible, you will be obliged to pay the tax on your income—the income you had prior to registering and for which you didn't collect GST or PST/HST. So obviously, it's much easier and more advantageous to register from the outset.

On top of that, the $30,000 exclusion is not for the calendar year, but for any succession of four quarters of business that add up to $30,000. Let's assume that your business is going smoothly with an average turnover of $6,000 per quarter, or $24,000 per year. But suddenly, in the last quarter of the year, you make $10,000. Don't worry: your annual total is $28,000 (6,000 + 6,000 + 6,000 + 10,000). But if in the first quarter of the following year, you still earn $10,000, then the total of your four quarters is

$32,000! (6,000 + 6,000 + 10,000 + 10,000). This kind of fluctuation is sometimes difficult to predict: again, it's better to collect the taxes right away and not worry about what you'll have to do if business takes off.

4. Tax for export

GST (Canadian) and PST (provincial) or HST only applies to sales made within their respective territories. However, you are still entitled to deduct the tax paid on your expenses. Borderline case: if you draw 100% of your income from exempt sources (foreign who do no business in Canada), the government will reimburse taxes paid on expenses in Canada in the form of a nice cheque each quarter. This reimbursement will then be added to your income (so, taxable itself), but it's still better than having to pay the taxes up front. The logic is the same for interprovincial business regarding your provincial sales tax.

Choosing the right "method"

You don't need to be incorporated in order to register to collect GST and PST/HST. The only thing you need to be is yourself. It doesn't cost anything. There is a simple form to fill out. You will receive the numbers in a few weeks and, from then on, you, should include them on all your bills and charge them. When your registration is confirmed, you will receive an instruction booklet that explains what is deductible and how to make the calculations.

One decision you have to make when you fill out the form is how you will calculate your GST and PST/HST contributions. You can do it one of two ways: using the regular or the quick method. It's an important decision because it will affect how you keep your accounting records (Chapter 21) and how you report income and expenses (Chapter 20).

In a nutshell, the quick method is really more advantageous to most self-employed workers, but you need to meet a number of criteria. You need to have been in business continually for the 365-day period prior to using it and your revenues can't exceed $400,000). There is also a list of business that cannot use the quick method (e.g. bookkeeping and accounting services, non-profit organizations, charities). You can only change calculation methods once a year.

- If you opt for the detailed calculation method, you will have to add up the GST and PST/HST paid on each of your expenses and subtract it from the taxes collected to determine the amount you have to pay. You must do this for each receipt. It can get a little tedious when it comes to small amounts, but this calculation method is useful if your taxable expenses are proportionately high, amounting to roughly more than 50% of your income (more on this later).

- The quick method, which is available for businesses with sales under $400,000, is much simpler. In the case of GST, you pay only 3.6% from the 5% collected. For HST (e.g. Ontario), you pay 8.8% from the 13% collected. Even better: under certain conditions, the government offers you a 1% credit on your first $30,000 of gross revenue! This reduces your GST rate to 2.6% and the HST rate to 7.8%. You don't have to keep a detailed accounting of the tax paid on every pencil you buy, quarter by quarter. At the end of the year, when you file your income tax return, you just add to your revenue the difference between the taxes collected and the taxes paid and voilà!

The advantages of the quick method

To understand why the quick method is almost always more advantageous, compare the case of Georgina and Ruby. Georgina uses the detailed method. Ruby uses the quick method. For the purposes of examples, they both have incomes of $30,000, their expenses are $10,000 and they collect 13% HST.

Georgina (detailed method):

HST collected at 13% (on revenue she bills): $3,900
Taxes paid on her expenses (at purchase): $1,150.44
Taxes paid to the government: $3,900 – $1,150.44 = $2,748.56

Ruby (quick method):

HST collected at 13% (on revenue she bills): $3,900
Taxes paid on expenses (7.8% from the 13% collected): $2,340

As you can see, Ruby pays $408.56 less in taxes to the government than Georgina does on the same amount. However, to balance things, the government wants Ruby to add the difference between the taxes collected and the ones paid to her revenue. How much? It's $3,900 minus $2,340 for a total of $1,560. Because Ruby will declare her deductible expenses *with the tax included*, she will pay some income tax on this extra amount, but never as much as Georgina. Plus, Ruby will have had less accounting hassles.

So, which is better: the quick method or the detailed method?

For cash flow reasons, and especially if you're dealing with big sums, the detailed method may be better for you. Specifically, this is the case if the proportion of your taxable expenses exceeds half of your gross income. A good accountant will be able to advise you on which choice is best, but the quick method is almost always the most advantageous if you are just starting out, or if your income is modest.

The spreadsheet

Your GST and PST/HST must be remitted quarterly, in the month following the end of the quarter, so before January 31, April 30, July 31 and October 31.

If you have opted for the detailed method, you will have to make the exact calculation of what you owe. That means that you need to make a detailed calculation of your income and expenses. If you are using the quick method, all you have to do is pay Revenue Canada according to a simple formula based on your taxable income.

Whichever method you use, quick or detailed, you must extract the taxes from your income. If you only do business in your province, that will be quite simple.

If you do business elsewhere than in your province, it becomes a little more complicated because the rates vary. Abroad, there is no sales tax that applies to your calculations. Certain goods or services, such as medical or insurance goods or services, are also tax-exempt (the rate is then zero). In Canada, the GST is 5% everywhere, and the QST is 9.975% in Quebec. But in Ontario, everything is consolidated into a single harmonized tax of 13%. In the four Atlantic provinces, the HST is 15%. Manitoba and Saskatchewan have a provincial tax of 10%, British Columbia, 12%. Alberta and the territories have set their provincial sales tax at 5%. (And these percentages vary if your business is reselling purchased goods.)

In practice, it's rare for a self-employed worker to do business with clients in many different tax jurisdictions. But it does happen.

To separate taxes from income, we use a spreadsheet in Excel to keep track of revenues and expenses in all categories. A spreadsheet will only do the work that you ask of it, and we ask a lot of ours. You (or your accountant) can easily set up your own spreadsheet adapted to your own needs.

The main job of the spreadsheet is to automatically separate the gross income, the net income and the applicable taxes. Our model includes a column for zero-rated (or exempt) income, including income generated abroad, for example. We then have four columns, respectively, for income taxed in Quebec, income taxed in Ontario and two other categories. The main thing is that you have to adapt your spreadsheet to your situation.

To help us with our accounting, we've also added a number of rows. Instead of putting everything into one consolidated income, we separate it into journalism income, book royalties, conference and consulting fees, and translation fees. Our spreadsheet, in the revenue section, has a line for "refund" and another line for "manual reimbursement." The reason for this last line is that some expense claims have a wide variety of rates (when they involve travel abroad, outside Quebec or outside the country). As a result, the total of the invoice and taxes does not correspond to any existing equation. In this case, which is rare, we have to enter the number manually in each of the boxes of this rather special line.

Other columns to the right add up the various tax rates and give the total results gross or net of taxes. These nuances are sometimes useful. It sounds terrible, but many accountants using the best accounting software on the market still prefer to manually transpose their figures into a spreadsheet to extract taxes. It's not as onerous as it sounds. It can be done in a matter of minutes.

If you use the detailed method, the bottom part of the spreadsheet is what you need to calculate expenses. If you use the quick method, you just add everything up in the first column, since the government asks you to report your expenses with taxes included. For the detailed method, if you are not using an accounting software such as Quicken, the numerous columns of the spreadsheet will be particularly useful. Simply group your invoices by category, add up the total, enter it in the right column and presto!—the desired data will come out.

A little help for making calculations

You can easily create your own spreadsheet using a few simple equations you learned in high school.

Extracting the GST and PST/HST from revenue and expenses sounds complicated, but the government's instruction book provides the equations you'll need in the spreadsheet.

For example, if you pay $22.60 for a book and you want to know the net amount without HST (13%), you multiply 22.60 by 100/113. It will give you $20. To find out the HST, multiply the original amount, 22.60 by 13/113 and it will give you $2.60.

Of course, there are other ingenious fractions you can use to extract taxes separately or in combination. They can be found in detailed government documents, but your accountant knows them too.

20

The final word on taxes

Your rights and obligations with respect to revenue agencies

Myth # 20: "I can just store my receipts in a shoebox."

Tax authorities are watching you. But tax authorities are also *watching out* for you. In other words, tax authorities have two roles: they are enforcers and enablers. They can be strict, but they can also be surprisingly accommodating towards people who create wealth, i.e. business owners like you.

The general principle of calculating personal income tax for self-employed workers is a simple one: your business's profit (the difference between your gross income and your expenses) becomes your personal income. The freelancer's tax return can be filled out fairly quickly: all you need is an extra line or two on the general form—don't use the simplified version, which paradoxically will complicate your life for nothing. Since you have no employees except yourself (remember, contractual freelancers are not your employees), you don't have to pay any of the payroll charges or various taxes on payroll, for example. As a result, your case is pretty simple.

The self-employed worker's tax is special in three ways: workers must provide a statement of income and expenses, make instalment payments and keep records.

The income statement

This document is used to distinguish your net income from your gross income and expenses. A standard form is attached to the professional income tax form, but it contains categories of deductions that won't necessarily apply to you. You can create your own financial statement (see the box on the next page). You won't have any problems as long as you are precise. You can use footnotes to explain the calculation methods you have chosen to use.

If you use a good spreadsheet (as we explained in Chapter 19), you should have no trouble producing this income statement, with all the right amounts. Obviously, depreciation calculations are a little more complicated, so we advise you to let your accountant do them.

The following is an example of a self-employed worker who uses the quick method: the gross income is net of taxes but expenses include taxes.

Income statement

Paul Trunk, horticultural adviser
4654 Clover Street
Rosebud, New Brunswick E1A 0A3
HST #: 123456789

CONSOLIDATED REVENUES AND EXPENSES
As of December 31, 2022

Gross income (1)
Fees $63,000

Refunds (2)	$7,000
Total gross revenues	$70,000
Expenses (3)	
Professional fees	$519.00
Office supplies	$1,300.00
Telephone fees	$2,000.00
Travel expenses	$1,500.00
Interest and bank fees	$350.00
Advertising	$2,400.00
Documentation	$800.00
Training	$1,000.00
Tool maintenance	$1,200.00
Conferences	$1,800.00
Miscellaneous and dues	$500.00
Depreciation (4)	$743.00
Motor vehicle expenses (5)	$2,698.00
Rent (6)	$5,031.00
Meals (7)	$630.00
Total deductible expenses	$22,471.00
Net income (profit)	$47,529.00

NOTES

(1) All expenses are net of tax.

(2) Reimbursements paid by customers for long distance, miscellaneous transportation and travel expenses in the performance of contracts. These invoices have also been recorded as expenses.

(3) All expenses including taxes (HST).

(4) Calculation of depreciation:

Category: automobile (acquired in 2020)
Value at the end of 2020 $2,900.00

Depreciation 2021	$870.00
Residual value	$2,030.00
Rate: 30%	
Portion for professional use 75%.	
Depreciation	$456.75
Category: computer (acquired in 2022)	
Value	$955.00
Rate: 30%	
Depreciation	$286.50
Total depreciation	$743.25

(5) Calculation of motor vehicle expenses:

Gasoline	$1,800.29
Repairs	$1,297.00
Insurance	$500.00
Total	$3,597.29
Non-deductible portion (25%)	$899.32
Total deductible	$2,697.97

(6) Calculation of the rent:

Gross rent	$17,263.84
Electricity	$820.00
Gas	$500.00
Insurance	$300.00
Maintenance, household	$1,243.42
Total	$20,127.26
Non-deductible portion (75%)	$15,095.45
Total deductible	$5,031.81

(7) Meals: is 50% of the total $1,260.

The income statement has to have three components:

- **Gross income.** Equal to the sum of all the fees received. Do not count as income the amount of taxes collected such as GST-PST/HST, which are calculated separately each quarter. Do not include here amounts you receive outside your business, such as your employee salary (if you have a job) or various types of child benefits you might receive. Also, don't include fees for which a client produced a T4. These amounts appear on other lines of the general form of your personal income tax return.
- **Expenses.** The annual total for each category of deductible expenses should appear here. There's no need to include copies of each of your 1,500 receipts (although you should keep them in files): the tax authorities will only ask to see them if they decide to audit you. The amount you indicate depends on several things.

1. If you collect GST-PST/HST and you have chosen the detailed method, you must indicate your expenses *without* sales tax. The spreadsheet described in the previous chapter makes it easy to extract the taxes, regardless of the various tax rates or exempt amounts.
2. If you use the quick method for GST-PST/HST or if you do not collect sales taxes, you must indicate your expenses *including* sales taxes. Write the total amount, including the amount of taxes.

If you are producing a good, not a service, you must divide your expenses into two categories: operating costs (necessary for production) and administrative costs (expenses incurred for sales, management, etc.). Tax authorities ask for these to be separated so they can better control the expenses that are being deducted. Production costs, in terms of equipment, can be high. Separating them from administration costs (which should be relatively similar for all companies) makes it more difficult to conceal unreasonable administrative expenses (e.g. extraordinarily high "consulting" fees).

- **Net profit.** This is the difference between gross income and expenses. A normal business would pay tax on this amount, but the self-employed worker's net profit becomes their personal gross income as a taxpayer.

  To this income you will add, on your tax return, other income, such as that from a job or from allowances, to which all personal credits and deductions (RRSPs, health expenses, etc.) then apply.

If you collect GST-PST/HST using the quick method (and only in this case), you add to your income the difference between the taxes collected on your income and the tax paid according to the pre-established formula explained in Chapter 19. For those who are curious about why it is done this way, the explanation is simple: the net tax amount will be adjusted as for the detailed method, but inside your income tax return. How is this possible? Simply because your expenses include all taxes. This is what makes the quick method not only quick, but also simple to apply.

According to the business logic that guides self-employed workers, it is possible for you to record a loss some years: you might have invested a lot in a new project, for example, and had very little income from it, or a client suddenly dropped you. This has happened to Esso, so it can happen to self-employed workers too. If you have a net loss, you don't pay tax. You can also carry this loss forward in whole or in part to a subsequent year, or even spread it over several years, which will reduce your taxes in those years, but let your accountant handle this. However, take note that while this can happen to you one year, or even two, if you try it five years in a row the tax authorities will probably start to wonder where the "expected profit" is that justifies the expenses (and continual losses).

Instalments

For the self-employed worker, taxes are not withheld on your pay cheque, at the source, but tax authorities won't wait until April 30 every year for their money. So, you will have to pay your taxes by instalments quarterly on March 15, June 15, September 15 and December 15 (these dates do not correspond to the quarters for the calculation of GST-PST/HST). The amount for the instalments is always calculated on the previous year's income tax paid and payment must arrive on time; otherwise you'll be subject to penalties. The tax threshold at which instalments become mandatory varies. Federally, it's $3,000 but in Quebec it's $1,800.

These instalments are just a provision: the actual total tax payable will be adjusted when you submit your tax return. In the first year, an accountant will be able to help you make these estimates. As we said, the CRA will send you what you need the following year after receiving your income tax return. The form is simple: you don't have to show calculations, just enter the amount to be paid and deposit it in the bank.

The required tax instalment system does have one flaw. The amount for the instalments is based on the amount filed in your previous year's income tax report. Most self-employed workers' income fluctuates from one year to the next. You need to keep this in mind while you are paying your instalments. If your income increases with respect to the previous year, it's a good idea to increase the amount you pay in your instalments accordingly or at least increase your tax reserve. Otherwise, you will have to pay extra tax when you file your income tax return (which is fine and legal, but harder to manage, trust us). On the other hand, if your income drops sharply in a given year, you may be caught having to pay instalments based on your higher income from the previous year. You might not be able to afford to wait for the government to reimburse you for the excess tax it is collecting. Fortunately, the tax authorities allow you to reduce your instalments as long as you can explain it. If you collect GST-PST/HST, the government can easily check whether your income actually fluctuated.

A word of advice: unless you're very disciplined and have all the cash reserves you need on hand, don't wait until April 30 to pay all your tax for the previous year. Resisting the temptation to spend your tax reserve is difficult. When Jean-Benoît first started out, he found himself in this situation more than once. He had just finished school and had had a good year, which felt better than it actually was since he went ahead and spent the money he would later have to pay in taxes. He recalled having a very rude awakening in January when he added up his year and realized he would certainly have a hefty sum to pay on April 30. That was painful enough, but then he realized he would also have to start paying tax instalments on March 15, then on June 15. In all, he ended up having a ninety-day period to pay taxes for a year and a half of work. He learned his lesson.

Paying taxes in foreign countries

If you do business abroad, you should be aware that you may be subject to different tax rules, particularly for real estate and royalties for intellectual property. In almost all countries, the royalties you earn (on your copyright, patents or trade mark) will be subject to an automatic 33% tax.

But don't (necessarily) panic: tax treaties exist between Canada and about 100 countries that allow you to avoid paying foreign taxes on those. Roughly speaking, the procedure involves providing them with proof that you pay taxes in Canada. This is your country of "tax residence."

In the United States, you must first obtain a seven-digit number called ITIN (Individual Taxpayer Identification Number) from the IRS (US Internal Revenue Service). This number registers you in their system as a Canadian tax resident and exempts you from paying US royalty tax. It can be obtained in two ways: either through the IRS agent at the US Consulate or by going to the nearest IRS office—in the IRS office closest to your border. Not fun. But here's the good news: you'll have your ITIN for the rest of your life, and it will come in handy every time US authorities want to snatch a piece of what your client is paying you. However, each new client with whom you use your ITIN will ask you to fill out another form called a W8-BEN, which frees them of the obligation to deduct tax at source.

The ITIN applies to an individual. If you are doing business as a company, other rules apply and it is preferable that you speak to an accountant who is familiar with them.

The general principle is the same from one country to another, but the paperwork and procedures differ. In the case of the UK, you have to produce a Canadian tax residency certificate which must be renewed every five years. With France, it is another system of forms that must be renewed every year.

Keep your records

Unfortunately, when it comes to keeping archives of your receipts, there are no clear rules to guide you. You are required to keep all of your receipts for seven full tax years and records of bookkeeping indefinitely (including bank statements). But since tax inspectors may ask you to justify any transaction, you should also hang on to your agendas, project-related correspondence and invoices. That will put you in a better position to provide explanations if you are required to do so. No one loves boxes of archives cluttering up their office (or in our case, our basement), but when you are self-employed, you really don't have any choice. You have to hang on to a certain amount of paperwork just to cover your you-know-what.

Our tax specialist also advised us to keep, in a separate envelope, all of our receipts for nondeductible personal expenses. The reasoning is: in the event of a thorough tax audit, we will be able to demonstrate that we are not deducting *all* our personal expenses, but only the ones we deem to be reasonable and legitimate. The more you stretch the elastic as to what is reasonable and legitimate, the better idea it is to have some record of your personal expenses to back you up.

In 2011, Julie received a letter from federal tax authorities asking why, in 2007, she had not declared $114,200 in copyright royalties from our agent in France. These international royalties are subject to tax agreements between countries (see box Paying taxes in foreign countries) and the authorities ask to see them because those who pay them also have to produce special slips. We had never received such an outrageous amount of money from our literary agent. The actual figure was about $11,000. We asked our accountant to discuss it with the tax authorities and then we demonstrated that there was an error on the slip. To do this, we had to show them the details of everything we had collected and a few photocopies of bank accounts to demonstrate that had we had simply never received a deposit of $114,200—but only one a tenth of that amount. Since we keep our accounting in order and file papers scrupulously, it was relatively simple to demonstrate our good faith, so we had no problem, but it did take time and cause anxiety.

The moral of the story: keeping your papers in order won't prevent misunderstandings over income tax from happening, but it will make them much easier to solve.

Common sense may tell you to keep your papers in order, but the government will really make you do it. That requires a minimum level of organization. You can't afford to just stuff your receipts in a shoebox and forget about them. And in any case, you have a financial interest in filing them carefully and systematically: when your affairs are in order, the services of an accountant end up costing significantly less (they charge by the hour).

Tax authorities are usually looking for big fish, not minnows. They don't care much about tadpoles with $30,000 in sales. But if, one morning, you receive a call from Revenue Canada, there's no need to buy a one-way ticket to Cuba. You won't have any problem as long as your financial statements are clear, your numbers add up, you have been obeying the law and your figures respect certain benchmarks—a reasonable level of expenses, an expectation of actual profit, restaurant costs of less than 1% of your sales figure (see Chapter 18) and so on. In any case, you greatly benefit from keeping rigorous and honest accounts and being able to justify any expenditure you declare. If you are ever required to undergo a tax audit, don't hesitate to consult a chartered accountant. If the situation ever gets out of hand, this professional will be better equipped to make your case for you.

With tax authorities, it pays to be honest, but don't be naive. Always ask your accountant to talk to civil servants first. Good accountants are known and respected by tax officials. What's more, your accountant will be better able to figure out quickly, exactly what the tax authorities' beef is.

Your audit will be one of three forms: questions by letter, questions in person, or a thorough audit. Most of the time, the tax authorities detected something odd and just want an explanation. The first step is to determine whether you are credible and if your documents are clear and orderly. If you have cut corners and have difficulty answering some basic questions, you will look suspicious. The inspectors will then ask for a sample of your receipts so they can take a closer look. If something is amiss, they will then proceed to look through all your records. If you are confused about these notions, get your accountant to explain the process to you.

Don't even think of offering far-fetched explanations for expenses you can't justify. Tax officials have heard it all, including the one about the famous windstorm that blew all your papers away and the one about the ex-husband who moved out with the box of receipts and didn't leave a forwarding address. With tax authorities, the best story is the truth.

This is exactly the situation we found ourselves in with Julie's 2011 experience, mentioned above. When we redid our calculations, we discovered we had indeed made an accounting error of a few thousand dollars. For a minute we wondered what to do: bury the error and hope that the authorities wouldn't dig any further? But if they had searched—which was likely, given the justification they were asking us for in the first place—they might have realized that we were trying to conceal a mistake. So, we chose to come clean and admit the problem voluntarily. As it happened, the forgotten sum was something subject to a very advantageous tax credit in Quebec (professional artists can deduct their first $30,000 of royalties), so forgetting to claim it would not have been in our advantage!

Probably because we had demonstrated our good faith this way, we did not end up having to pay any penalties except the tax arrears with interest. That hurt a bit, but less than if we had been caught cheating red-handed, in which case we might have had to pay a penalty. We got out of paying a penalty by arguing that the amount we had forgotten was a genuine oversight. We backed this up by showing the mistake did cost us because we were entitled to at least the tax credit for this type of royalty. In the process, we discovered that tax inspectors are actually quite open to discussing things, as long they know you aren't trying to hide something.

21

Advanced management skills

Handy administrative tips to simplify your life and make your sales figures talk

Myth #21: "I'm not good at numbers."

If you read the last three chapters without stopping for a break, you either love numbers or you're an accountant (so you love numbers). For most people, reading about management and administration is either sleep-inducing or terrifying. Fortunately, the main thing you need to manage your business well is just common sense. You don't need to be an accountant to understand what we're about to explain.

Accounting is one of the tasks a self-employed worker can most easily delegate to someone else. However, beware and tread carefully if you do delegate. Bookkeeping is not just about numbers. It's also about putting your paperwork in order and getting a clear picture of how your business is doing.

That said, even if you opt to hand over managing your accounts to a third party, you need to be able to master basic accounting skills. At the very least, you need them in order to supervise the accounting work that's being done for you. And again, it really is not that complicated.

The basic math kit self-employed workers need is pretty simple. Any self-employed worker—like any citizen, really—must at the very least be able to divide percentages and convert them into fractions, or proportions. You don't have to master advanced skills in statistical calculation. If you have been able, up until this point, to estimate the price of your product or your hourly rate (see Chapter 5) and negotiate contracts, you have all the math skills you need.

If numbers don't scare you, you are under no obligation, legally, to delegate bookkeeping to a third party. In principle, all you need in order to produce a complete set of accounts is an income box, an expenses box, a general ledger and separate journals for payroll, accounts receivable, purchases and inventory. For complicated cases, hiring an accountant will probably cost $2,000 to $3,000 a year. If you are just starting out or you are in the first few years, have low sales and no employees, a simpler general ledger accounting system will probably do the job. The average person can handle this, especially since there are plenty of good software options out there to help you, as we'll see a little further.

But even if you hire the best accountant in town, in the eyes of the law, you're still responsible for what they do. That means that you have to stay on top of things no matter what, even when someone else is doing the legwork.

Choosing the method

Whichever path you take, you will have to choose one of two accounting methods early on: cash or accrual. And then stick to it.

What's the difference? The accrual method reports all expenses and revenues that are billed but not necessarily paid, which means you need to have a column for unpaid accounts payable. The cash method compiles exactly the same data, but only when payments have been received (as opposed to when you send the invoice) or made.

We use the cash method. The cash method, which is much simpler and perfectly fine for most small businesses, corresponds to cash flow. But not all self-employed workers can use it. Lawyers, for instance, are required to use the accrual method because they manage money remitted by some of their clients (i.e. trust accounts), which requires them to follow the highest accounting standards.

Another choice in method that you will have to make early on is whether you will completely separate the business side of your life from the personal side. This would mean you would have to have a bank account, credit card and credit line that are totally dedicated to your business. And you will pay for groceries, medication, medical or school fees from your separate personal bank account, credit card and credit line.

We must confess that we have never been able to do this, partly because we never made that choice from the start. And also because, very often, the decision to count one expense or another as deductible is made after the expense. Which means that for 35 years, much of our accounting effort has been just about separating our personal and business expenses.

Opening accounts

A self-employed person running a business in their own name can operate quite well without having a special business account. There's no need to have a business account unless you are operating your business under a different name than the one your parents gave you. A standard personal checking account will do the job. It's one of the reasons we don't use a bookkeeper. They handle the business side of accounts. Once we have already separated the business and the personal expenses, there's not much left for a bookkeeper to do.

We have a second bank account that serves as a cash reservoir for the money we set aside for taxes and or savings. The third account is the credit line, though for many years the only credit we used was a credit card. The issue of credit is a personal one and also a matter of your personal circumstances. But having at least two bank accounts—one for operations and one for reserves—to manage things is no luxury.

For years, we tried to run our business with a single personal account under the mistaken belief that it was simpler. It wasn't. The gymnastics of keeping track of what funds were earmarked for taxes, versus what were our personal savings, just became too much to manage. It made it almost impossible to be disciplined about how much we were spending or saving.

Using a separate account for taxes makes it a lot easier to ensure there will be enough money there to meet our obligations when we need to. All you have to do is systematically transfer a predetermined percentage of each cheque you receive into the tax account when you get it. We find that putting aside between 33% and 40% usually covers what we have to pay in all taxes (personal, GST-QST, property and school taxes). What is not spent on taxes is our savings.

If you're just starting out, 10% or 15% might be enough. But bear in mind that since taxes are progressive, you have to increase the proportion of payments you put in the tax reserve as your net income climbs. The more you earn, the more you pay. So if things go well, you may have to adjust that percentage in the course of the year.

File away!

Rigorous, regular bookkeeping allows you to quickly figure out what your GST-PST/HST payments should be, as well as your year-end income tax return. It's a good habit to get into. With regular bookkeeping, you compile information as you go along instead of putting it all off and having to wade through mountains of invoices and receipts in a panic with a deadline looming over you. Yes, tracking down bills and putting papers in order can seem tedious at first and be frustrating at times. But you're better to spread the pain out evenly over your week or month, as opposed to drowning in a paper mess every March or April. The other advantage of keeping on top of things is that it makes it easier to quickly identify expenses you can bill to customers. That means you can get reimbursed more quickly—sometimes even before you have to pay the balance of your credit card.

There are two methods for compiling your data: you can use a system of folders and envelopes, or books of accounts. The latter used to come in the form of ledgers, but today generally come in the form of software.

If your business is small and simple, you'll be better off not complicating your life with unnecessarily elaborate bookkeeping software. A well-maintained system of folders and envelopes (paper or electronic) will probably do the job, at least when you're starting out and probably for some time.

And in any case, even if you use an outside bookkeeper or accounting software, or both, you will still need to develop a good paper filing system that lets you store receipts and invoices so you can pass them on to your bookkeeper at some point. And in case you need another reason to file receipts: it will reduce your bookkeeping fees, which are charged by the hour. Folders and envelopes do the job marvellously.

For our whole data compiling routine, we use about a dozen paper folders that we arrange in order inside an old-fashioned brown accordion file folder (you can still buy these at Staples for around $30). We have a folder for each of the following:

- Invoices sent (accounts receivable)
- Bills to pay (accounts payable)
- Reimbursable expenses to be invoiced to our clients
- Receipts and transaction records for the business account
- Receipts and transactions for the personal chequing account
- Transactions in the tax savings account
- Receipts and transactions on the personal credit card
- Receipts and transactions on the credit line
- Receipts for cash expenses.

We make an effort to put all our receipts and bills promptly in the right folder. It helps reduce the clutter in our wallets and on our desks. As for reimbursable expenses, we make photocopies of them right away and put them in the reimbursable expenses folder. We send the photocopies to clients and hang on to the originals, which are filed in the appropriate folder depending on which bank account we used to make a payment. Dividing income and expenses up this way makes it possible to locate documents quickly and easily. Since the documents are filed chronologically as they come in, it usually only takes a few hours each quarter to do the bookkeeping.

When we receive (or print up, as the case may be) bank statements, we match the receipts for every transaction to the statement for each account to make sure they are accurate. Banks don't make mistakes very often, but whenever they do, they work in their favour. Matching receipts to transactions is also a good way to spot deductible transactions for which you forgot (or neglected) to get a receipt. There is usually a way to get your hands on the receipt, especially when it was for a digital transaction, the ones we most often forget to get receipts for.

The other thing we do is write the nature of each transaction directly on the bank statement—unless it's totally obvious. For instance, if we received or made a bank transfer, we write down which account it came from or went to. This system also helps us keep track of what cheques have been cashed. It's a bit tedious and irritating to do all this when you are starting out, but it becomes a habit and you learn to appreciate over time the many ways it actually simplifies your life (especially when you have to check something months or years after the fact). You need to accept that keeping track of expenses is part of your work. Trust us, bills do get lost and sometimes you really need them. Cyber fraud is also on the rise so it's a good idea to make sure you have your receipts for online credit card purchases.

About every quarter, when it's time to make our GST-QST payments, we simply divide all the cheque stubs and divide receipts into income and expense categories, tally up the total for each category and then put our totals onto a spreadsheet. When this is all done, we just staple the stacks of receipts together and stuff them into an envelope (each account has its own). And then we forget about them.

Since we use the quick method for GST-QST, accounting for expenses is quite simple. If you collect GST-PST/HST using the detailed method, you absolutely must subdivide each expense category according to tax levels (the rates vary by province). The spreadsheet described in Chapter 19 can help you do the math.

It's probably a good idea to actually consult an accountant, as we did, to find out what is best for you. For many self-employed workers, especially those just starting out, the very simple approach we use will work fine because their business, like ours, is pretty simple to begin with. We have a dozen or so clients, no employees, no inventory and we only handle around 100 receipts for deductible expenses per month.

If you have employees or inventory (because you are selling a product), our method will not be enough. You will have to use more sophisticated bookkeeping about which we are completely ignorant: talk to someone else in your business to find out what they use.

Choosing the right software

We eventually opted for a more elaborate bookkeeping software because as life got more complicated (with the arrival of our daughters, for example) we felt the need to keep better track of where we were overspending for business, but also on personal items—restaurants, impulse purchases and so on.

Bookkeeping software also gives you superpowers. You can use software and advanced accounting methods to determine all sorts of financial indicators—some simple, some complicated—that will give you an idea of how your business is doing. You can use a bookkeeping system to see what your bank balance is, check the status of your accounts receivable, figure out how long you've been waiting to be paid for a good or service, calculate what your weekly, monthly or yearly sales were, see how much profit you made, or what your losses were and calculate how much you owe to the Canada Revenue Agency.

Good accounting software makes your life easier in a number of ways. First, it adds and subtracts correctly on the first try so you don't have to double-check your calculations. Secondly, it automatically tracks and matches transfers from one account to another. For example, if we pay a $200 membership fee for our provincial writers' association with our Visa card, then reimburse the amount from our chequing account, the software registers this, not as an "expense," but as a movement of funds from one account to another. Nothing is lost, nothing is created. The software also labels each income or expense according to its category, which makes it possible to automate data compilation. Finally, good accounting software makes it easy to analyse, sometimes in detail, what is happening in your accounts, like how much you are earning or spending per month, or quarter.

Software and spreadsheets cost less than hiring an accountant, but you'll have to master a number of concepts and equations in order to use them. Machines only know how to count: they don't actually think; they don't read newspapers and therefore don't know that laws change. They also have no judgment. As an engineer friend aptly said: computers do everything faster, including making mistakes!

Have no fear, there are a lot of good accounting software options out there, including Quicken (which we use) and Sage 50 (formerly Simply Accounting). But none of them is perfect. Quicken, which we know well because we use it, is a bit awkward for calculating taxes, but very good for messy situations like ours where there is no clearcut line between personal and business accounts. Sage 50 has other limits.

But even with their limitations, these software packages are great simplifiers (once you've done a little self-educating to master them). You can download your bank account into them, including credit card statements and even your line of credit data and the amounts will go straight into a spreadsheet. That considerably reduces the amount of scribbling and fiddling you have to do in a month. Because the software makes it possible to assign a category to each income and expense, it is very easy to make monthly, quarterly and semi-annual calculations and therefore to analyse specific things, such as whether your level of expenditure has increased over a given period.

Bear in mind that accounting software is basically a glorified spreadsheet with colours that handle bank information easily. Any accountant can create a spreadsheet to respond to your exact needs. They will also be able to explain to you how to download data from your financial institution.

In order to make his life easier, Jean-Benoît (who does the data entry) customized out accounting software with a fairly detailed list of categories (see box below) he uses to keep track of expenses and income of different categories and separate deductible from nondeductible expenses for taxes. A custom-made spreadsheet could do the same thing.

Our income categories (for the quick method)

Income

01d-Honorariums

01h-Honorariums

01q-Honorariums

02d-Royalities

02q-Royalities

03d-Conferences

03h-Conferences

03q-Conferences

04q-Consultation

06-Rent

07-Awards

08-Interest

09-Government allowances

10q-Script-writing

11-Gifts

18- GST collected

19-QST collected

Deductible expenses

20-Advertisement

21-Office supplies

22-Telephone, Internet

23-Travel

23p-Personal travel

24-Transportation

24p-Personal transportation

25-Fees, membership

26-Documentation

27-Office insurance

28-Banking charges

28p-Personal banking fees

29-Maintenance

30-Equipment

31-Training

32-Honorariums

33-Conferences

34- Restaurants

34p-Personal restaurants

Car expenses

40d-Car-payments

41-Car-gas

42-Car-maintenance

43-Car-permit

44-Car-insurance

Home office rent costs

50-Rent interest on mortgage

51-Rent-hydro

52-Rent-gas

53-Rent-miscellaneous services

54-Rent-insurance

55-Rent-municipal + school taxes

60-Mortgage payment

61-House-personal

Miscellaneous (personal expenses)

70-Groceries

72-Daycare fees

73-Health expenses

74-Children school + activities

76-Entertainment

77-Personal transport

78-Clothing and beauty

79- Personal care

80-Personal insurance

82-Donations

87-Sports

90-Tax instalments

94-Personal taxes

98-Sales tax

We use numbers 01 to 19 for income. The small letters that follow each number (d, h, q) are for the tax system that applies to each article of income: d is for zero-rated; h is for harmonized tax (13%) and q is for Quebec (including GST and QST). The numbers from 20 to 39 are for deductible expenses. Those with a "p" correspond to the personal (non-deductible) expenses of the same type. Categories of car expenses (e.g. gas, parking, insurance) are between 40 and 45. Categories for deductible expenses for the home office are between 50 and 56; 60 to 65 are for the home. The range of 70 to 89 is used for categories of personal expenses (e.g. groceries, personal care, entertainment). The 90 to 99 numbers are for various categories of taxes paid. Sounds a bit complicated, but once it's rolling it's easy to use and very helpful for seeing at an eye shot how much you spend and where.

Remember that despite its advantages, software is basically just a robot and it's only as good as what you do with it. If you decide to use the detailed method of accounting for GST-PST/HST, you will want to extend these codes to expense categories to automate their compilation. If you don't like ready-made formulas, a good accountant will be able to create a personalized Excel spreadsheet for you that does exactly the same thing as standard software. It really is the same. If you run a business that produces goods, you'll need to separate your expenses into two categories: operations and administration. The first refers to whatever is necessary to produce the good, while the second refers to sales and general administration. This division allows you to better evaluate what proportion of your budget goes to administrative costs and what share goes to production costs. If you are making major investments and need to take your assets and liabilities into account, you should consult an accountant.

Counting your hours

There are all sorts of instruments you can use—some simple, some complex—to measure how productive you are. One of the simplest tools is a clock. To know if you're making good use of your time, you first need to determine how much time you are using to get things done.

It sounds obvious, but people overlook this most basic measure, particularly when they are starting out.

Your first contract will definitely take longer than you expect, or wish. This is normal. It's part of simultaneously learning how to be chief negotiator, customer service manager and chief operating officer of your business. You should start seeing a difference by your second, or maybe third contract, which will already take up less of your precious time to execute. How do you know you are making progress after that? There's only one way: self-employed workers have to keep track of what they are doing and keep statistics on their use of time.

A colleague of ours has been keeping rigorous statistics on how much time he spends doing individual tasks for some twenty years now. He counts every quarter of an hour and documents its use using a code system (like the one we have for our bookkeeping). He even adds up his volunteer time, management time, the time he spends developing ideas and the time he spends doing sales. With these detailed statistics, he can see how his income evolves on an hourly basis—which kind of jobs pay off and which don't. He can evaluate the time required by each contract, set his own rates, set limits on how much time he'll devote to projects and negotiate fees on an objective basis with any client.

A less time-consuming method is to assign a number to each contract and take a few minutes at the end of each week to calculate the amount of time you spend on each project. You can also assign a number to your administrative tasks to help you figure out how much time you spend on them. An even easier method is to separate productive (billable) time from non-billable time (what you spend doing sales, management, in discussions with your banker or haggling with your Internet provider, etc.).

As writers, our work is somewhat divided into "passion projects" and "work that pays." We tend to focus our time-calculating energy on the work we do more specifically to make money, like translation contracts. For the passion projects, it's more a matter of estimating if we have enough money to be able to afford to spend the time we want doing the work. For instance, we have a good idea what kind of book advance we need to be able to survive long enough on it to finish the work. The amount of time spent writing a journalism article can also vary a great deal. Basically, we make sure we are paid enough per word or per page to make this work viable, i.e. not a huge drain on our overall financial performance. But for things like short translations, editing jobs, conferences and any kind on non-journalistic writing, we are more careful about counting our time to make sure it pays off—and whether it's worth continuing to do it for a specific client.

Ratios that speak for themselves

Bookkeeping has other uses beyond just keeping track of bills and paying taxes. It generates information about your overall financial situation. We all know that time is money, but so is information.

If you ever decide to do an MBA, you will definitely do at least one course on "mathematical decision-making." This involves learning a ton of equations and then figuring out which one will enable you to make the right decision in the midst of the chaos of everyday life. But if you don't want to go to business school, there is still simple information available that can help you make decisions about your business. For example, an income statement adds up your monthly, quarterly, semi-annual or annual income, subtracts expenses and shows you your net profit (see the box below for some definitions). Watching these figures and comparing them from year to year, or quarter to quarter, allows you to measure how your business is evolving and decide what needs to be done to make it grow, or remain viable. In order to make the numbers speak, you will need to master eight key concepts.

Eight key concepts in financial jargon

Current assets. Cash or assets that can be sold or converted into cash in less than a year, such as accounts receivable, but also your financial reserves, prepaid accounts and temporary investments.

Long-term assets. What is necessary to carry out your production operations and what you cannot sell without hurting your business. They include both tangible (equipment, machinery, building) and intangible (intellectual property) assets.

Current liabilities. Debts that are due or will become due within the next year. Includes accounts payable, loans, the current portion of long-term debt and taxes payable.

Long-term liabilities. All debts with terms of more than one year—minus the portion of that debt that you have to pay off within the year.

Net assets. The difference between your assets and your liabilities, current or long-term.

Balance sheet. A portrait of a business on a given day. It shows the assets and liabilities. This compilation excludes revenues and expenses (see next).

Income statement. It compiles all revenues and expenses over a given period. The difference between revenue and expenses is the net income (positive or negative) before taxes. This is the number you need to file your income tax return. Assets and liabilities are not included in the income statement (see above).

Financial statements. This includes the income statement, but also the balance sheet. It shows whether you make a profit or suffered a loss, and how this affects your assets.

Over the ages, accountants have come up with dozens of different business analysis models. Different tools are necessary because one ratio can't provide the entire picture of a business. Ratios can even be misleading if you look at them at any given moment, taken out of context. For example, $3,900 in advertising seems enormous for a self-employed worker, but if this figure only represents 1% of total sales of $390,000, it's not unreasonable!

Ratios are the preferred tool for analysing business management. Ratios are most often expressed in fractions or percentages. They are almost always obtained by dividing one number by another. There are about fifty ratios used in business management analysis, linking all sorts of data. The most useful ones are the following:

1. Your *net profit ratio*, which tells you if you are making more profit than you did before and whether your expenses are disproportionate to your total sales. It is established by dividing net profit by total revenues. You can make this calculation monthly, quarterly or at the end of each year. The result varies from one area to another. A journalist, who spends very little on materials, should logically have a higher rate of net profit than, say, a bronze sculptor (unless the journalist has to buy a lot of new equipment and travel extensively in the same year, which happens). But on the whole, you should be able to compare your net profit ratio with that of individuals working in the same field, or with your own ratios from previous years to see how your business is doing. If your net profit ration is going down, you may not be charging enough or you may be losing control of some expenses.

2. The *payback period* is used to determine whether the collection of your accounts is accelerating or slowing down. Take the total of your accounts receivable and divide that by your annual sales figure. The higher the fraction, the more precarious your situation is. This means you will likely run out of money and that your line of credit will be maxed out, or will be soon. Take steps to speed up the payment of bills that are owed to you. If necessary, reread Chapter 17 on bad debts.

3. The *working capital ratio* is a way to predict when you will run out of money. It is calculated by dividing current assets by current liabilities (terms defined in the financial jargon box). A ratio of less than one means that the sum of your liabilities will exceed your cash flow. In short, even though your business may be running in full swing, paying your debts is draining it. So it's probably time to ask clients to pay the money they owe you.

4. The *debt ratio* is used to establish your vulnerability to creditors. You get it by adding up the total of your debts (total liabilities) and dividing this by your total assets (everything you have). The higher the ratio, the more vulnerable you are in the long run. Your working capital ratio may be very good, for instance, but you'll have trouble making your payments over time—maybe because you've borrowed too much. A creditor could then force you to liquidate an important asset, the sale of which would put you at risk. You can correct this situation by injecting more capital (by using some of your RRSPs, for example), by teaming up with a more solvent partner or by increasing sales without increasing your investments.

If you are new to this, these fours radios may seem complicated, but you will soon get an intuitive grasp of them. What's more, they may be all you need to run your business for quite some time.

Remember that it's pointless to only consider any single one of these ratios on its own: you have to look at a number of them together to get the whole picture of how your business is faring. A pilot who navigates on instruments in the middle of the night has to constantly watch the altimeter, the trim indicator and the compass. If they ignore a single one of these, their plane will probably crash. So, when you start making ratios, make several at the same time. Otherwise, you might crash too.

Also, when one of your ratios is cause for worry, analyse it. Let's take the simplest ratio, that of the net profit ratio. If it drops from 65% to 50%, you should be concerned. But what caused the drop? Was it because your sales decreased (while your expenses remained the same)? Or because your expenses increased because of an investment you made in a new (and necessary) piece of equipment? The two situations do not have the same long-term consequences, nor do they call for the same corrective actions.

As you can see, it's good to make your numbers talks, but don't expect them to give you all the answers. For that, you need to employ some good old-fashioned human judgment and some plain old common sense.

22

To insure or not to insure

How to make sure you're properly covered

Myth # 22: "Insurance is too expensive."

It's fair to say that French war correspondent Paul M. Marchand (1961–2009) was addicted to risk. He started his career in Beirut, then moved on to Sarajevo at the height of the Bosnian war in the 1990s. Feeling invincible, he drove a Ford Sierra with "Don't waste your bullets. I am immortal," scrawled on the back trunk. One morning, a sniper fired a shot straight into Marchand's hand. It was not pretty: bones shattered, massive haemorrhaging. The authorities transfered him to France, where doctors managed to save his hand for the handy sum of one million francs ($175,000). The problem? As a freelancer, Marchand wasn't insured. He had assumed his clients automatically covered him for the kind of risks he was obviously taking on their behalf. He wasn't and none of his clients would reimburse him for the surgery.

When it comes to insurance, self-employed workers need to remember that life is a kind of movie stunt that always ends badly. Even if you work in front of a computer and the biggest risk of your day involves walking your cat, you should still consider getting insurance. Ordinary working folk like us are bound to get sick or injured, sometimes on the job, sometimes in the comfort of your own homes, or just by getting rear-ended driving home from a gig. It happens to the safest of drivers.

However, when it comes to insurance, whether professional or otherwise, self-employed workers are in a less advantageous position than, say, unionized employees are. Still, there have been considerable improvements over the past decades in private policies on the market and government coverage.

In the early 1990s, when we started out, it was hard to find income replacement insurance. The few office insurance plans that were on the market invariably excluded self-employed workers. Things are much better now mostly because more companies have caught up with the times and the reality of the labour force and now offer different types of insurance.

Understanding risk

You probably think insurance is terribly expensive and you're not entirely wrong. It's not cheap. But having no insurance can end up costing you a lot more. Your tolerance for risk is also a factor to consider: it might be worth spending money for some peace of mind up to a point. Luckily, there are some fairly objective ways to figure out what kind of insurance you need, how much is enough and how much is too much.

The key to the puzzle is understanding risk.

Jean-Benoît's grandfather Joseph was not a rich farmer but nevertheless made the strange decision to take out life insurance for his ten children (which was strange because the children didn't contribute to the family income, so while losing one would be emotionally devastating, it would not hurt the family's finances). On the other hand, Grandpa Joseph didn't bother to insure his house, which then burned down. What was Grandpa Joseph thinking? He wasn't. He appears to have been overly sentimental and wanted to insure the things that were the most precious to him.

What we're saying is, the decision to buy insurance should not be guided by "feelings." It should be determined by risk assessment. According to Grandpa Joseph's (poor) financial reasoning, the only way to be compensated for his house burning down was if his children died in the fire—which fortunately wasn't the case. We don't feel good recalling Jean-Benoît's grandfather in these terms, but there's no getting around the fact that his insurance purchases were idiotic—especially given how much more likely it was that he would lose his house than all his children.

Since insurance covers risk, the first thing you need to do is decide if there really is a risk. As a mathematician friend explained to us, risk is probability multiplied by cost. For example, it is quite likely we will break an arm or a leg in life (Julie has already broken a number of bones). The probability is high. However, what's the cost of breaking an arm or leg? In Canada, where everyone has universal health insurance, broken bones don't have a price tag, at least not a direct one. The cost in most cases is a few days or work lost and some discomfort. What's more, for people like us who spend most of their day sitting in front of a computer, even the risk of loss of work because of a broken bone is relatively low. The cost is even lower when you are young (when she was fourteen, Julie spent two weeks in a coma and two months in the hospital and still managed to finish Grade 9). Even today, we could still work in wheelchairs if we had to. If we broke an arm or injured a hand, we'd have to type with one hand for a month, so our productivity would decline. But is that enough of a risk to merit taking out insurance to cover arm injuries? Definitely not. Low cost means the probability, though relatively high, is not worth insuring. The question, of course, would be quite different if we were professional pianists or guitarist and the use of our fine motor skills in both hands was critical to our ability to earn a living.

So, what situations have a high cost, then? Let's look at an extreme case. Say a giant asteroid crashed into Earth and destroyed all civilization. The cost would be quite high indeed. But it is quite unlikely that many people would survive, including our insurer. From the perspective of this example, although the cost associated with this risk is enormous, the probability is so low that the overall risk is really zero.

We can also look at cost from another angle. Jean-Benoît's grandfather was not entirely crazy to insure some of his children at a time when children worked on farms and contributed to its profitability. Given the rate of child mortality of the time, there was a high probability he would lose one. But the likelihood of losing them all was very small. Given that the youngest were obviously much less productive than their older siblings, maybe it would have made sense to insure the older children. But insuring the house should have been a no-brainer. The cost of rebuilding a house was enormous and the probability of losing a wooden house in a fire was high. In short, he should have insured his house rather than his children.

Moreover, if you have property that is irreplaceable and precious, the best insurance in the world will probably not be as useful as a good safe, or even a good vault. Those will undoubtedly cost less than buying insurance, which would require you to put everything in a safe anyway!

In other words, you need to weigh probability versus cost to assess risk before you come to a decision to get insurance.

Take note that the cost of probability is measurable—insurance companies base their fees on hard numbers of likelihood. You should consider thinking the numbers through for yourself. Jean-Benoît's life insurance company offered him a "special" one time: for a 10% increase in his premium, they would cover up to $100,000 more in the event of his accidental death. It seemed like a good deal: he would pay 10% more and the policy would increase his coverage by 20%. But that got us thinking about the insurance company's motives. Why would they offer 20% more for an additional cost of only 10%? The key was in the probability of an accidental death. In our entire circle of professional and personal acquaintances, we only know of one person who has died in an accident. We checked with Statistics Canada and it turns out that only about 4% of deaths in Canada are accidental. And for people doing office work, like us, the probability is even lower. Aha! That's why the insurer could afford to offer this juicy increase in coverage! However, the low probability of Jean-Benoît (or Julie) dying accidentally made the deal suddenly look a lot less interesting: we would pay 10% more to insure against something that only had a 4% chance of happening. It wasn't worth the cost.

Your decision about what to insure and for how much will be made through different processes of reasoning depending on whether you are buying personal or professional insurance. Personal insurance should be taken out as early as possible in life, preferably at a fixed rate for a long period so the price will be affordable in the long term (the price charged tends to rise with the age of the applicant). General insurance, such as office insurance, on the other hand, should be taken out as late as possible, only when your business is established and you have something to lose.

The only nuance we would add here is: get insurance before something goes wrong. Like banks who refuse to loan money to people who have no property for collateral, insurance companies are not going to give you a good price when you are in the middle of cancer treatment. (If we return to the risk equation of cost and probability, the fact that you already have cancer raises the probability to 100%.) The insurer only offers decently priced policies to people who are young and in reasonably good health. All of which is to say, take out your insurance before you start having problems. Unfortunately, this is not when people are most likely to be thinking of insurance.

An insurance company is basically a legal betting scheme. The actuaries who work there use a battery of equations to evaluate different risks. And they use a battery of questions to make their bet on insuring you or your property is a sure one. Who can blame them? If you were trading horses for a living, you would do the same thing. It's not nice, it's business. A life insurer bets on your life; a health insurer bets on your health; a home insurer bets on your home. Their questions are designed to figure out whether or not you are a good bet. And then there are plain old probabilities that have nothing to do with you. Maybe you take good care of your home, but if your roof is more than twenty years old, the statistics say it's more likely to leak. You might walk systematically for an hour a day, but if you keep smoking after forty, the statistics say you won't live as long. You might know some smokers who lived long lives, but there are more who don't.

Group insurance is cheaper for the simple reason that the risk is spread over many people. Self-employed people do not qualify for most group insurance. But many self-employment groups and professional associations offer their members insurance packages through outside brokers or agents and these usually have competitive rates. These offers are generally worth considering and are often your best option, particularly when you are starting out. However, in the long run these offers may not fit your situation precisely, especially if your business does well. So you should be on the lookout for something better.

We recommend doing business with a good insurance broker to help you make the right choices. We got ours through a professional reference and have never regretted it. There are a lot of different types of insurance out there and a broker can help you weed through them, but also help you understand nuances you might otherwise miss.

Two important questions to consider

■ Agent or broker?

Agents mainly sell the products of the company they represent. The most autonomous of them can sell products of other companies when their own company does not sell a competing product. Brokers are less common. Since they are independent of any insurance company, they are able to compare insurance products. They can help you make the best choice between different companies. There are good agents and there are bad brokers, but generally speaking, a good broker is more independent.

■ Is the policy guaranteed?

A guaranteed policy is always more expensive because the insurer, when signing the contract, has verified that you are eligible, insurable and that your statements were accurate. In the event of a claim, the company offering this policy will not dispute your state of health at the time of signing (twelve years earlier) nor start asking you how much you were earning at the time of the claim. The guaranteed policy insures a pre-agreed, non-negotiable amount. The non-guaranteed policy is cheaper because the insurer promises you a certain amount of coverage based on your statements. When you ask for compensation, the insurer will then proceed to fact-check information you gave a year or twenty years ago. Among other things, for wage-loss insurance, it will ask you for your income at the time of the claim. If you earn less than the amount originally purchased, coverage will be adjusted to your current income, which may be a disadvantage if your income has recently decreased.

Insuring yourself: Seven options

We've organized this chapter into personal insurance and equipment insurance and arranged them in order of usefulness. As you'll see, our definition of equipment includes anything that doesn't affect you personally. (To see whether the premiums paid for these insurances are deductible, go back to Chapter 18, where we discuss tax deductions.)

1. **Salary or disability insurance.** This protects your income in the event of illness, disability, temporary or permanent. It is the most important insurance self-employed workers can take out. According to statistics, one in three Canadians will suffer a six-month disability before the age of sixty-five. Note that this type of insurance does not cover time off during pregnancy or after childbirth, except in the case of complications that would make you unable to work. Parental leave benefits—which have been available to self-employed persons in Canada since January 2006—will cover you for this (we discuss those in the next chapter).

   For a non-smoker under the age of thirty, a salary or disability policy will cost less than if you are a sixty-two-year-old smoker. So it's in your best interest to take out this type of insurance as early as possible in your career. Getting approval for a guaranteed (and therefore verified) policy, not surprisingly, is a long and involved process: the insurance company is betting on your health over a period of forty years. If you have a choice, always opt for the non-cancellable contract that is guaranteed renewable. The premium will be fixed with no conditions. A good company that insures your salary will not cancel your payments after two years of disability, even if you are able to do another type of work. Nor will it challenge your status as an insured person, even if you were on social assistance at the time of the accident or illness, as long as you have paid your premiums.

If possible, choose a standard salary insurance policy for the payment of which an insurer won't ask you whether the disabling action took place at work or not.

Workers' compensation: An option to consider

One alternative to private disability insurance for your salary is subscribing to your provincial Workers Compensation Board by paying the employer's contribution (you are the employer). This is not mandatory for self-employed workers unless you practise a specific trade or profession, like construction workers.

WCB insurance has the advantage of costing much less than private insurance and will pay up to 90% of your salary from the first day of your absence. In addition, the insurance lasts as long as you subscribe to it. If your problems recur frequently, you will remain eligible—except that if the same problem occurs too often, an inspector will show up to see whether you are deliberately injuring yourself.

This insurance is only valid for work-related disabilities, so it would be difficult to convince an agent that your lawnmower exploded and scarred you while you were talking on the phone with a client. On the other hand, you could easily have caught pneumonia while inspecting electricity towers, if that is your line of work.

2. **Health insurance.** Always expensive, this insurance reimburses all or part of the cost of medication (in Quebec, it reimburses what is not covered by the government drug insurance) and various services like chiropractic treatment, prosthetics and convalescent homes. Dental care is optional, but this part of the premium is particularly expensive and the insurance company may require a contract for a minimum of three years.

   We had extended health insurance for many years but recently decided to drop it. We added up what we were spending on our health insurance premiums and compared it to the actual cost of the services our insurance was reimbursing us for, partially or entirely. We mainly used the insurance to cover physiotherapy and an occasional MRI. But even in a "bad" year the amount we spent for these services didn't come close to what we were paying for insurance to cover them, so we dropped the policy. We understood that insecurity was driving our desire for insurance, not actual risk. We feared disaster and thought having insurance would somehow stave it off. But when we stepped back and thought carefully about it, all of the real costs of a "disaster" (hospitalization) would be covered by the public system, anyway. We also realized that the travel insurance part of the health insurance was not nearly as good as the one offered by our credit card company (for free).

3. **Critical illness insurance.** This can be a supplement to, or substitute for standard health insurance. It gives you a lump sum—$75,000, $100,000 or $150,000—in case you have one of ten or twenty serious illnesses, like cancer, a heart attack or stroke, defined in the contract. The amount is paid to you immediately after diagnosis. You can then use the money to get any type of care you deem necessary, depending on whether the condition is chronic, or requires treatment in a special clinic. This insurance costs less than health insurance, but it can be a good lifeline. If the coverage in your disability insurance seems low, this insurance can become an interesting complement. On the other hand, it is worth researching whether you have a real chance of being affected by the illnesses that are the subject of the contract. For example, the probability of heart disease is as high as cancer. If your

insurer covers some types of cancer, but excludes others, the policy becomes much less interesting.

4. **Travel insurance.** This makes sense for self-employed workers who have to leave the country, or even the province on a regular basis for work, personal business or holidays. You might want to check the rules of coverage of your province before purchasing this. Permanent travel insurance, which covers any trip of less than fourteen days without notice, might be included in your health insurance policy. However, your credit card also might include thirty-day travel insurance. Check the fine print and make sure you understand the rules of this. For instance, some companies insure you for more than ninety days of travel per year, but never for stays of more than fifteen days at a time. Always check the exclusions, especially if you travel to places that are the least bit risky. For example, in 2004, we travelled to Israel while doing research for a book and we were covered, but our insurer made it clear that we wouldn't be covered for any risk in the occupied territories (considered to be in a situation of permanent low-grade rebellion). Regardless of the territory or travel insurance, you will not be insured if you participate in a war, riot or rebellion anywhere. And even if you are going to a country considered relatively low risk, such as Mexico, make sure your salary and travel insurance cover all parts of the country, or at least all the parts you'll visit. Insurers read the news, too.

5. **Life insurance.** This will cost you about $200 a year for $75,000 coverage in case of death. Of course, you can pay more for higher coverage. Life insurance also includes optional clauses in case of mutilation. But paying for life insurance is pointless if you don't have anyone who depends on you. You don't need it if your children or your spouse are not dependent on you to meet their needs, or if you have salary insurance that protects you in case of a disabling injury. If you plan to have children after the age of thirty and they will be dependent on you until you're old enough to retire, it may pay off to take out fixed-rate life insurance early.

6. **High-risk insurance.** This was what our war reporter Paul M. Marchand really needed. If you are doing contract work for an NGO in Haiti or if you are a supplier of drone equipment in Ukraine, it is

necessary. This insurance will cover you in situations where all other policies become void, such as an act of God, a rebellion or a war. Not surprisingly, this insurance costs an arm and a leg—at least several thousand dollars per year. The client who sends you to work under these conditions should compensate you for the risks they are asking you to take. They often pay for the insurance themselves, but don't make the mistake Paul Marchand made. Check before you leave.

7. **Mortgage insurance.** This is without a doubt the dumbest insurance scheme on earth. It's so dumb it's surprising that governments even allow it. Mortgage insurance is a form of life insurance that covers the outstanding value of your mortgage. Most people take this insurance out because it seems like a bargain for what it covers. But consider this before you open your wallet: as time goes by, the probability of your death increases while the amount of mortgage payment this insurance covers *decreases* (because you've been paying your mortgage off all those years). The more you pay, the less you're covered, and yet the insurance premium stays the same. It's truly the insurance racket of the century. Temporary life insurance for the duration of your mortgage is a better idea: the premiums will be higher, but at least you'll be insured for the full amount, even as time passes. It also makes more sense, when you think about it, since you're more likely to die with age.

Employment insurance: An affordable option

Since January 31, 2010, self-employed workers in Canada have had the option of taking out EI on a voluntary basis. But this insurance does not cover you in the event of "unemployment." The list of what is covered is actually quite limited:

- Maternity benefits: Fifteen weeks
- Parental benefits: Thirty-five weeks
- Inability to work for medical reasons: Fifteen weeks
- Compassionate care: Twenty-six weeks

- Family caregiver for children: Thirty-five weeks
- Family caregiver for adults: Fifteen weeks

In 2022, the maximum weekly payment was $638/week. It is not the El Dorado, at least not for self-employed workers in Quebec who are already covered for the first two cases. But it could fill in for disability insurance. The main advantage is that the periods covered can be repeated several times during your working life, a bit like parental leave, which does not have a fixed limit on how many times you can use it.

However, if you earn relatively little, EI has the advantage of being cheap. For Canadians (excluding Quebeckers), you pay $1.58 per $100 earned, capped at a maximum (in 2022) of $952.74 per year. For Quebecers (who have maternity and parental benefits through their own provincial scheme) the amount is $1.18 per $100 of income, to a maximum of $664.34 per year. But Employment Insurance comes with strings: if you sign up, you will have to subscribe to it throughout your career as a self-employed person. There's only one loophole: you can opt out if you have never claimed benefits.

There are also all sorts of conditions for qualifying. There is a fixed annual income as a self-employed worker that you must exceed: in 2021 this was $7,555, but was lowered to $5,289 in 2022. You must provide a medical certificate for yourself, or for a loved one to "provide medical proof showing that a seriously ill family member needs your care or support." You can earn some income during the benefit period, but there are all sorts of limits on this and it will reduce your benefits, even if you receive income that was billed long before the claim. In short, this insurance is really a last-resort wage or disability insurance for people who are not otherwise insurable.

For full details about this insurance, see the "Employment Insurance Special Benefits for the Self-Employed" section of the Service Canada website.

Insuring your tools: Six options

1. **Car insurance.** This is compulsory. However, it costs more to insure your car for commercial use. Many self-employed workers save money by taking out non-commercial auto insurance, but then you have to be careful not to get caught in the event of a work-related accident. If you use your car a lot for your business (we don't), you should consider getting commercial insurance.

2. **Home insurance.** It's not mandatory, but we regard it as essential, especially if your office is in your home. However, it might be a good idea to add home office insurance to it (see next point). Ask your broker about this. If you are a tenant, you should be aware that your landlord's insurance will not cover any losses that are related to your business.

3. **Office insurance.** For an office that occupies about 20% of our living space, office insurance costs us 20% of the home insurance. This is more than fair when you consider that the office insurance also cover the costs of running an office, which are often excluded from home insurance—including things such as accounts payable, but also loss of income, overhead, business interruption—in addition to compensating you for moving and office reorganization. It can also allow you to set up a temporary office in a few hours.

   Since policies vary considerably from one insurer to another, don't try to save money by taking out bargain home insurance with one company and bargain office insurance with another. These policies may not match, which means you find yourself in the crossfire between two competing insurers squabbling over "who should pay for what" when your business computer overheats and burns down your house.

   Some office insurance policies will cover your equipment if you're on a business trip, even if you spill coffee on a client's computer. However, make sure you check the territories that are covered. Some companies only cover North America (as if it were riskier for your computer to be in Europe?) If you find yourself in this situation and you have a problem in Europe, your home (not office) insurance will cover you, as long as you are just a tourist (through your home insurance).

If you opt against taking out office insurance for your home office and you make a claim, your insurer may refuse to pay out if they find out that you are using the room where the incident occurred to earn income of any amount. The insurer will react by concluding—unfairly, but justifiably—that you should have taken out office insurance. We decided a long time ago that we might as well just pay a little more for office insurance and go to bed not worrying whether an electrical problem will ruin us.

Naturally, if you have a home office full of sophisticated telecommunications equipment for which you are claiming compensation from your home insurance, your insurer may rightly wonder what these things are doing in a home (even though, of course, ordinary homes do have a lot of sophisticated audio-visual equipment these days). The same logic will apply to musical instruments: home insurance will cover them, as long as you don't say that you are using them for commercial activities. In the case of expensive musical instruments or tools, you may need to take out specific insurance (see next point).

4. **Equipment insurance.** This is necessary if your office, trade, craft or art requires a lot of sophisticated specialized appliances, instruments, machines or tools in it. However, if you only have one piece of equipment (like a computer), this insurance may be unnecessary and more expensive than it's worth. Be especially wary of insurance offered by distributors or manufacturers. A few years ago, Apple offered us a three-year insurance plan worth $100 per year for an $800 printer. That's $300 in insurance. We stopped and thought about it for a second. The most expensive part that breaks—and it rarely breaks—would only cost us $350 to replace. Manufacturers make huge profits cashing in on consumers' insecurity by getting them to pay in advance for repairs that they probably won't need within the insurance period, anyway.

5. **Third party and professional liability insurance.** This protects you in the event of a professional mistake that results in damage (e.g. the bridge that you designed falls down). This kind of insurance, which is mandatory for engineers, lawyers and doctors, is prohibitively expensive: around $5,000 a year. When we were starting out

as journalists, we considered getting professional insurance to protect us from libel suits. It would have cost us $7,000 a year. We decided against it because we just couldn't afford it. Sure enough, over our thirty-five years in the business, we've heard from plenty of unhappy readers but no one has ever threatened to sue us for libel, not even once. So we figure we saved $175,000 by not getting libel insurance. Being cautious turned out to be the best insurance policy.

That said, a client or financier may require you to have professional liability protection as a condition for doing business with you, particularly if you work in the United States. Americans are quick off the block when it comes to threatening lawsuits. If you opt for this insurance, don't forget to factor the additional cost of it into your fees.

6. **Special risk insurance.** This is the kind of insurance that a film producer takes out on a major player in case the latter is unable to play the lead role due to illness. Actors can also insure themselves for acne, and pianists for their hands and fingers. You can also insure the life of a particularly profitable or productive associate—also a classic plot twist in a murder mystery.

Remember: risk = probability multiplied by cost.

23

Time off

Why it's important to take breaks and how to make sure you do

Myth # 23: "I can't afford to take time off."

If you want to last, you have to pace yourself. If you won't take our word for it, then listen to public health experts who agree that the reason people live longer today than they did a century ago is not just that we are cleaner, eat better and have better health care. It's because we don't do as much physical labour and take holidays and weekend breaks.

So far, we've talked a lot about how to work. Now we're going to talk about how to not work. If you want your self-employed career to last, you have to know how to stop, take vacations and relax. Of course, the same is true for permanent employees. However, when it comes to taking holidays and relaxing, the self-employed workers have a special set of obstacles, both material and psychological, that they have to overcome.

Talent and energy, alone, do not guarantee long-term success in your chosen field. You also have to stay healthy, eat well, sleep enough and know how to unplug from work. There's no way around this. People who cut corners here pay later. It happens all the time. Talented self-employed workers forget the basic rules, mostly out of insecurity. They think the only way to succeed is to work more. Of course, beginners do have to work harder to acquire skills, but one of those skills is learning when to stop. Self-employed workers need to learn to set their limits early on, or they risk fizzling out fast. There's no better excuse for customers to take advantage of you than assuming you're "always on."

If you are the type of person who believes freedom means the right to work more, then you *really* need to keep reading.

Setting your own policies about vacations is a good start. We've always worked hard, but we rarely work evenings or weekends, only when it's really necessary. Carefully delineating time on and time off is part of our routine. Occasionally we have to dip into the "down time" to finish a project or meet a deadline but we have always been careful not to let it become a habit or a lifestyle.

First, a basic truth: when you work from home, it's hard to stop working. There's only a door separating you from the office and no one else is there to lock it. Employees who work in offices get into their car, a bus, subway or onto their bike at the end of the day. The only thing many self-employed workers do at the end of the day is close a door, so you have to use some imagination in order to feel like you are really "leaving the office." That starts with rituals that replace the transport ritual: take a bath or grab a book, go for a run, crack open a beer, pour yourself a glass of wine. Since we are parents, we generally finish the day by filling the dishwasher and starting dinner. But since only one of us cooks at a time, whoever is not cooking has to do something else to mark the end of office hours. Julie, for instance, plays the piano for a few minutes. It helps her switch gears, takes her mind elsewhere (of course, we love reading, but picking up a magazine, unfortunately, takes us straight back to work).

As we said above, one of the main reasons that freelancers fail to unplug is insecurity. Beginners almost always take on too much work because they think that if they stop working, they will run out of work. You need to learn to embrace the slow times, even savour them. They are a great opportunity to read and get on top of filing, paperwork or bookkeeping. We often get great ideas for new projects during these little interludes. Your brain is more creative when it is not focused on a stressful task, but, rather, "floating" (that's how we refer to these moments).

The tricky part for self-employed workers is that we have no authority figure or peers to dictate when to work and when not to. We don't have preset holidays, no official office hours (after which the office doors are locked) and no scheduled weekend. This is why it is so important to learn to say no. You shouldn't be working your heart out on Boxing Day (or any statutory holiday for that matter). Your client probably isn't working and probably doesn't expect you to, either. If they do expect you to work after hours, you should at least ask them why. Sure, you can make occasional exceptions for something that is really worth the trouble. But on the whole, if you can't muster the strength to say no when enough is enough, you will end up paying for it with your health and your social and family connections down the line. Ask yourself: is it worthwhile killing myself in order to live better? The answer, as you can see, is in the question.

One great reason for not working too much is being able to spend time with those closest to you; spouses, parents, siblings, kids, nieces, nephews, close friends. But even if you are a relative loner, you still need to take downtime. A coal furnace actually runs more efficiently if it never stops, but not humans. We need a lot of down time for maintenance, both physical and mental. We have to stop to eat, exercise, daydream, read, watch TV and sometimes, just do nothing.

You have to get over the idea that taking a holiday will hurt your business. It won't. But you may have to compromise on the timing. The best time to take time off, is when business is slow. Almost every business has a season that is a little (or a lot) slower than others.

On the other hand, there is no universal recipe for what makes a great holiday. Everyone should take the holidays they need. Jean-Benoît is often tired of being on holiday after about ten days. However, he has taken three full weeks when he was really worn down and didn't regret it. Julie is usually ready to head home after two weeks but there have been exceptions as well. When our daughters were preschoolers, we once spent an entire month with them in France. It was a situation where we were mixing business and pleasure: Julie took advantage of being there to do some book research and interviews for a food article she was working on. That also helped cover our expenses. Being self-employed allows you to come up with creative ways to do what you want to do.

Some self-employed people manage to accumulate enough surplus over the course of the year to take extended periods off, but normally in those cases there is more to the destination than just holidays (like our month-long trip to France). Or they just take their work with them (which we've also done).

Making the financial wiggle room

That raises the question of how to afford holidays when they aren't "paid for" by an employer. There's a good trick: build up a surplus of money to pay for time off. This is where the "10% profit" on your hourly rate comes in handy. If you already take 25% of each cheque you receive for taxes, why not add another 5% or 10% for holidays? You can put the amount straight into a TSFA to make sure you don't spend it on a new kitchen floor instead. To do this, you must remove the money immediately and systematically for each payment as soon as you receive it. If you wait, the money will be gone before you get a chance to redirect it to your vacation account.

You don't need make a budget to save money for holidays. We have tried to do this a few times and just found it complicated and hard to stick to. Our advice it to just make up your mind not to touch the amount you set aside except to pay for holidays or cover emergencies. It requires a bit of discipline but you get used to it. We find we can generally get by fine on what's left after skimming our cheques this way. To be honest, we don't even think about it anymore.

The real obstacle to taking holidays, in our experience, is not money, but time and other responsibilities. Every week of holidays has to be made up, somehow. So for self-employed workers who can't pass responsibilities on to anyone else, this means doing additional work before and after holidays to make up for lost time. If it's any consolation, from what we have observed, conscientious salaried employees have the same challenge before they leave for holidays and when they get back. Deadlines are deadlines, and clients are clients. Whether you work for yourself or someone else doesn't change things. The difference is just that self-employed workers never have the option of passing work off to colleagues—although we have occasionally found another freelancer to take a contract we can't do because we'll be away. We generally prefer doing extra work before our holidays so we don't undo the benefits of taking holidays by having to tackle an insurmountable pile of work on our day back, or during the holiday.

Whatever formula you choose, there's no getting around the fact that you have to prepare for holidays. When you leave, your accountant, president, the sales team and credit manager (they're all you!) leave too. There will be no one left to collect your accounts receivable while you're gone, no one to call new prospects, no one to cash cheques. Some of these things can be managed with automatic payments. And honestly, customers are more understanding than we generally think they are. They take holidays too. And if you're good, they won't forget you after two weeks. They will want to keep doing business with you. If you have an accounts payable schedule, it will be easy to anticipate what's coming, even over long periods of time and pay everything in advance.

Parental leave

Self-employed workers in Canada who have registered for EI are eligible to receive benefits for parental leave. In this case, they have two options: they can take standard or extended leave. Standard leave is for thirty-five weeks within a fifty-two-week (one year) period; extended leave covers sixty-one weeks within a seventy-eight-week (eighteen months) period. For standard leave, you can receive 55% of your declared income up to a maximum of $595 per week. The maximum insurable earnings you can use for this is $56,300 (2021). For extended leave, you receive 33% of your income up to a maximum of $537 per week. This leave will not work as a last-minute solution in case of a surprise pregnancy: you will have to wait twelve months from the time of your confirmed registration before applying for EI benefits of any type.

Quebec has the benefit of offering distinct parental insurance separate from EI. Self-employed workers have been eligible for it since 2006 (the very year we adopted our twin girls!) It is more generous than what EI offers, both for the number of weeks covered and the amounts paid.

All parents are eligible and it's covered by taxes so there is no special contribution involved.

When failure looms

It happens to us all. Projects don't get off the ground. Circumstances change and it is possible that something that was working just fine suddenly stops working.

In some cases, you imperceptibly sink yourself deeper and deeper every year without realizing it, until it's too late. In some cases, you may actually have to declare bankruptcy in order to get on with things.

If you find yourself in that situation, don't feel ashamed (yes, we know, that's *much* easier said than done). But it actually did happen to a close friend of ours. We'll call her Sylvie. After working twenty-five years as a self-employed creator, she was forced to declare bankruptcy. Sylvie worked in a sector that was literally replaced by robots and offshoring a lot of work, so her business had been declining steadily for seven or eight years by that time. Unfortunately, she racked up an income tax debt in the interim. Despite of her best efforts, she just couldn't figure out how to make the business turn a profit.

At the advice of a local financial aid association, she went to see a bankruptcy trustee. The representative there asked her a series of questions. He then told her to stop kicking herself about it. He assured her she had done everything humanly possible to try to save her business and that the reason the Bankruptcy and Insolvency Act exists is to give people a shot at getting the upper hand on things quickly when things are going badly, instead of dragging their plight on pointlessly for years.

So Sylvie went ahead and declared bankruptcy. The main challenge immediately after that was that she had to make do for a few years without having access to credit. But she found a job quickly and still works on contracts in her field one day a week, for a little extra money (and satisfaction).

What impressed us the most about Sylvie was how Zen she was about the whole thing once she made the decision to just declare bankruptcy and then get on with her life. She had lost a lot of sleep in the months leading up to the decision and was relieved just to be moving on. Sylvie even managed to adopt a healthy attitude about the whole experience.

We've never had to declare bankruptcy, but we have had our share of bad years, projects that never got off the ground after we had invested a lot of time and money in them and what we'd call "half-successes" (in a way, worse than failures because we have to carry on with something that didn't turn out the way we expected it to). But the truth is, some of our most spectacular successes came after equally spectacular failures. It took us almost a year to sell our first book together, during which time we ate a lot of frozen pizza. When we finally got a book contract, the advance was pitifully low. Then it became a bestseller. Over the years we have learned to get over things quickly and not to dwell on setbacks.

Money for a rainy day

As we explained in Chapters 20 and 21, managing your business should include getting into the habit of putting a percentage of your income into special accounts or funds. That serves to pay for holidays and works as an emergency fund, or savings for retirement, as well.

To build up a holiday fund or safety cushion, again, withdraw certain amounts or percentages of your income every month and put them in a holiday fund somewhere. These amounts don't have to be huge: if you set aside $50 a week for holidays, you will have $2,600 at the end of the year. That's $2,600 less to pay on your credit card when you buy airline tickets or reserve hotels.

The important thing to do is put systems in place to make sure the money comes out of your operating funds and goes into savings of some sort. One idea is to open a fourth account in a mutual fund, where you place savings above a certain threshold, say $3,000. The return will be better, but more importantly, it will be harder to withdraw funds on impulse. You may have to wait a few days to get them. That will give you some time to mull over whether you really want to withdraw the money or not.

Financial advisors recommend having a savings "cushion" worth three months of income. But it's not easy to get there. Financial advisors tend to push the importance of building your savings. However, we find it best not to push too hard. Sometimes it's more important for your business to spend, say, on developing a new project than it is to build your personal savings. In our experience, people who save at all costs usually do so because they want to retire early, or earlier than normal. But early retirement does not have to be your goal. It's not ours. We love our work and want to keep doing it for as many as years possible.

But, of course, you still have to save money to retire. It catches up with all of us eventually (or hopefully, anyway). In the popular book The Wealthy Barber, author David Chilton advises readers to systematically put aside 10% of their income. Per week, per month, you wonder? Doesn't matter. It's all the same. The simplest thing is to put aside 10% of everything that comes in, as soon as it comes in. If 10% is too much for you, start with 5% or even 3%. The most important thing, according to Chilton—and we agree—is to not put it off. When you collect a client's money, take some out of your pay and put it into your savings right away. Once you're into the habit, you may find that going from 3% to 5%, and then 8% is easier than you thought.

Should I make a budget, you might ask? If you want, but it's not really necessary. We've never made a budget and probably never will. That's because we use the "wealthy barber" system. We set aside a planned amount, make do with the rest and deal with unexpected circumstances with our savings. When expenses pile up, we slap a moratorium on credit cards. We just don't use them. (It's amazing how much we use credit cards for things we really don't need!) That usually gives us time to get back on top of things and figure out where we were going wrong. It's really, really, not rocket science.

Use your credit well

Although financial planners are uniformly opposed to acquiring debt, owing money can be a good thing if it produces a desired result. Just think of student loans or mortgages.

When you think about it, any form of credit amounts to "reversed savings." Instead of saving all your life for a house for which—by the end of your life—you will have no use, credit allows you to borrow to buy the house, pay for it as you use it and then keep using is after it's paid for. The difference is that instead of receiving interest on your savings, you pay interest on your loan for a higher premium.

There are all sorts of forms of credit; mortgages, credit lines, credit cards and personal loans, to name but a few. Each has a separate cost but they all allow you to get something for which you will pay later (at extra cost). The financial validity of taking a loan depends on your capacity to repay (and you need discipline to do that) and the interest accrued. But more importantly, it depends on your purposes and whether what you gain will repay the debt.

So, borrowing to pay for a good holiday (provided it's affordable), or some training, or your RRSP or to take six months off to develop a new project, might make a lot of sense. As long as you can pay back the loan or live with the consequences if things don't turn out as expected.

The retirement question

But, of course, it's still important to save for the long-term, what most people call retirement. We use the word figuratively, since we hope we'll be able to keep working well into our Golden Years. If we were lumberjacks, or Pilates instructors, we might look at the situation differently, but for writers, getting physically older isn't really a problem. Besides, many people dream of publishing a book when they retire. At some point, of course, we'll probably stop working "for money." And to enjoy our last years at their fullest, we recognize we'll probably want more resources at our disposal than what the government provides. That's why we've been putting money into RRSPs since we were in our early 20s. Self-employed workers are wise to start this when they're young, ideally before they have too many other financial obligations (e.g. children's braces, windows to change) that interfere with saving.

For that matter, you should try to use your RRSP benefits to their fullest—meaning both the tax deduction and the actual savings. Unfortunately, when it comes to RRSPs, self-employed workers are at a certain disadvantage, again, with respect to employees. The maximum contribution limit for RRSPs is based on your net income. An employee who earns $50,000 can invest 18% of this amount, i.e. $9,000. But a freelancer with a turnover of $50,000 and expenses of $20,000 has a lower taxable income (in this case, $30,000) and as a result, can only put a maximum of $5,600 into an RRSP (18% of $30,000). That's the downside to declaring expenses in order to lower your net (taxable) income. It's also a good reason to go easy on the deductions. (On the other hand, do you know any employees who earn $50,000 and actually invest $9,000 a year of that in a retirement fund? Probably not.)

At any rate, as we've said, for self-employed workers, the secret to saving for retirement is quite simple: start early. Mr Early puts $2,500 a year into an RRSP between the ages of nineteen and twenty-seven. He therefore contributes a total of $22,500 before the age of twenty-seven. Meanwhile, Ms Late starts contributing the same amount to her RRSP, $2,500 per year, but only starts at age twenty-eight. She continues to contribute this amount (at 9% rate, like Mr Early) until she is sixty-five. In total, Ms Late will have contributed $95,000 over the course of her working life. That's four times more than Mr Early contributed. Who comes out ahead? It depends a bit on their investment strategy and rate of return, but if we suppose that they both get 9% per year, by the time they retire, Mr Early will have $940,000 (for an original investment of $22,500) while Ms Late will only have $770,000. Yes, Mr Early has $160,000 more! The explanation? It's the miracle of compound interest. At a 9% return, Mr Early's annual interest at age 28 had already exceeded the total amount Ms Late invested that year. At a 6% return, Mr Early would have to contribute six more years, until the age of thirty-three, to get the same result. Assuming that Mr Early continues to buy more, he will still be able to stop saving earlier to have the same retirement amount as Ms Late.

In other words, time is money. But money needs time.

Conclusion

A few last thoughts on the meaning of freedom

We always laugh when people idealize the freedom we have as self-employed writers. Yes, in some ways, we really are free. We can work in our pyjamas all day (or at least we could before Zoom invaded our space). We can take time off in the middle of the day, or the middle of the week to go cross-country skiing, or to the pool for a swim, or for a walk in Montreal's Botanical Gardens (a five-minute drive from our home). No one blames us for not answering the phone, for getting to work late, for chatting in the corridor, for not checking out emails, for taking long lunches or not submitting our expenses on time.

Yes, we enjoy all these "freedoms"—in theory. The reality, of course, is that many of these freedoms are cancelled out by great responsibilities that come with being self-employed. We rarely indulge in many of the freedoms at our disposal, with the notable exception of long lunches to go for walks, swims or skis (a must for us). The fact is, if we were to let comfort, pleasure and spontaneity rule our decisions, we wouldn't get much work done and the bills would start piling up quickly. Freedom has its limits, starting with the responsibilities that go along with it. If we don't perform, we don't bill clients. When we leave for holidays, we have to make sure we're not leaving clients hanging and wrap up last details on projects first. Our income is not conveniently spread out over fifty-two weeks, or even twelve months of the year so we need to manage it carefully; it comes in dribs and drabs, or sometimes in big batches with long, drier spells in between. We also have to deal with being a little outside the norm: bankers are still sceptical when we tell them we are freelance writers. And then there are the special distractions that come with the home office. Our desks are very close to the cookie jar (but also, the washing machine, the dishwasher, the garden tools . . .). Our daughters walk in to our office while we're working to pick up documents from the printer, or water the plants, or ask us for help with a homework problem, and naturally we want to stop and ask them about their day. In short, we have to resist temptations, tolerate interruptions and grapple with a certain amount of prejudice every day.

Which requires—in a word—discipline.

But does this mean we're actually not free? It's the wrong question. When you make big decisions about what to study, where to work and whom to love, that's when you want to be really free. Afterwards, you just juggle the consequences of the decisions you've already made. You try to get a free hand to make the small decisions you need to make to keep things running, to keep moving forward in your work, or in your life. That's about as far as freedom goes in this life. In order to do what you want for a living, when you want to do it, you have to attend to a thousand other needs and contingencies that may prevent you from . . . doing what you want.

There's a great line in the film Before Sunrise where two young lovers, Jesse and Celine (played by Ethan Hawke and French actress Julie Delpy), are wandering the streets of Vienna. Jesse remarks: "You never hear somebody say, 'With the time I've saved by using my word processor, I'm gonna go to a Zen monastery and hang out.' I mean, you never hear that." His point is, machines have definitely freed us from much of the drudgery that occupied us in centuries past. You only need a thermostat to heat your house now; you don't need to split logs and bring in firewood. There are no more trips to the well; water just runs straight into our houses. The text on the screen is already laid out in pages as you type it and customers will receive it with the click of a return button instead of a trip to the post office. The list of modern conveniences is endless. But it hasn't really given us freedom. It's mostly made us able to get more done in a shorter period of time.

Some studies have shown that we actually laugh less than our ancestors did. Maybe that's because we are doing more. The work that we do today also demands more of our mental attention. And with the web becoming a constant presence in our every waking moment, we are constantly being interrupted. The mobile phone rings in the middle of a walk in the park. We surf the web when we should sleep. We communicate more effectively and more, but not necessarily better. And, of course, there's the car, which we drive at 100 km/h to go to the gym for exercise. Why the hurry?

The "old" constraints of our working lives forced us to slow down in a way we don't today. At the beginning of the 20th century, workers in lumber camps took an hour to eat lunch and rest every day. It wasn't a perk their unions negotiated for them. They didn't have unions. The reason they stopped was that their horses needed an hour to digest their lunches before they could work again.

There's a time when the animal in us wants revenge on the machines we created. Automobiles are a miracle, but we still need to walk and not just to get from point A to point B. Our bodies need to move and our minds need to wander. Machines will not free us. Only we can do that.

Why all this philosophizing? Just to make our point: if you want to become self-employed to have more freedom, don't over-idealize the concept. There will still be plenty of things tying you down. You may feel like the decision to become self-employed was the last thing you did when you were still free. Our advice? Make the most of the freedom self-employment does give you, so you can do what you really want with your life.

Acknowledgements

This book started out as a COVID-19 pandemic coping mechanism.

Like many, many, self-employed people, the uncertain days early in the pandemic translated into a sudden shortage of work for us (fortunately, it was temporary, in our case). Like many creative people, we knew that the best way to cope with financial uncertainly was to start a new project. So, we took a look at our "backburner" projects and decided this was the right one. For years we had been thinking of translating and adapting Jean-Benoît's French-language *Guide du travailleur autonome*, originally published in 1998 (now in its 3rd edition).

As self-employed workers, we know how fortune often hides in misfortune. Because some contracts vanished overnight at the beginning of the pandemic, we became eligible for a limited number of CERB payments. That slight financial relief gave us the peace of mind we needed to start working on translating *Le Guide*. As a result, we would like to first thank the federal government for stepping up when we—and a host of other self-employed workers—really needed them.

We would also like to thank the publisher of the original French version of this book, Québec Amérique, for agreeing to revert the English-language rights of *Le Guide du Travailleur autonome* so we could translate and adapt it for Canadian self-employed workers. We are also grateful to Québec Amérique for having believed and invested in *Le Guide* for over two decades now.

Writing a book like *Going Solo* would have been a remote—probably impossible—goal for us, had we not benefitted over the years from the help, advice and encouragement of Jean-Benoît's father, Yvan. As the youngest member of a poor, working-class family who went on to found a large engineering company, no one knew better than Yvan how important it was to do what you love. Passing that belief on to us, was one of his greatest gifts.

We would also like warmly thank Irina Rakhimova, CPA, CA, Senior Manager, Tax at Ernst and Young who took time out of her busy schedule to help us untangle a few tax concepts.

And of course, we are grateful to our publisher, Kenneth Whyte, for embracing *Going Solo* so enthusiastically and to the team at to Sutherland House for getting it onto book shelves. We also feel very indebted to our literary agent, Evan Brown, at Transatlantic Agency for helping us to create a successful book proposal with such skill and helping us navigate the early stages of the book's life with such aplomb.

Finally, we owe a great debt to all our self-employed colleagues—writers, editors, filmmakers, architects, shop owners and many, many more—and to the participants of our workshops on self-employment and freelancing over the decades. Their insights and questions have not only helped us better understand the challenges of being self-employed, they have constantly reminded us of the great benefits of living life without a boss.

In short, if there's one thing you learn as a self-employed worker, it's that you can't do it alone!

About the authors

Julie Barlow

Julie Barlow grew up in Hamilton, Ontario and has been working as a freelance writer since 1995. She writes for magazines and newspapers in Canada, including Chatelaine, Report on Business and *L'actualité*, and has published in *The New York Times*, *USA Today* and more. Author of eight books, including her latest, The Bonjour Effect, Julie is presently developing a TV documentary series based on her book The Story of French, written with husband and partner Jean-Benoît Nadeau. She lives in Montreal with Nadeau and their two daughters.

Jean-Benoît Nadeau

Born in Sherbrooke, Quebec, and a political science graduate of McGill University, Jean-Benoît Nadeau once held a job for a total of 29 days and has been self-employed for 35 years. A regular reporter and columnist to *L'actualité* (Canada's main national French magazine), he is also a past contributor to the *Report on Business Magazine*, and has signed papers for various American, Canadian and French publications. His freelancer status has allowed him to live in various venues like Phoenix, Toronto, Paris and Montreal as well as undertake radio, film and book projects, some of which with his spouse and partner Julie Barlow.

Index